W9-BJV-511

THIS HILL, THIS VALLEY

American Land Classics

Charles E. Little, Series Editor

American Land Classics is a quality paperback reprint series that makes available again books with the stature of classics in the literature of landscape, nature, and the American "place." Each book is a facsimile reprint of the original edition and is handsomely produced on acid-free paper for your permanent library.

THIS HILL,
THIS VALLEY

by HAL BORLAND

with drawings by Peter Marks

The Johns Hopkins University Press • Baltimore

A part of the material in some of the chapters of this book first appeared, in
another form, on the editorial pages of the *New York Times*, 1941–1955.
Originally published in a hardcover edition in 1975 by Simon and Schuster,
Inc., New York. Reprinted by arrangement with Barbara Dodge Borland.

Johns Hopkins Paperbacks edition, 1990

The Johns Hopkins University Press
701 West 40th Street
Baltimore, Maryland 21211

∞ The paper used in this book meets the minimum requirements of
American National Standard for Information Sciences—Permanence of
Paper for Printed Library Materials, ANSI Z39.48-1984.

Library of Congress Cataloging-in-Publication Data

Borland, Hal, 1900–1978.
    This hill, this valley / by Hal Borland : with drawings by Peter Marks. —
Johns Hopkins Paperbacks ed.
        p.   cm. — (American land classics)
    Reprinted. Originally published: New York: Simon and Schuster, 1957.
    ISBN 0-8018-4020-1 (alk. paper)
    1. Borland, Hal, 1900–1978—Homes and haunts—Connecticut. 2. Authors,
American—20th century—Biography. 3. Naturalists—United States—
Biography. 4. Natural history—Connecticut. 5. Country life—Connecticut.
6. Connecticut—Biography.
I. Title. II. Series.
PS3503.0563Z47   1990
508.746—dc20   89-43554
                                                                          CIP

To my Barbara

Preface

Most of us know the world around us *rather intimately during our growing-up years; then we lose sight of it in the haste of a busy life, now and then catching a quick glance from a superhighway or a coast-to-coast plane. We urbanize, or we make a tentative and nostalgic compromise and suburbanize and try to recapture a lost sense of belonging. And occasionally we get a second chance to see and try to know exactly where we live.*

Five years ago I was taken to a hospital and partook of a miracle. I went there dying of a ruptured appendix and advanced peritonitis, and I came back alive. I went there while Winter was passing, but I was not aware of that for in a hospital there is neither wind nor weather, sunrise nor moonset, but only a strange intermediate stage between life and death.

Preface

I came back to March, and even its gusts and gales, its snow and slush and rain, were full of wonder. Its gray skies were pussy-willow gray, not leaden. Its chickadee song was as gay, if not quite so loud, as that of a May oriole. The sound of March melt, trickling down the hillsides, was full of laughter and Spring just offstage. March and I were alive, getting acquainted with each other all over again. To see daffodils budding was to know, as for the first time, a magnificent wonder. To see buds open into new leaves was to see, suddenly, a marvelous facet of that big miracle which each Spring stirs the earth and all things thereon.

I saw and felt, and it was like feeling my own strong pulse again, sensing my own growing strength. I was a part of some universal magnificence, as I had not been for a long time.

March passed, Spring strengthened, and I knew that I, too, had come to a new season in my life. Almost half my life had been spent in a daily job, a good part of it at a desk in a city. Because of some urgency in myself, I lived most of those years at the edge of the country, near woods and open fields. I spent evenings and weekends there. Then I quit the city job and moved to the edge of the country for good, to write what and when and where I might. But for eight years I was coming and going, to California, to Michigan, to Colorado, to Florida, to Mississippi, wherever an editor sent me, making a living at my typewriter.

All that time I had made occasion, at least once a week, to renew my acquaintance with the trees and flowers, the weather and the wind. However, I felt the need to remain close to the city, never more than an hour away. The habit was deeply ingrained, and though I compromised by owning a few acres of hillside and brook and coming to know them intimately, I was being trapped by suburbanization, which in its own way is worse than urbanization.

Then I went to the hospital and came back, and it all seemed more of a compromise than a man should make. Reappraisal was inevitable. Barbara, who is my wife and who had known that I would come back when others doubted, agreed

*that there were things more important than an assignment in
Maine or Tennessee. She, too, felt that a self-chosen assignment
on a hillside of my own choosing was the important thing now.
So we sold our suburban acres and moved to Weatogue, to
live, to write, to see and feel and understand a hillside, a river
bank, a woodland and a valley pasture.*

*We came here, not to a cabin in the wilderness but to a
farmhouse beside a river. So far as the legalities are concerned,
we bought and own a hundred acres, one whole side of a mountain and half a mile of river bank. I have spent the months and
years since, living with this small fraction of the universe and
trying to know its meaning—to own it, that is, in terms of
observation and understanding. There is no other way to own
a piece of land. We have been away briefly, on one errand and
another, some of them a continent's span away; but this is
home, this is the source, this is where I live and work the year
around. I have written of many things during my years here,
but the continuing topic has been here in my own dooryard, six
miles from the village, a hundred miles from the city. I was
granted a second chance to know this earth of my origins, and
I have found here in Weatogue a good vantage point from
which to examine it.*

*Weatogue is a strange word to the unaccustomed tongue.
It is of Indian origin. In the Mahican tongue it meant "The
Place of the Wigwam." Or, more simply, "Home." As late as
1740, when the first white settlers had come here, there was an
Indian village of 70 wigwams not far from where my house
now stands. Not a trace of that Weatogue remains, though
flint arrowheads and other stone implements were found for
years in a field just down the road. There is a post office called
Weatogue forty miles from here, but locally the name means
only the valley where I live, a valley less than four miles long.
We pronounce the name we-a-tog.*

*This book is not the story of this valley, of Weatogue,
specifically. Rather, it is an account of one man's seeing and
thinking and his attempts at understanding. It follows the pattern of the year, Spring to Spring, because that is the nature*

Preface

of time, all the time man has known. It is the story of a man and the universe he knows best; and perhaps in that sense it is the story of Man and his World. The same sun rises here as in Miami or Chicago or Seattle, and the same moon, and the same star patterns. My river, like all rivers, flows from an upland to the sea. My mountain was once a new upthrust on the surface of a restless land. My valley, like all valleys, has a hill on either side. Mine are global winds, and my rains and snows come from remote sources. My rabbits and squirrels and deer and porcupines are no strange, antipodean creatures; my robins and orioles and wood thrushes and mourning doves are known in the Carolinas and in Ohio and in Arkansas. The equinoxes and the solstices are as faithful in coming here as elsewhere. I came here to live with these verities and to search for understanding of them. I shall never know all there is to know about them, but what I have set down here is an interim report.

H.B.

Weatogue
Salisbury, Connecticut

THIS HILL, THIS VALLEY

SPRING

Iwelcome the vernal equinox as a signpost, but nothing more. It says that Spring lies ahead, the Spring we know and recognize in rising sap, opening buds, returning birds. A Spring day in March is as rare as the proverbial day in June, but today I seem to sense the cleanliness of change. Winter's debris still litters the roadside and murks the river, but the brightness of new growth is not far away. Already there is a touch of green beside Millstone Brook and Springhouse Brook in the pastures, where flowing water has leached the frost away, and here in the dooryard I find tentative daffodil tips showing and the white-veined lancets of crocuses.

But the equinox is a matter of celestial mechanics, and terrestrial seasons follow it only approximately. One year the equinox found us with two feet of snow on the ground and the river still iced in. Another year it found me tapping the maples on a day so mild I shucked my coat and sweated in shirt sleeves as I carried pails of sap and fed the fire under the syrup tub. This year it is somewhere in between, remnants of drifts in the woods on the mountain and the temperature in the low 40s.

If there is integrity in the soul of man it must reveal itself when Spring turns the year. I may fuss and delude myself all Winter, but come Spring and I must face my own truth if there is truth in me. I must know that there is faith that transcends creed. I must believe in eternal things. I understand something of the flow of life and time.

The big issues of this world are between man and man, not between man and his environment. If man could only live at peace with his own kind he would have no reason to quarrel with the world around him. I find no vindictiveness in nature, and I am as aware as anyone of hurricane, tornado, flood, drought and earthquake. Man's morality and man's codes have no more application to the sun and the seasons, the rain and the earth's fertility, than do his esthetic concepts to the pattern of a sunset.

I went out tonight to stand and watch the stars, and a sense of peace came over me. I felt a part of the universe, a sentient but lesser part; and that feeling is fundamental to the dignity of man. I am, somehow, a part of the great rhythm that flows through this universe. There is my source, my origin. My own pulse is such a rhythm, and quite probably the rhythmic impulses in my brain, which constitute thought, are also a part of something far greater than the individual. I am not sure of the purpose of man, any more than I am sure of the purpose of the stars; but here we are, and there they are, and among us there is discernible order, a continuity. Recognition of that is perhaps enough for me during my tenure here.

A FLOCK OF ROBINS has come to the valley, as they come each year within a few days of this date. This morning the whole flock is in the pasture behind the house; I counted fifty-two, and quite likely that is a conservative count, for they were too busy for an accurate census.

The life of a robin, or of any early migrating bird, must be full of adventure and surprise. The things that can happen to a bird that comes north with the best of expectations while Spring is only a promise would make most of us humans turn and run in panic.

Worse things can happen to a robin, of course, than to come north through balmy skies and get caught in a snowstorm or a sleety rain. But to a non-robin such an experience would be the ultimate of frustration. What does a robin do about it? He gets wet, he gets cold, he takes shelter under a pine or a hemlock, and he pokes around for something to eat. Food is scarce, but if the sun comes out the next day he fluffs his feathers and begins to sing.

Robins seem able to take March on its own terms, possibly because some race memory or instinct says that after March comes April, which may be worth knowing intimately. Robins make out pretty well in April, and by May they are doing very well indeed. March is simply the price they pay for May.

There are benefits, of course, for the early arrivals, such as robins. Firstcomers get first choice of nesting places and feeding range, so it must even out. If it didn't even out, the robins wouldn't keep on coming north so early. They know what they are doing, whether non-robins know or not.

I LIVE BESIDE A RIVER. It is my nearest neighbor, just there beyond the dooryard. According to the scientists, such water as this was the womb of mankind. In some primordial time of development and elemental curiosity, evolving creatures of the water crept up on oozy banks and grew lungs to replace their original gills. Eventually one of these creatures also grew legs and arms and eyes that see better in the air than in the water. He even developed a brain that was more than a node of ganglia. He became a man.

Millions of years passed. Man became a creature of family, of tribe, then of race. He went through a centripetal stage of social development, during which he built massed cities; and from that stage he at last entered a centrifugal stage of redistribution, migration from the cities back to the open country, to the mountains, the valleys, the woodlands. What he did with that environment is another matter, but I have a haunting wonder if man will ever learn to live with the world on its own terms rather than try to impose his own narrow terms upon the world. In any case, here am I, once more dwelling on a river bank, a modern throwback to the company of frogs and salamanders and fish.

Whether it is an antediluvian instinct or not which brought me here, I have not yet decided. But I know that my river is a comfort and a satisfaction. It is movement and change in a primal sense, and that movement gives me a sense of per-

manence. Here I live, planting and harvesting, and there flows the river, fecund and ever changing. Long ago my kind came out of such water to stand erect and stride the land. I have come back to contemplate myself and my beginnings.

OURS IS A RURAL VALLEY and our neighbors are farmers who have lived on the land all their lives. Of the eight houses on this four-mile stretch of valley road, only one belongs to Summer people. The rest of us live here, work here, the year around, intent on weather, crops, markets.

The first white settlers came here in the 1730s and found parts of this valley even then being cultivated, primitively, by the Indians, who harvested corn on the silted bottomlands. To the west rose the ridge now known as Tom's Mountain and Miles Mountain, and five miles away to the east rose the long, rugged ridge of what we know as Canaan Mountain. The valley itself was at least as old as the retreat of the last glaciers, perhaps 25,000 years ago. The river, a mountain

stream both above and below here, was and still is a placid stretch of wide, deep water.

Over Tom's Mountain, to the west, lie two lakes, Washining and Washinee on some old maps, simply Twin Lakes to most people now. From up on the shoulder of Tom's Mountain I can see a clustering of mountains ten to fifteen miles away which rise 2,600 feet, Bear Mountain, Mount Everett, Mount Ashley, Mount Race. And to the north our valley widens as it reaches up into Massachusetts, to Great Barrington, to Pittsfield and beyond, flanked always by high hills and low mountains.

This is old land, peaceful land. In Summer it is full of corn and alfalfa and pasturage, and dairy cows. In Winter it is often full of snow, and the river is a winding band of ice. Spring comes slowly here, and Fall lingers, often until Christmas. It is a quiet valley and, in miles, it is remote from the city, three hours by rail or car. But what place is remote now? One can achieve a degree of peace and privacy, but even those who try cannot escape the world. The highway, three miles from our door, is jammed on holidays and many weekends; fortunately, ours is a back road, leading nowhere in particular and little trafficked.

Two villages, full of friendly folk and convenient services, lie six miles away in opposite directions. Both are venerable villages, dating back to the days of first settlement here. Albert and Ruth, our nearest neighbors, live half a mile down the road. A mile in the other direction are Charley and Elitha. Both are farm families and the best of neighbors, which is to say they are always there when you need them, with help and friendship and understanding. Albert and Charley are dairy farmers and wise in the ways of living with the land.

Our farm is still known as "the Proper place" (pronounced with a long *o*), after the farmer who owned it twenty years ago, though we are the third owners since that time. A few of the older people in the village speak of it as "the Barnum place." It was owned by a Barnum about fifty years ago. Thus slowly do things change in this valley. I am glad for the persistence of the past in such matters. Some things should not be forgotten or easily discarded. The name of a farm, after all, is of little consequence. Everyone who has ever lived here has been a tenant, in a sense, and a transient, for the valley was already old when the first Indians saw it. I am only the latest in a long line of settlers on this land.

I DOUBT THAT ANYONE denies the wonders and magnificence of astronomy, one of the great sciences which endure as monuments to man's powers of reason and observation. But at this season of the year I am always aware of hidden forces so accurate and so sensitive to time and the astral sequence that any human science seems to pale at least a little by contrast.

Man has known for a long time the fixed sequence of star and planet, earth, sun, moon and tides. But how can a seed "know" when to begin to sprout? How can sap at the roots of a tree "know" when comes the proper time to start that mysterious upward movement toward twig and waiting leaf-bud? What moves a bulb to send up shoots to catch the sunlight and begin to manufacture food for the plant? What mysterious force prompts one seed to wait in its sprouting until all danger of frost is past, while another sprouts at that exact moment its stem and leaf can survive ten degrees of frost but not twelve or fifteen?

We have answers, of a sort, in terms of warmth and length of daylight; but those are, in final examination, observations of response, not of ultimate cause. We have elaborate apparatus to measure sun warmth and soil moisture and even sap

pressure; but how does a grass seed measure such critical conditions? Somehow they are measured by all living things which spread leaves and manufacture chlorophyll. They "know" when they should respond to the arrival of Spring. Man doesn't know until he has watched a clock and studied a star, and even then his knowledge is approximate at best.

SURELY IT IS NO ACCIDENT that the chlorophyll of the leaf and the hemoglobin of the blood are chemically akin. Man is more than a vegetable, but he lives under the same sun as the tree and the vine, and he responds to the seasons, senses them in the very depth of his being, in his blood stream, in his emotions, in the seat of his understanding when he takes time to understand.

Man's quest for the meaning of his place in the universe has deeper roots than we usually admit. We all need, physically need, a sufficient link with our environment to be at ease in it. Extend and substantiate that ease and you approach the state we should call civilization. Automatic furnaces, automobiles, television, and vitrified plumbing no doubt have a purpose in some of the processes of civilization, but only insofar as they provide ease from the vicissitudes of existence and thus give man time to wonder and speculate and explore his own mind and his habitat—to achieve ease and acceptance in his environment.

Perhaps that is one reason we all look forward so eagerly to the end of Winter, because nature herself then eases the vicissitudes. I know that I need the renewal of Spring as much as the trees need it. My mind requires the quickening, the replenishing, the photosynthesis in whatever form it manifests itself in the human body. Besides, it is much easier to be friends with one's environment in temperate weather.

THERE IS A SUCCESSION in the days, now, that quickens the heart. Whether they are gusty days or days of calm, chill days or days of deepening warmth, they have the air of change. Today is gusty. Yesterday was calm. I await tomorrow.

8

Spring

The weeping willow beside the old milk barn has an amber glow, as though golden sap were pulsing just beneath the thin outer bark. Beside the river the red osiers are ruddy as though blood were just beneath their cambium layer. The daffodils are well up. Hyacinths and early tulips have broken ground. Crocuses begin to spread their color to the temperamental winds. Flower buds are fat on the forsythia. Iris sends up its green bayonets.

I walked through the garden, still bare as Winter itself, and I saw these things, and I walked along the river bank and I noted them. I looked up Tom's Mountain, which rises just beyond the pastures, and I felt the same slow but certain pressure of succession, the slow, certain urge of change. Growth is there in the earth, at the grass roots, at the twig-ends. The green world is in the making, already waiting where the mysterious chemistry of sap and chlorophyll has its origins. April whispers from the hilltops even as March goes whistling down the valley.

BARBARA, MY COLLABORATOR not only in much writing but also in marriage and living, is a vegetable gardener. She was out in the garden plot today, poking in the soil with her hands. And up the road our neighbor, Charley, who is a farmer, was out in his fields, walking, pausing now and then to take up a handful of soil. Gardeners and farmers must feel the soil, literally feel it, now. They know full well that you must plant in season, but they also know that you plant in the earth; and they must touch the soil, feel its grit and strength and thus renew contact with the source of all good and growing things.

I watched Charley as he strode across the field this sunny afternoon. He scuffed the soil with his heel. He crouched down and picked up a handful, feeling the fine roots lacing through it. He made a ball of it, a miniature earth. There in his hand he held the stuff that nourishes corn and oats and grass. Out of such soil sprang the timbers of his house, the shirt upon his back. Out of it grew all the flowers that ever pleased an eye or nose.

It was no mere chance that inserted into primitive folklore the recurring tale of how the first man was created from

the soil of the earth. The ancient people knew the soil intimately, even though they were hunters and herdsmen. From it
sprang the substance of life. It was Mother Earth. And Mother
Earth it remains, no matter how far we travel. When the time
of planting comes we shall, as always, bow down to Mother
Earth as we plant.

THE CHILL HAS RETURNED, a raw, windy chill
that ripples the river and whistles and moans in the big Norway spruce outside my study window. It is a proper reminder
that Spring takes its time, no matter how the human heart may
long for its coming. But I still take comfort in the willows and
the osiers, which are as vivid and as vital as they were a week
ago. Even though I shiver in the wind, I see new life in them.
There is no pulse in them, of course, beyond the mysterious
processes by which sap moves from the deepest root to the highest twig; but I feel the larger pulse, the bigger rhythm, which
is almost visible in them. I watch them, and I know that this
chill wind will pass. But I put my faith not so much in the trees
and shrubs as in the season itself, of which they are only a part,
even as I am.

WE WENT TO THE VILLAGE TODAY to do a couple
of chores, and as I walked down the street and looked in the

stores I had the feeling of mid-May. There wasn't a snow shovel in sight, and the coarse salt and wild-bird seed were hidden by racks of brand-new spades and hoes and rakes and weeders. And bags of patent fertilizer, and grass seed, and clover. And stands of bright new seed packets, pretty as a flower garden in full bloom. And work gloves.

I went on down the street and around the corner, past the implement store. There was the same thing, on a bigger scale. Tractors, big and little, plows, harrows, seeders, cultivators, hay balers. And busy men assembling, tuning, repairing such machinery. And at the siding near the railroad station were boxcars and farm trucks, men unloading lime and phosphate. Farmers saying, "Tomorrow," or "Next week," or "It's almost dry enough, except in that bottom land."

Then we came home and looked at the vegetable garden. And in five minutes we knew it was planting season only in the stores. Maybe we can plant a few peas next week, with luck, but that's all. I got a spade and tried to turn up some soil, and found it cold and frosty less than a spade-length down. I found two angleworms, tightly curled into pink balls, and they didn't give much encouragement to thoughts about fishing. It won't be fishing time till it's almost time to plant garden and mow the lawn and hang the screens and tend the early flowers.

Then I remembered that there wasn't a bottle of muscle liniment in sight at the stores, no sunburn lotion, no mosquito repellent. And I went in for a warmer jacket and decided to stay indoors a few more weeks.

THE PONDS WERE SCUMMED WITH ICE again this morning, but by noon the temperature had risen to fifty. A few more days of this and we shall be hearing the peepers and seeing frog eggs in the shallow woods pools. It is time for the tadpole cycle to start again. Frog life, though brief in the individual, is long beyond belief in the species, and it gains its length by the fertility of the animal in conditions that would wipe out warm-blooded creatures.

How old frogs may be, as a distinctive form of life, no

one can say with certainty. Fossils that seem to be almost identical with the frogs of today have been found in the Eocene deposits of France, and the Eocene era is estimated at fifty million years ago. Certainly the frogs saw the uplift of this land we know as America. They watched it slowly emerge from the sea and no doubt croaked and greeted the season's change while sitting in the vast marshlands that have become the great valleys of today. How long ago they learned to climb trees, as the hylas of today climb, and to trill their tremulous peeper notes, is anybody's guess.

The swamp maples prepare to open their florets, relative newcomers among the world's trees. Skunk cabbage, a venerable species, unfurls its brownish hood to reveal its primitive flower stalk. Bees, at least as old as frogs in this world's history, come buzzing for the first taste of pollen. And man, not long here himself, hears the buzz and trill from the bogland and says, "These are the sounds of Spring." They are, the sounds of Springs untold, of the very Springtime of life.

ALBERT, THE DAIRY FARMER down the road who leases my pasture land, came up today with his truck to get a few boards. Like most of us hereabout, he takes out a few loads of logs every Winter, lets them season until a slack time, then hauls them to the mill and has them sawed. He stowed a pile of lumber in my big barn last year. My barn is a kind of community warehouse, open to anyone who lacks cover for tools or feed or gear. It now shelters hay, straw, lumber, a wagon, a hay baler, a hay rake, a cookstove and a plow, none of them mine.

Albert put his boards on his truck and we sat beside the barn in the sun and talked crops and weather. I asked what he was going to do with the field where he had such a good stand of oats and mustard last year. He smiled. "That is a good mustard field, isn't it? I'm putting it into corn. That'll keep the mustard down. This year. But when I put it in oats again it'll be half mustard, as always. It's been that way ever since I was a boy. Can't get rid of it. And it's the only field on the place that has any mustard to speak of."

Spring

He got up to leave and looked up the mountain toward where the birches have taken over a whole hollow. "Beautiful stand of birches up there," he said. "Birches are the prettiest trees there are." He frowned and got in his truck and drove away. If I hadn't known him I would have thought he was annoyed at my mention of the mustard. He wasn't. He's just sentimental about birches and hates to admit it, even to me.

IT HASN'T REALLY warmed up yet, but when we went for a walk this evening we heard the first few peepers and we knew the silence has ended. The silence which began with the last scratchy note of the last katydid, progressed through the brittle-dry rustle of leaves on the road, deepened into the echo of the owl hoot and the fox bark. At its greatest depth it was a silence so profound that I could hear the whisper of snowflakes nudging each other as they fell. Now it has ended in the rush of flowing water, the quack of black ducks and American mergansers on the river, and the tentative trill of the hylas.

These, of course, are only the obvious voices. So, too, are most of the bird songs which precede the great chorus. The robins already sing a little at dawn, and so do the song sparrows, but their songs seem a little hoarse and hesitant. But at the marsh down the road the blackbirds, both the red-shouldered ones and the rusties, newly arrived from the South, are in full voice at midday.

The subtler voices call for other listening, however. I feel them with all my senses, listening with my skin, as insects listen. Then I am aware of the outriders of the great insect hordes—the ants, the first hungry bees, the first wasps, the earliest beetles, the minute flies which tap the opening buds. They are barely humming, but I know that back of them is the whole season's insect life and loudness. The silence will not return until frost bites deep in another Autumn.

APRIL

I HEARD A CARDINAL'S WHISTLED CALL this morning, over-riding the wind and declaring that this is a good time to be alive. If I had said a few years ago that I heard a cardinal here in this valley the bird watchers would have thought, even if they refrained from saying so, that I didn't know a bird from a bee. Cardinals just didn't come this far north. But we have had half a dozen of them here this past Winter, duly authenticated. Cardinals do come here now.

Birds keep changing their ranges. Forty years ago the evening grosbeaks were unknown in the East; now they come to this area in flocks every Winter. A few weeks ago a man not far from here said he had seen a mockingbird. I was skeptical. I have never seen a mockingbird as far north as Philadelphia. But this man may be right. Pehaps our next unusual migrants will be mockingbirds.

I am especially glad to have cardinals here, for the redbird is as good to look at as he is to hear. He is Mr. Redbird, from his cocky crest to his jaunty tail—and don't forget the Mister! The redstart, who will be along a bit later, is a beautiful bird, but he can't hold a candle to the cardinal's brilliance. The evening grosbeak has a vest that would knock your eye out, but he, too, must take a back seat sartorially to the cardinal. The oriole is flashy, and the goldfinch is beauty incarnate, but they, too, are somewhat lesser birds than the cardinal. This opinion, of course, is subject to discount; I am a little like the man who told his wife she looked beautiful in any color dress, just so it was red.

Spring

THIS IS A SEASON when I can listen only so long to a recital of the world's shortcomings. Then I must go outdoors and see the world itself. Last night I heard a long harangue by a man who is full of the world's ills, and today I took a walk up the mountainside and found that though a hundred things may be wrong, a thousand things are right and completely in order.

The right things are so obvious. Water still runs downhill, making brooks that sing and rivers that flow seaward. Grass still sends up green shoots in the pasture. Robins strut the lawn and sing their mating call from the trees. Daffodils come to blossom. Maples begin to open wine-red bloom. Bees are busy at their Summer's search. The newly turned soil of the fields is full of fertility. Farmers and gardeners prepare to plant, knowing that the earth is still good.

These are simple, obvious things which I have seen every April of my life. If they happened only once in ten years we would wait breathless and put aside our worries and our quarrels to watch for their coming. Instead, they are commonplaces and taken for granted while men bandy words and dispute ideas. The trouble is that too many of the words are empty and too many of the ideas are sterile.

The world is all right. The quarrels are among men. Men who forget that ideas have their roots in one of two places, in the earth or in the stars. April invites a conference on the open hillside to investigate the state of affairs at their common source.

THE NIGHT TURNED COLD and today is raw and windy. The lead-gray river is as full of wrinkles as an old man's forehead frowning at the chill. Barbara, who was happily inspecting her garden soil yesterday and talked of planting beans, though she knew such a venture would be absurd, asked me to light a fire in the Franklin stove. That gave the living room a fine glow; but, like so many actions, it had an opposite reaction. The living-room temperature rose. The furnace thermostat, which is in the living room, cut off the furnace. The remainder of the house grew cold.

One might labor a point and come out with a splendid parallel, but to what end? Our mechanical contrivances give us comfort and convenience, and if we violate their mechanical laws we change our comfortable balance. But we usually can restore that balance by flipping a switch, turning a faucet, replacing a fuse or a light bulb. I have little patience with those who say in direful tones that we have become slave and prisoner of our machines. That is nonsense. Unless nature takes command, of course, and knocks out power lines with sleet or wind.

To make my study comfortably warm, I turned up the thermostat and the furnace went quietly to work again.

Spring

I DOUBT THAT WE WOULD have bought this place if electric power and a telephone line had not been available. I see no need to revert to the utmost of simplicity. If that were my purpose I should have moved into a cave on a hillside, a move I suggest for those who harp on the evil complications of labor-saving and exalt complete simplicity as the means of human salvation. I never see these fine theorists taking to a cave to subsist on berries.

Any country place is somewhat at the mercy of storms. We are fortunate to have spring water fed to the house from high on the mountain. It comes into the upstairs bathroom with enough pressure to knock a glass from your hand. We cook and heat water with bottled gas, another weatherproof system. Our furnace burns oil and is run by electricity, but if it is disabled we can heat a habitable part of the house with a wood fire in the Franklin stove. We have a couple of kerosene lanterns and a stock of fat, utilitarian candles. We couldn't live comfortably forever without electricity, but we could get along for quite a while.

Our country road is on a tank-truck milk-collection route, so it is plowed out after snowstorms. Now and then a snow or sleet storm makes it difficult or unwise to get the car out, and I walk a mile and a quarter to our rural mailbox. In any emergency I could walk, cross-country, to the village in less than an hour. We are no more than usually at the mercy of the weather, and when all goes well—as it does most of the time—we live quite happily with our machinery.

BEFORE THE SEASON PROGRESSES another hour, I must make an appraisal. Another week and I shall be so engulfed in the season that I shall lose most of my perspective.

Spring is one thing that man has never had a hand in, no hand at all. It is as remote from man as sunrise or the phases of the moon. This may be difficult to believe when you have a gardenful of daffodils and hyacinths and tulips planted by your own hand. But none of us can fend off an April frost, and none of us can make a tulip bulb grow and come to blossom by

17

holding it in our hands. We have to commit it to the earth and trust to forces beyond human power or control.

Spring came before man was here to see it, and it will keep on coming even if man isn't here to see it some time in the future. It is a matter of solar mechanics and celestial order. And for all our knowledge of astronomy and terrestrial mechanics, we haven't yet been able to do more than bounce a radar beam off the moon. We couldn't alter the arrival of Spring by one second if we tried.

Spring is a matter of growth, of bud and blossom. We can alter growth and change the time of blossoming in individual plants; but the forests still grow in their own way and the grasses of the plains haven't altered measurably in a thousand years.

Spring is a magnificent phase in the cycle of nature, but man really hasn't anything to do with it. He just happens to be here, to enjoy it and benefit from it. This is a good time to admit it. By the time May arrives we shall be in a mood to say that it is all ours, our own achievement.

MAN IS AN ITINERANT CREATURE. It is a question whether economic necessity—which is to say hunger—or simple curiosity drove him over the hill and into the valley beyond his birthplace when he first began to wander. But I know this: Man didn't invent the wheel merely to help tote a burden. He made a wheel so he might build a cart in which to carry a few possessions to a new dwelling place. He didn't hollow out a log merely to go out in the middle of a lake and fish. He contrived a boat in which to go somewhere. He remained a herdsman as long as he did because his flocks wandered the hills and he could follow them. The explorers have all been men consumed by curiosity rather than by hunger.

What I am doing, of course, is rationalizing my yearning to go somewhere, get out of the house and see what is beyond the bend in the road. I am saying that my foot itches because the sun shines and there is a bright, clean line at the horizon. And I have been a staid householder long enough.

18

Spring

I WENT SOMEWHERE. I walked up the road a couple of miles with Pat, the dog. We found that the celandine is flourishing and that the rabbits are numerous. Pat investigated the rabbits. I surveyed the celandine.

Celandine is a perverse and undemonstrative member of the poppy family. It is also cousin of the bloodroot, though you'd never know it at a casual look. Like all its family, celandine flowers bear pollen but no honey, so it lures the bees for its own purpose and sends them away short-rationed. The flower is technically a poppy, yellow and four-petaled but small and undistinguished. It blooms in May and keeps on blooming all Summer.

The plant's distinction is in the yellow juice which oozes from any broken stem or leaf, as a similar juice does from all the poppy family. Celandine juice is bitter and astringent, was used by the old herbalists, and still has a place in medicine. It will inflame a sensitive skin, and it was once recommended as a wart remover. It was also used to treat jaundice and as a purgative. In large doses it is poisonous.

Its name comes from the Greek for swallow, the bird, and it is sometimes called swallowwort. By nature it is a biennial and it winters with a large rosette of lower leaves persistently green even under snow and ice. Late Winter, and it burgeons with new leaves as though trying to hurry Spring. Two things distinguish it—this early vigor, and a beautiful name. Otherwise, it's nothing but a roadside weed.

This Hill, This Valley

PAT ADOPTED US the first Winter we lived here. He arrived in the midst of a snowstorm, he and a black pup, both of them rib-thin and wary. They spent two nights on our front porch and refused to leave the place. You can't let even a tramp dog starve in such weather, so we finally fed them and gave them sleeping room in the woodshed, hoping they would move on when the weather eased. They didn't. Nobody in the area had ever seen them before and they had no identification tags. Eventually the black pup became a nuisance and we transferred our nebulous title to a family ten miles away. By then Pat had made himself at home with us.

Pat is every ounce a gentleman and he has a good but unknown background. He is a handsome black-and-white dog, probably a foxhound with some beagle blood. He is an excellent rabbit dog; but someone also taught him impeccable manners both in the house and out. He has had, from the beginning, a reserved and almost distant dignity, especially with guests. He has three privileged places in the house: in front of the living-room fire, on the Navajo rug at the head of the stairs, and in my study. He knows that bedrooms and the dining room are out of bounds, seems always to have known it. He knew from the beginning, too, that Barbara's study, just across the hall from mine, is forbidden to him. He does not snitch food. He stays off the furniture, with one exception—the chaise longue that stays on the porch in Summer. He and Barbara wage persistent war over the chaise. He knows it is forbidden to him, but he can't resist its soft comfort; and he always is chagrined when she catches him on it.

Pat owns the valley and everyone knows him, but he has only a few intimate human friends. I am his man, and Barbara is his woman; apparently she is the first woman he ever liked. In his other life he must have known maids or housewives who broomed him, for a broom is the one thing he fears. Charley stands next to me and Barbara in his affections. Bobbie, who visits us from time to time, is the only other woman he seems to regard as more than a casual acquaintance; Bobbie prowls the mountainside with him.

Spring

Pat loves to hunt. Charley calls him the best rabbit dog in the area. He will go hunting with Charley any time, and he would hunt every day and all day with me if I would go. But the only other person he will hunt with is Georgie, Charley's teen-age grandson. All Summer Pat wages his own war on the woodchucks, the only wild animals I have ever known him to kill. Last Summer he caught and killed seven woodchucks in one two-week span. He also likes to go fishing with us. We go in the boat and he prowls the banks, swims the river, startles frogs, herons, rabbits, an occasional fox, and makes a splendid outing of every trip.

Twice Pat decided to live with Charley, who indulges him more than we do; but each time he changed his mind—Charley calls him a notional dog—and came back here to live. Now when we have to be away for a few days, Pat moves up to Charley's till we come home, then comes back here and is wholly content.

Pat has made his peace with life, even our kind of life. As I write these words he lies here in my study, drowsing, occasionally looking at me with one dark eye, waiting for me to finish and go up the mountain with him. I wish I knew half as much about that mountainside as Pat does, but I know I never shall.

THE YEAR HOLDS ONE MOMENT, which may last for a week, when tree and bush and vine are on the breathless verge of leafing out. It is then that one can stand on a hilltop and look across the valley and see the scarlet and orange maple blossoms like a touch of pastel crayon across the treetops.

I saw such a generalization today and I knew that breathless moment is here. Then I began to look for particulars. The pear tree beside the garden is dressed in green lace, its leaves no larger than my little fingernail. The lilacs are tufted at their stem-ends, each twin leaf cluster tipped with faint brownish purple and not a leaf among them as big as a squirrel's ear. The wild raspberries beside the river have scarlet tassels not half an inch long, each tassel an unfolding group

21

of leaves whose form can be faintly seen. The early apple trees have silver gray nubs at their twig tips; when I drew down a branch to look I could see each nub as a young leaf cluster emerging from the bud, each leaf the size of a ladybird's wing and each red-tipped as though blushing. The bridal-wreath bush is green at every joint with little green rosebud leaves.

These things are here now, this instant. Even an hour from now all will be changed. Tomorrow it will be still different. This is the trembling moment when life stands between bud and leaf, promise and achievement. A new world is in the making on these old, old hills. I am an observer while Creation is taking place.

I AM GLAD WE CAME here to live, and my satisfaction is not compounded of a fine April day and a savory breakfast. It goes deeper. We came here because we thought this was a place where we could feel at home, which is to say at ease with ourselves and the things around us. Not until weeks after we had moved in and settled did we see, consciously, that this area reminds us in many ways of a certain foothill region in Colorado which means much to us.

Spring

I wonder how many people who have their own choice of a living place choose an area that reminds them of some pleasant memory. I suspect that is a greater factor than any of us know or admit. We feel at ease there, in a state of friendship with our environment. Man is a restless, sensitive creature and is happiest when he is at ease in that sense, when he feels that he belongs where he is. We belong here. The land just happens, by the turn of an economic factor, to belong to us. Had not that sense of belonging to the land been present, we would never have been at home here no matter how long we stayed.

VIOLETS, MARSH MARIGOLDS, Dutchman's-breeches and trilliums will soon be brightening our woods and meadows; but until these natives spread their petals I am thankful to the Mediterranean basin for April color. The bulbs now beginning to brighten the lawn and garden are, with few exceptions, natives of the Mediterranean area.

The big hyacinth, for instance, which especially delights Barbara's heart, came long ago from the lands which stretch eastward from Greece into Asia. The name comes from the Greek, and there are at least two versions of its origin. One is that the flower sprang from the blood of the tragic youth, Hyacinthus, when he was slain. The more likely origin is in the ancient name for a precious stone thought to have been a sapphire, in which case it would be another of the many color-names of flowers.

And the narcissus, in its various forms, is native both to the European and the African shores of the Mediterranean. Most of the narcissuses we cultivate today are of European origin. The varieties are almost countless, but they fall into three broad groups: the poet's narcissus, with shallow cup and broad petals; the jonquil, which bears two to five small, fragrant blossoms on one stem; and the trumpet daffodil. The name "daffodil" is closely related to "asphodel," a standard topic for English nature poetry a few generations ago.

All these flowers are migrants, even as so many of us

are. If they spoke a vocal language, if they had a religion, if they competed on the labor market, we probably would find some excuse to dislike them. Since they are flowers, not people, we accept them at face value and think they are rather wonderful.

PERHAPS ONE REASON I am so fond of trees is that I grew up in a treeless country. The plains of eastern Colorado have a few valleys with watercourses lined with willow brush and an occasional cottonwood tree; but both the watercourses and those trees are rare. During my early boyhood I never made or even saw a willow whistle. Then I spent a summer in the mountains and learned about pines and spruce and aspens and oaks.

When I first owned a few acres of woodland, years later, I couldn't bear to chop down a tree, even for firewood or to clear a driveway. I left so many trees around the house that it was dark and damp, and I marveled at the way seedlings sprang up everywhere, even in the tomato patch. I suppose that a Sahara Arab would have the same awe of green grass.

I still dislike to cut down a tree, though this land of ours is well timbered, timber on a whole mountainside above the pastures. When I walk there I watch that I do not step on a seedling pine, no matter how slim may be its chances of ultimate maturity. And when they cut trees along the river to widen our road I objected vigorously, even though I had to eat my words when the cutting had opened up a new and magnificent vista from our front porch.

I watch the trees now, the way the white pines put forth each annual whorl of five branches, the way the sugar maples open their leaves, the way the pear tree keeps shooting up, untrimmed, until its fruit is beyond reach of hand or ladder. I am childish about these matters—not childlike, but childish, sentimental, unreasonable. I remember when and where there were no trees.

OUR HOUSE GREW ON THIS LAND, literally grew here. The farmer who built it lived for years in a small white house just north of where the present house stands. Countrywise, he built a big barn and ample outbuildings before he lis-

tened to his wife's desire for a new house, but when he gave in he gave in completely. One Winter he went up on the mountain, chose the trees, felled them, trimmed them, cut them to length and skidded them down to a hollow just above the middle pasture. He cut oak and chestnut and white pine, and when the weather was right he brought in a sawmill. For days the mill must have chugged and whined, and the whole valley must have been sweet with the fragrance of fresh planks and boards. Then he stacked and seasoned his lumber.

The next year he built this house, and built it well. The subflooring is white pine. The beams and rafters are oak and chestnut. The trim and stairs are chestnut. There is a full basement, poured concrete, spacious, dry. When he had finished the house he moved in and tore down the old one, some of the boards of which probably went into a new chicken house. But he never got around to leveling off the old cellar hole. It was a two-foot hollow in the lawn until last Summer, when I filled it in and planted grass.

At the foot of the mountain the dark pile of moldering sawdust still remains. On up the mountain are the stumps, big stumps now surrounded by trees a foot through. Every time I walk that way I glance at the old sawdust pile and nod to the big stumps. That is where my house grew.

EVER SINCE MAN first was aware of Spring he has stood at this season with awe in his eyes and wonder in his heart, sensing the magnificence of life returning and life renewed; and something deep within him has responded, whatever his religion or spiritual belief. It is as inevitable as sunrise that man should see the substance of faith and hope in the tangible world so obviously responding to forces beyond himself or his accumulated knowledge.

For all his learning or sophistication, man still instinctively reaches toward that force beyond, and thus he approaches humility. Only arrogance can deny its existence, and the denial falters in the face of evidence on every hand. In every tuft of grass, in every bird, in every opening bud, there it is. We can reach so far with our explanations, and there still remains a force beyond, which touches not only the leaf, the seed, the opening petal, but man himself.

Spring is a result, not a cause. The cause lies beyond, still beyond; and it is the instinctive knowledge of this which inspires our festivals of faith and life and belief renewed, our Easters of whatever name. Resurrection is there for us to witness and participate in; but the resurrection around us remains the symbol, not the ultimate truth. And man instinctively reaches for that truth. He reaches, like the leaf itself, for something beyond, ever beyond.

EVERYWHERE THAT SPRING COMES now we look out across the hills and meadows and fields and lawns and say, "How good it is to see a green world again." And thus we pay tribute to the grasses of this earth, which are even more widespread than the trees and, in some ways, even more closely linked with mankind's life. Grass is not only the ubiquitous green of this world; it is the life-giver. Grass, which grows everywhere there is even moderately dry land and an even intermittently hospitable climate for man or beast.

Of all green-growing things, grass is one of the most humble and at the same time one of the most persistent. There are about 5,000 species of grass, some of which grow in the hottest of the tropics and others of which can be found well inside the Arctic Circle. Grass finds a foothold where nothing else but lichen can survive. It asks only a little rootage, a scant foothold, an occasional taste of moisture.

Few areas are more amazing than the vast plains where grass stretches mile after mile, native grass which was there before the first man saw those plains. Few things are more beautiful, or more taken for granted, than an eastern meadow green with Spring new-come. And who can travel the Midwest and fail to be astounded by the horizon-wide fields of that giant grass called corn? Our corn is grass, as are wheat and rye and oats and all our grains, and sugar cane and sorghum and all our forage, and even bamboo. Few of us are vegetarians, but none of us would have meat if there were no grass; our meat animals are vegetarians, grass-eaters.

Looking at my pastures this morning I could see in their live green grass the substance of milk, butter, cheese, beef, leather and a dozen other items in my wardrobe and larder.

WE FOUND MARSH MARIGOLDS TODAY. We had to wade, almost up to my boot tops, to pluck a handful. Even to find them, for that matter, for they grow in the swamps and boglands by preference, and occasionally on the banks of a slow stream, where the wild iris will be blooming in June. We found ours in a marsh beyond the river.

Only the first of them are opening bud. The flowers are like giant buttercups, with the same lacquered golden look to the petals. The resemblance is no accident, for the marigold of the marshes belongs to the same family as the buttercup of the meadows. The Latin name, *Caltha palustris*, means cup of the marsh. The marsh marigold leaves are heart-shaped, like big violet leaves.

Some call them cowslips, for no understandable reason. The true cowslip belongs to the primrose family and has no resemblance whatever to the marsh marigold. And of all the flowers of Spring, only the buttercup itself can rival the marsh marigold in color. Its waxy petals, however, are big as silver half-dollars, dwarfing even the biggest buttercups.

The place to find marsh marigolds is where the giant marsh violets grow, preferably where slow-flowing water warms their roots. They grow in shallow water or at the oozy margin of a bog and make late April a heart's delight on a brisk day. Some country folk use them for cooked greens. They have a mild flavor, not too unlike spinach, but it seems a shame to pot them. Only the first few were in bloom today, but ten days from now the bog will be carpeted with them. And before they are gone the bog will begin to turn purple with violets.

TODAY WE LOOKED FOR HEPATICA but found none, for some reason. We did find many leaves and a few blooms of bloodroot. And all over the mountainside the anemones are in blossom, both the wood anemones and their daintier cousins, the rue anemones.

Anemones are early risers among the debris of Fall and Winter. They have a life cycle to complete, leaves to spread, delicate white-petaled blossoms to open, bees to welcome, seeds to ripen and root to strengthen. Another month and there will be little sun where the anemones now stand thick, for the ferns will shadow them, the viburnum will be in full leaf, and the oaks and maples and birches will be reaching for the sun with their full leaf heads. So this is the anemones' time, now, while the April wind is still chill and the warmth of fermenting leaf mold is just beginning. Now they must get their heads above ground and open their petals, all in what amounts to one gesture, to lure the sluggish bee and get their life cycle past dead center. A month from now would be too late. Even a week from now would be dangerously late.

The anemone is a flower—one of the few—whose popular name is a literal translation of its botanical name. It is often called windflower, particularly the big wood anemone or *Anemone quinquefolia*. *Anemone* comes directly from the Greek and means "wind," the same root as the word *anemometer*, which is an instrument for measuring wind.

29

This Hill, This Valley

T. S. ELIOT SAID SOMETHING ABOUT APRIL being the cruelest month, which suited his purpose but is something less than the truth. April is cruel only as it stirs some cruel memory.

April is newness and eagerness and urgency; but all those are qualities in the observer rather than in the season. April brings newness in an old pattern, eagerness as eagerness always is, and urgency to accomplishment. Come to mid-April and you are already forgetting March and thinking ahead to May.

One year we went to Florida and back in April, and as we drove up through the Carolinas, homeward, April was almost poignant. It was a little breathless, it was so beautiful. Not only to the eye, which by then was accustomed to pristine leaves and Spring flowers, but to the skin. The touch of April was the feel of perfection. Today was like that, though squills and hyacinths and a few early tulips were the only flowers out. The temperature was in the high 50s and April was a joy to know.

ON SECOND THOUGHT, maybe Eliot was right. The sap flies are here.

My entomology is by no means conclusive, but I know that two types of insects are damned with the sap-fly name at this time of year. One is the tiny bloodsucker often called No-see-um and scientifically one of the *Culicoides*, related rather closely to the pesky but relatively painless midge. No-see-ums are also close kin to sand flies, which have a vicious bite. The other variety is the larger *Simuliidae*, the black fly and the buffalo gnat; their vigor as attackers seems to increase as the square of their volume. They can drive an unprotected man insane.

What we have here just now are the smaller ones, the No-see-ums. They always appear in swarms when the birches are leafing out, and when I walk in the woods I have to wear a handkerchief dangling beneath my cap to keep them out of my ears. I am tempted to wear goggles, too, for they get in my eyes. Their life span is brief and their stay a matter of only ten days or two weeks, but for that time they are the epitome of persistent annoyance. Spring isn't Spring without them; but Spring can't be enjoyed with them, either.

THE SAP FLIES ARE STILL HERE, but I went out today and avoided the woods and found other insects by the hundreds. Grasshoppers are swarming out of the moss clumps, or seem to be, egglings no more than half an inch long. Ants are busy again and on the predatory march. Beetles come ambling from their hiding places to sort over the Winter's litter, persistent hordes of endless variety and countless number. Most of those I saw are carrion beetles, members of the *Scarabaeidae*, the scarab family which includes the tumblebugs that fascinated me as a boy. I make no pretense at knowing more than a few beetles. Men have devoted their lives to that study and still not covered the ground, for something like 22,000 beetle species are known in America alone. I am quite sure, however, that if this world is ever inherited by the insects, the teeming legions of armored beetles will be the ruling class.

But one must look for these groundlings. Just now, when buds are opening and leaflets gleam with pristine wax, it is the winged hordes that make themselves noticed. Winged ants come swarming from rock crannies and earth tunnels to dry their gossamer and test the air. The larger bees hover at daffodil trumpets and myrtle stars and grape-hyacinth clusters. Butterflies not much larger than my thumbnail flash in the sunlight like gray and white and yellow and blue particles of confetti. I feel dazzled, but a bit consoled when I try to look them up in a handbook and find that "they puzzle even the professional," though most of them seem to be of the family known as *Lycaenidae*, a strange name for a butterfly since it comes from the Greek for she-wolf.

WE WALKED IN THE PASTURE at the foot of the mountain last night to feel and smell the season, having the notion that those senses are quickened in the darkness. But my eyes accommodate swiftly, and while Barbara was using her nose and her ears I was looking. Finally we sat down on a big rock and waited for the night to come to us. An owl flew overhead, a swift, silent shadow against the stars. In the trees up the hillside a bird called softly, almost sleepily; it sounded like a robin. There was a rustle in the grass ten feet away, and I could make out the small, dim form which watched us for a moment, then hopped away, clearly a rabbit with his white tufty tail. Then there was nothing but the soft wind and the smell of greening grass.

We watched the stars, still glittering with Winter's brilliance. The Big Dipper swings higher in the evening now than at any other time of year. We had to look high to find it, the inverted bowl well above the Pole Star. The Big Dipper, Ursa Major.

Astronomers have called it the Big Bear for thousands of years, but in the time of Homer it was also known as Mamaxa, the Wagon. A little later the Romans called it Septentriones, the Seven Plowing Oxen. Both these names came down through the years to England, where for a long time it was known as the Wagon of Charlemagne, or Charles's Wain, and where today it is usually called The Plow. Ancient Arabs saw the constellation as a coffin followed by a funeral procession; but the Arabs left little imprint on popular astronomy in the West.

American Indians had various names for Ursa Major. In one Indian legend it is a bear followed by three hunters, and in one version it is said that the middle hunter—the middle star in the Dipper's handle—is so sure of a successful hunt that he carries a cooking pot on his shoulder. Anyone with sharp eyes can see both the hunter and the pot, a large star and a small star very close together, stars which the astronomers have named Mizar and Alcor.

We saw the Indian hunter and his cooking pot tonight, for the sky was dazzling clear and there was no moon, not even a hair-thin line of a new one. Then we came back to the house, pausing at the quiet pool in Millstone Brook to watch the slowly dancing stars reflected in it.

Spring

MILLSTONE BROOK HAD NO NAME when we came
here, and it is too small and too seasonal to justify more than a
private naming. It rises halfway up the mountain in a series of
springs that make a boggy little bottom all the year around,
and it comes tumbling down a rocky hollow to spill out across
the pasture in a flow that we can step across except after a
heavy rain. It cuts across a corner of the vegetable garden, a
convenient source of water when we are setting plants, and it
goes through a culvert under the road and spills into the river
beside a huge old willow stump. It usually dries up in July and
August, but the other ten months of the year it makes a continuous chuckle where it plunges from one rocky pool to another on the mountainside, a pleasant night companion of
which we are seldom aware in the daytime.

Two Springs ago, after a heavy snow-melt and a week
of rains which made it a minor torrent and spread it over half
an acre of pasture, I went up the brook's mountain bed and
found a strange rock there. A rock peculiarly rounded, circu-
lar, with a square hole in it. I pried it loose and found it to
be a millstone, a small one, only fifteen inches in diameter and
less than three inches thick. One face of it still showed the
original grooves cut to speed the grinding. It was made of
native gray granite.

I lugged it home and asked everyone I met if there had
once been a mill on that brook. None remembered such a mill,
even in the old stories. Its size indicates that it was probably a
hand mill, or at most a mill for one household. No one around
here has ever seen one like it, and I have never found its mate.
But from it the unnamed brook got a name.

RAIN TODAY, A SLOW SPRING RAIN that gurgles
in the downspouts and drips from the big Norway spruce outside my window and makes pools beside the road. I can almost
see the hourly change in the color of the pasture, which will be
a warm green by tomorrow night, at this rate. And I can hear
the patter in the maples out front, an index to their leafing out

—there are now enough leaves, and enough leaf-spread, to make a patter in the rain.

I sit and watch the river, the way the rain swishes across its surface, and I see as one seldom sees on land the gusty way even a quiet rain falls. It comes not as a solid sheet or a steady downfall, but in waves which swish first downstream, then upstream, each swish of rain followed by a space of calm, a rainless interlude, then by another swish. These rainless pockets, as I think of them, are constantly on the move. Air currents, of course, which concentrate the rain in certain areas, gusts that whip the drops to one side or another. The action is graphic when seen on the surface of the river.

When I went down to the mailbox after lunch there was the feel of **Spring** in the rain itself as it touched my face. March rain is **cold**, biting, almost sleety. Today's rain was not warm but it **was** not uncomfortable, either. It had no sting. Albert's cows, standing out in the rain in his barnyard, chewed their cuds almost contentedly, not even moving back under the shed to escape it. I doubt that any cow has enough comprehension to know that this rain means fresh pasture soon, but if any cow can apprehend cause and effect, those cows did.

THE RAIN STOPPED EARLY last evening, but today the brooks are roaring. Barbara declared she was going to work in the garden, though it was so wet she practically

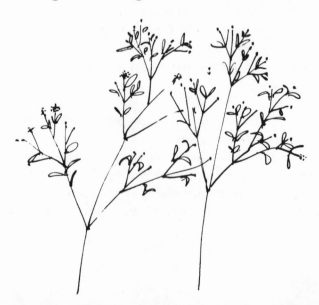

bogged down. Her peas are up—so thoroughly up, almost washed out, that they need attention. She was out there an hour, seeing that the drowned peas had their roots covered again, and she came in beaming, and mud from red cap to blue sneakers. She found new chives and thyme and winter onions, and her parsley bed is full of new shoots. She is certain that the asparagus will soon be up. Right now she is in the bathtub.

When she gets out of the tub I must tell her about Russell and his beans. Russell was a city man who wanted to know what country living was like. One year he rented a country cottage and planted a garden, by the books. A week later, making his inspection rounds before dashing to the commuter train, he saw all his beans in sight. He didn't know that a sprouting bean thrusts down a root and pushes up the bean itself which opens above ground to release the primary leaves. He saw all his beans above ground, and he hurried down the row and thrust them all back in. And wondered later why they didn't ever sprout.

A FLOCK OF CANADA GEESE went over last night. We had eaten dinner and had gone outdoors to get the feel of the dusk, and I heard the thin, distant gabble. I looked up, searched the sky, and saw them high above our valley, so high they caught the last light of the sun. They were like a thin, wavering, penciled V against the depth of the sky. We watched and listened, and they disappeared in the thin light before the sound of their gabbling was lost. It came back, a faint echo, even after they were gone. They probably are in Canada today and sometime this afternoon or tomorrow they will begin seeking out nesting places.

Geese have been persistently maligned. The old saying, "silly as a goose," has little basis in fact. Few animal groups show more wisdom than wild geese, and few birds have a more strongly developed family sense. My craft, of course, owes an enduring debt to the goose, whose quills were used to set down some of the most enduring words in the language. The word *pen* comes from the Latin *penna* through medieval English *penne*, which meant feather or quill, and the best quills were always those from the goose. Goose feathers also feathered the arrow, and thus indirectly the goose won the battle of Hastings, one of the major turning points in English history. The goose feather on a longbow arrow was, in 1066, as epochal as uranium in a bomb today.

I AM GLAD TO KNOW that the mockingbird is enlarging his range northward, and I hope the report that one was seen a few miles from here proves to be true. I'd like a few mockingbirds for neighbors. Every time we go south we hear the first mockers in Delaware or Maryland. By the time we get to the Carolinas the mocker's song is loud and persistent. In Georgia the mockingbird sings all night, and in northern Florida he sings twenty-four hours a day.

As a songster, the mockingbird is a joy and a delight. He is a whole flock of birds rolled into one. He may start off with the piercing whistle of a cardinal, play with it for a time, then go on to the robin's matin song. From that he may turn to an oriole's or a grosbeak's song, and always he makes the imitation a·good one, sometimes even better than the original. He may toss in a few jeering notes to remind one of his northern cousin, the catbird, but not too often. The mocker is too full of music for that. But as a mimic he may imitate a cat, a whistling boy, or a surly seagull.

Twenty years or so ago a pair of mockingbirds arrived one Spring in a little town I know well in eastern Colorado. It is in treeless country, but the townsmen early planted their streets with maples and Chinese elms. The mockers chose a maple and raised a family. The next Spring they came back with friends. For years the mockers came to that town each Spring and made it loud with song. Then a severe Summer hailstorm swept the town. It stripped the trees and killed many nestlings and some adult birds. Those which survived sang sad songs the rest of the Summer, then migrated. And they never came back, not one of them:

How long the days have become. This evening the sun did not set until almost six-thirty, and that is not strictly accurate because the sun sets here behind a mountain. It rose this morning at a quarter of five. I didn't see it rise, but I was up soon after. We keep country hours.

Each man's schedule should be his own business, if he can so manage. We happen to like the early hours to be awake. The world around us wakens then and gets about its business early. We catch an early-morning news and weather report on the radio and wait for late afternoon to read the morning paper. Weeks pass with the radio silent except for that dawn report.

I spent a good many years watching news tickers and reading each edition as it came from the presses. Newspapermen do that as automatically as they eat cold sandwiches and drink coffee from waxed paper cartons at their desks. But I eventually resigned that habit, along with the job, and both the world and I seem to continue unimpaired. Whether I have achieved any larger view this way I cannot say, but I am sure I have a longer view than I used to have. And if I haven't got a good many things, including my own life and place in the world, into better perspective, I have wasted many early morning hours.

I always knew that news is relative. Now I know that time is relative, too.

APRIL NEARS ITS END and the old poetry about April and Spring seems just as trite as ever. Maybe a little more so, except that of Chaucer. I know that Wordsworth and his imitators rubbed a good deal of the sheen off Spring for me, because they seemed to deal in platitudes instead of with the sweet and sentient season I could see all around me. I doubt that Wordsworth was trite when he wrote, as he seems now, for he was seeing things and saying things that few of his contemporaries saw or said. But he couldn't really capture Spring, because Spring is a vast and complex poem in itself. The old words have been worn smooth by rubbing against one another, so smooth that only the birds can warble about the season now and not sound like a parody. Man-made poems about Spring seem to be all violets and triolets, May and roundelay, buzzing bees and whispering trees. The birds do it better, much better.

WE WENT OUT THIS EVENING to welcome May which is just over the hill to the east. The dipper hung so high

we had to tilt our heads to see it and Cassiopeia was down on the horizon, half hidden by the mountain. Pegasus was out of sight in the west and Aquila had not yet risen. The evening was young.

Across the river the hylas were shrilling, with the bass counterpoint of frogs in irregular syncopation. An owl hooted from the first pines on the mountain. A breeze, carrying a sweater-chill now instead of a coat-chill, whispered among the apple trees.

Our eyes became accustomed to the darkness and we walked out into the middle pasture. We could see the stark whiteness of the big clump of paper birches at the far corner. We came to the place where birdsfoot violets purple the bank of the brook by daylight, and their fragrance momentarily seemed to fill the air.

From down the valley came the thin voice of a pup proclaiming his right to challenge the mysteries of the night. Pat listened, then turned away, not enough interested to answer. We turned back toward the house and saw the white cloud of apple blossoms in the trees back of the woodshed. When we glanced at the sky again the clock of the stars pointed to five minutes till May.

MAY

BARBARA, AS I HAVE SAID, is the vegetable gardener. I am able enough at it, but she has genius. She talks to her growing things and they listen and respond. Hers is a combination of the practical and the emotional approach to gardening. I take the recommended varieties and grow satisfying crops. She makes her own choices, uses her own methods, and gets awesome results. The Summer we came here, the last week in July, we pulled knee-high weeds from a patch six feet square and she planted lettuce before we unrolled the rugs. By late August we were eating our own lettuce and by mid-September she had head lettuce bigger than a dinner plate. Anybody else would have had pindling little leaf lettuce or heads that bolted.

This morning she is out in the lettuce bed. She plants her lettuces in a small seed bed of pulverized soil and she plants them thick. As they come up, she thins them sparingly, just enough to give them growth room. As they grow, she thins almost daily, using the thinnings for salad: tiny lettuce leaves, chopped young chives, radishes sliced paper-thin. Then, on a warm, rainy day—the rain is essential—she transplants her lettuces, two dozen at a time, into ample space, setting them at least a foot apart each way. They grow like mad. She keeps her seed bed going all Summer and transplants four to six crops, in succession. She has head lettuce from mid-June into October.

OF HER LETTUCES, Barbara says, "You can't buy Oak Leaf in the market because it bruises easily in shipping. But in the garden it heads nicely and has the tenderest flavor of all. Penn Lakes heads magnificently all Summer, heads big as cabbage, and has a better flavor than Iceberg. Bibb, a Southern variety, produces beautiful little rosettes that I like to serve whole as individual portions. Salad Bowl will head if transplanted and given plenty of room; it is the most spectacular head lettuce of all with its delicate pale green. Deer Tongue is crunchy with a fine flavor and has become our favorite. I'll chance Boston only in Spring and Fall; it's apt to bolt or fire in hot weather. Romaine, or Cos, heads all Summer long. Most lettuce seems to head properly if transplanted in pouring rain and muddy ground."

She also raises garden cress, which has the tang of water cress. And mustard, which she picks as baby stalks to add to her salads. Her curly chicory and escarole grow all through the Fall and right up until deep frost and snow; she trusses their leaves when the plants are half grown to blanch them and protect them from early frost.

THE FORSYTHIA is now at its peak, the green leaftips just beginning to show, which means the blossoms will soon fall.

While I was inspecting the forsythia at the corner of the garage I saw the season's first catbird. He saw me first and began to jeer. It sounded like: "So you're still here! Well, well! A regular old stay-at-home, aren't you? How are the strawberries doing? Ha, ha, ha! Hear that robin across the river? He thinks he can sing!" And he went into a travesty of the robin's song. Of all the birds that ever uttered a note, the catbird shows the nearest thing to a sense of humor.

EVERY WEEKEND NOW and many afternoons I see the young fishermen out, the boys on bicycles pedaling down the back roads to favorite pools on the brooks and rivers. Seeing them, I wonder if that traditional boy with the willow pole, the twine string and the bent pin ever really existed. I doubt it. He sounds to me like the imagining of someone who never caught a fish. Certainly he is gone now, if he ever did live.

These boys I see, and those I have always seen, are not interested in being picturesque. The boys today usually have nylon lines, fiberglass rods, know their leaders and flies, and know the waters they fish. They know how to fish.

Country boys know fish and fishing almost instinctively. It's a part of their growing up. When I meet a middle-aged man in waders and talk with him five minutes I find that almost invariably he says, "When I was a boy" or "Thirty years ago," and he begins to tell me the exciting things that happened right over at that bend or at the mouth of the next brook. The other evening I talked for half an hour with a fisherman in his seventies and he spent twenty-five minutes telling me about the bass and pickerel he took, fifty or sixty years ago, in the coves near the mouth of the Blackberry. He also talked about the way the shad-blow bloomed in May, the way the sun came up in the morning mist, the sheen of sunlight on water, the things that only men full of years seem to discuss with little self-consciousness.

The boys are rather bashful about such matters. But they are accumulating memories just the same. I see it in the gleam in their eyes, I hear it in the tones of their voices. They, too, know that fish are only a part of the fishing.

Spring

FIDDLEHEADS UNCURL and bright new fern fronds begin to spread themselves in the corner of the garden and on the mountainside where Dutchman's-breeches and violets are in full bloom. There is something venerable and touched with mystery in the uncurling of a fern, probably because the ferns are literally as old as the hills. Their beginnings go back millions of years. Fern fossils found in the ancient rocks show little difference from those on my own mountainside. Counterparts of lady ferns and maidenhair and wood ferns and cinnamon ferns grew here in the days when Tom's Mountain was a mud flat washed by a young, restless ocean.

For generations men were baffled by the ferns, which bore no flowers and had no visible seeds, yet throve and multiplied. They were magic plants, and those who dealt in magic believed that if only they could find the seed of the fern they would have the ultimate in mysterious power. They never found a fern "seed," of course, for ferns multiply by a complex of spores and intermediate growth in the form of prothallium, a process that takes seven years from spore to mature fern. And the process goes on so quietly and so unobtrusively that few are aware of it.

The ferns were the only vegetation on earth between 50,000,000 and 60,000,000 years ago. Flowering plants, which probably evolved from ferns, didn't appear until about 30,000,000 years ago, or even less. So the ferns are really the ancients, the old-timers, the venerable ones.

SOME PLACES ARE OVERRUN by sunflowers, some by burdock, some by mustard. Our area is overgrown by dandelions. They yellow the pastures and gild the roadsides for a few weeks at this time of year, and we all seem to feel the same way about them. They're beautiful, but they are a curse and a nuisance. They can ruin a lawn and they crowd the grass out of a meadow in only a few years. They can be cleaned out by dusting or spraying with a 2-4-D mixture, but a good many other plants, most of them desirable, are killed by the same procedure. Clover, for instance. So the farmers suffer them to grow, and plow and replant the meadows every few years and are rid of them for a season or two. Then back they come.

The dandelion, viewed dispassionately, is a beautiful flower, pretty as a calendula or an aster. But a dandelion has so many offspring! How can so flimsy a little puff of down and so minute a seed possess so much vitality? Let one beautiful dandelion go to seed at the far corner of a lawn or garden to-day, and the next week you have dandelions all over the place. A dandelion will grow in a crack in a cement sidewalk. It will grow on an ash heap. Neither flood nor drought seems to discourage it. The lawn mower merely encourages it to greater effort. I spend a week every year dosing the dandelions on the lawn, individually, with a weed killer, and thus I keep them fairly well in check. But the pastures are full of them, and each year they seed the lawn again. Albert and Charley and all the other farmers curse them and fight them from time to time, but there they are, beautiful and as vigorous a pest as you will meet in a week of Sundays.

BARBARA CALLS HIM MR. DAFFODIL, but I call him Mr. Spring. Barbara called to me this morning, "Mr. Daffodil is here!" and I went to my study window and saw him on the garden fence, brilliant yellow and shining black, the first of the season's goldfinches. He sat there, preening in the sunlight, then came down on the lawn and strutted and took the attention from every other bird in sight.

The goldfinch comes to us just ahead of the warblers, which are the only other birds with so clear a yellow and so much of it in their plumage. He does, as Barbara says, rival

44

the daffodil in color, and his color is heightened by contrast with the black of his forehead, his wings and his tail. On a dark day, he is like a burst of sunshine. And when he sings to his more sedately colored mate it is with all the sweetness and fervor such a bird should possess. He is one of the relatively few brilliant birds with a really rich song. The name "wild canary," occasionally applied to him, comes from his song as much as from his color. And he sings a good part of the season.

With the coming of Autumn he changes his plumage to a kind of olive green, much like the color of his mate, and thus he travels to his wintering ground, full of seeds and throbbing with life. Friends tell me that goldfinches winter on Long Island, but I still think of them as long-range migrants. But migration and traveling clothes are far away from him now. Here he is, resplendent and busy and full of song. He wouldn't need to sing a note, however, to get our admiration. He even *looks* like Mr. Spring. Or Mr. Daffodil.

THE APPLE TREES ARE IN BLOOM, and a magnificent sight, breathtaking in their expanse of profligate blossom. Downwind I can smell their fragrance a quarter of a mile away. When I walk down the road and look back I think nothing can be more beautiful than this place with its dozen apple trees in full flower.

Once the pasture closest to the house was an orchard, I am told. But the trees, judging by the size of a few stumps remaining, grew large and old and perhaps a little weary. And the apple market waned. I am sure the deer enjoyed the windfalls and the grouse came down from the mountain in snowy Winter to feed on the buds. But the economic reason for the orchard vanished, and the trees were cut and burned and the orchard became another pasture. Someone, however, had the good sense to leave a dozen of the trees here at the edge of the yard. They are big trees, and they would make a modern orchardist turn away in disgust, for they have gone unpruned for years. But they are beautiful, especially now.

There was a small peach orchard, too, up the mountainside. The peach trees died out, all but two, long ago. Those two stand now in a natural open space among the white pines beside the path that leads to the springhouse, and in a few days they will be lush with pink. They never seem to bring fruit to ripeness, but their blossom is a delight, though one has to climb the mountain to see it.

And there were pears. When the orchard was cut down the axmen left four pear trees at the far edge of the home pasture, and they, too, are in blossom now. About one year in three they come to fruit. Last year I picked two bushels of fine, large, red-flushed pears from them. But the pear tree beside the garden is of another generation, younger and of a different variety, a small green pear that ripens to a faint yellow, halfway in size between the Seckel pear and the big Bartletts in the pasture. Our garden pear bears prodigiously, and just now it is opening into a blaze of spicy white bloom.

I would have fruit trees around me for their blossoms, even if they bore no fruit. Just now it is like being surrounded by giant bouquets, and Barbara says it is better than living in a florist's shop.

WE HEARD THE SEASON's first whippoorwill last night. The earliest I ever heard one here was April 24, and sometimes they don't seem to be around until the last week in May. The one last night sounded off only a few minutes, but come the warm June nights and he will make the darkness echo.

If the whippoorwill uttered its call as most birds do, pausing for breath and looking around between phrases, it would be only another bird. But it doesn't do things that way. It starts that three-note call and keeps on going with what must be the most repetitious bird call ever uttered. I listen to its start and wonder how long it will continue. I count, and just as I am almost hypnotized by the rhythm the bird skips half a beat, then goes on and on. One night, just before midnight, I lay and counted 187 calls without an interruption.

Maudie, who once had a whippoorwill nest in her side yard, tells me that the fledglings have to be taught the call, note by note. She listened to this educational process and says the youngsters got the notes backward at first, muddled the tones and became so confused that they merely gurgled. Then the parent birds, who set the initial example, set it again and the youngsters started all over. It was a week before the youngsters managed two or three successive "whip poor Wills," at which there was much parental to-do. After that came long practice sessions, which almost drove the listener mad. It was six weeks before the youngsters learned to say "whip poor Will" ten times in a row without a mistake.

The one we heard last night was so close we could hear the faint "uh" before each "whip" in the call.

TRILLIUMS ARE IN BLOOM, if you know where to find them, the purplish red wake-robins, the shy nodding trilliums with white petals and long sepals, the large flowering trillium, and the painted trillium with wavy edged white petals with a crimson *V* on them. Farther south there are dwarf whites, too, the earliest to bloom, but in my area there are only these four; and in the woods I know I find only two, *Trillium erectum*, the wake-robin, and *Trillium cernuum*, the nodding variety.

There is an inherent trinity about the trilliums that made them of special interest to early herbalists, who credited the number three with special significance. Each plant has three leaves whorled about its stem, broad, intricately veined leaves of rich green. The flower, no matter what its color, has three long sepals which open to reveal the three petals. And the flower in all its parts is threefold. The flower withers, in its time, and a berry, usually red, takes its place; and the sepals remain, brownish, papery ribbons at the berry's base.

Any of the trilliums are exotically beautiful on a sunny afternoon, their petals wide, or on a damp morning after a slow rain, the petals closed and the long sepals like protecting green fingers around them. But if you want fragrance with your color, keep the trillium at arm's length. The odor it has was designed to attract carrion flies.

THE LILACS' HEADY FRAGRANCE comes in the open windows from all directions this morning, for we are well shrubbed with lilacs, some of them bushes ten feet high which grew beside the old house that was torn down when this one was built.

Yesterday I saw the flash of lilac color on a brushy pasture hillside several miles from here and half a mile from the nearest house. It was an old bush, older than our oldest ones, and it grew beside a shallow depression, the almost vanished trace of a cellar hole from a house long gone. It was testimonial to a New England farm wife who once planted a lilac sucker beside her house and watched it grow and smelled its sweetness and probably died in her early thirties. She is long gone, but her lilac bush lives on, seen only by the placid cows and curious passers-by like me.

All across America lilacs are perfuming the air. We took this shrub to our hearts long ago and have kept it there through the years. In our latitude it is practically symbolic of May. It sweetens the breath of Springtime.

THERE WERE DESK CHORES this morning, but I hurried through the pressing ones and left the others and went out of doors. There is so much to see out there! I went down to the apple trees, with the bees, down to see my little roses, the apple blossoms, which are going fast.

Prehistoric man ate apples, on accepted evidence, and even cultivated them in Europe. And, being human, he no doubt enjoyed the beauty of their blossoms. I shouldn't be surprised if prehistoric woman wore apple blossoms in her hair.

Examine an apple blossom. It is, indeed, a small rose, five-petaled and full of fragrance. Its bud was almost the same as that of the wild roses, the pasture roses which grow beside the fence up at the foot of the mountain. As the apple blossom's sepals opened, the blossom had the same soft, lovely color on its furled petals that marks the wild rose which will be blooming next month. It, too, has many stamens, like the rose, each cinnamon-tipped. Its fragrance is like that of a wild rose

slightly spiced and—perhaps I am imagining—faintly touched with cider. And when the petals fall this blossom too forms a hip, a bulbous fruit, but far bigger and sweeter than any rose hip that ever reddened.

Our roses won't be opening for another month, but this morning I have had a special rose festival with my little beauties, my gigantic rose bouquets, my apple trees in blossom.

THERE ARE MORE CONSPICUOUS FLOWERS, plenty of them, but of all our wildflowers I think we look forward most eagerly to the showy orchis, *orchis spectabilis*, as the botanists know it. It blooms just after the big trillium, with the crab apples and when the bloodroot begins to fade. We found a dozen orchises in bloom today.

Anna, who knows all the wildlings and where they grow, showed us our first orchis on a hillside ten miles from here. But today we went to a rocky hollow on our own hillside, where hemlocks grow and where last year's ash leaves lie deep and moldering. Bloodroot grows there profusely, and the dainty wood anemones, and the ground is thick with the heart-leaves of wild ginger. Nearby is a patch of moccasin flowers. Even though we knew the orchises were there, we had to search. Last year they were beside this rock, close to that tree, over at the edge of the trickle from the seep spring. But still we had to crouch and part the bloodroot canopy to find them. There they were, the deep green twin leaves, broad and rounded and much like small moccasin-flower leaves. Between the leaves rose the flower stem bearing the purplish magenta hood, the white lip, the perfect flower, more dainty than a hothouse orchid. This orchis is small, no more than three-quarters of an inch across, and by no means spectacular; the casual searcher will overlook it completely, particularly if a few moccasin flowers are in bloom. But it is beautiful, a precious gem of a flower.

The best way for an outlander to find the showy orchis is to know someone familiar with every nook and cranny of the hills. And even that person must love the wildlings. You find such a person and ask about showy orchis. The talk pauses. The prospective guide sizes you up. If you have even a hint of the flower vandal in your look or manner the whole venture is hopeless. But if you are fortunate, if your integrity is obvious, you will be expertly guided to the place where the orchis blooms.

"What did you say your name was? Where are you from? Are you sure you mean orchis, not orchid . . . ? It's quite a climb, and maybe they aren't out yet. You'll probably get scuffed and muddy. . . . Oh, you want a bouquet. Come to think of it, there's a big tree down over the only path. No, you couldn't possibly find the place yourself. If it's a bouquet you want, take some of that yellow rocket over there. Or some violets. They're much prettier."

IT RAINED THIS MORNING and brought down a snowstorm of apple blossoms. The yard looked as though a fragment of January had struck it, leaving drifts of petals. But it cleared by noon and we went fishing. I forked up a plot where Barbara wants to put her next lettuce transplants and got a canful of worms.

Some fish by ritual, but we fish for fun and for the pan. We make it an excuse to get out on the water, relax in the sun and watch the slow flow of the river. As I say, we frankly fish for the pan and the freezer, though when we hook a trout or a big bass or a pickerel we have our excitement, too. Most of our catch, though, is rock bass and yellow perch, both good eating. They keep us in filets for chowder or for a baked-fish dish Barbara makes most of the Winter, thanks to the freezer.

With the boat, a 12-footer built for comfort rather than for speed, we fish several miles of the river. And our section of the river is a comfortable, hospitable stream, 200 feet or more wide, almost free of surfacing rocks, and six to twelve or fourteen feet deep. Its current is only about a mile an hour, for

our part of the stream is leisurely, much different from what it is ten miles lower down; with us it meanders over the flatland of the broad valley, but lower down it hurries and whitens through rugged hills and sharp valleys.

Because the river is so slow up here it responds quickly to storm, its level rising a foot after half an inch of rain; and in Spring and Fall, when the hard rains come and the snow melts, it sweeps majestically along in semi-flood, three feet over our dock.

The river's swift changes, its temperamental ways, keep altering its bed somewhat, scouring it here, lodging new snags and brush there, cleaning out one hole and gouging out another. So each Spring we have a new river, in a sense, to explore, at least in terms of fishing. One year the perch swarmed at Dead Cedar Hole. The next year we didn't catch a perch there. One Spring there was good bass fishing at Deep Hole; by midsummer it was deserted. So we have to investigate, see what is the state of the fish world and the underwater feeding, at the Big Bend, at Sunday Cove, at Snag Hole, at The Rocks, at King Bird Hole, and all the other places we have named.

Today we went up to Deep Hole, caught two big rock bass there, then drifted down to Dead Cedar Hole, and Barbara took two seven-inch bluegills. Drifting again, we came to the Channel Behind the Island and rock bass bit like mad, most of them little ones to be thrown back. On down to Apple Blossom Hole and the perch began to feed.

Trout fishermen will laugh in scorn at the perch fisherman, but we like perch, fileted and fried exactly right. That's the way they were tonight, and I am content with my world. A bit sunburned, too, on the back of the neck.

A FEW YEARS AGO I wrote a piece about a remote spot in Colorado that I have admired since I was a boy. Today I had a letter from Jim, who is a judge and has lived there for years. "Last week," Judge Jim wrote, "I went up to Lost Lake, the country you wrote about, and flicked a few flies over the water. Not a strike. I wonder what happened to all those big trout."

I first knew that country as a boy when I went with my father to Lost Lake, in the high country. We went in by saddle and pack horse and it was early dusk when we reached the lake. Father said, "I'll make camp. Suppose you see if you can catch something for supper." I jointed up a fly rod and strung a line and took the first leader in the box, one that had a Royal Coachman on it and a bare snelled hook on the second loop. In my haste I didn't even take off the snelled hook. I ran to the edge of the lake, cast, and instantly there was a rush that almost took the rod from my hand. I played my fish and was lucky, and since I had forgotten a landing net I dragged my catch up on the sloping bank. I had not one lake trout, but two, both good size though I am sure not as long as my arm, as I remember. One had taken the fly, the other the bare hook. The lake swarmed with trout and they were ravenous.

We gorged on lake trout that night and the next day, and we took enough of them back with us to treat all our friends in town. Father said it wasn't much fun, fishing that way, but it made me feel like Bucky O'Neil, the best fisherman in that end of Colorado.

And now Judge Jim can't even get a strike in Lost Lake. Maybe I'm not doing so bad here on the Housatonic.

Spring

THERE IS A NOTION, a persistent idea, that anything with a depth of meaning must be hard to understand, written in a difficult language and reserved for the knowledge of the few. Yet here is May, a time of tremendous fundamentals and miraculous matters, all of them spread before us and flagrantly demanding attention. May, which speaks a language as simple as a new leaf or a buttercup flower.

Here is the fundamental of life, the whole process of germination and growth. Here is flowering fertility and life preparing its own renewal. Here are sunlight and water being turned into food by a process called photosynthesis, which is even more profound than atomic fission. Photosynthesis goes on in every blade of grass, every leaf, every weed at the roadside, no more secret than sunlight. Here is abundance and growth and munificence, so much of it that the world seems hard put to contain it all. It constantly spills over, outreaching itself in abundance.

Therein lies another of May's profundities: One of the fundamental laws of this world is plenty, not scarcity; production, not destruction; growth, not stagnation.

SHOWERS TODAY. Transplanting weather. We were out in the garden transplanting lettuce and weeding everything but the beans and the peas. Beans should be weeded dry, and peas should be weeded lightly if at all. Barbara has a theory about peas. She believes that you should leave most of the weeds in the pea rows to shade and cool the roots on hot days. The roots of the peas are sensitive to both heat and disturbance. That's where the hot-day damage is done, to the roots. Pull all the weeds and you not only disturb the fine rooting but you leave the soil open to the scorching sun. So we weed the peas only a little, and we get big yields and get them for several weeks.

But elsewhere we weed vigorously, using the hoe only to loosen the soil and hill up the rows. A cut weed isn't even discouraged for long; but a weed pulled up by the roots and left naked for an hour in a hot sun is usually finished. Besides, weeding aerates the soil, keeps it from packing.

We are always tempted to plant corn earlier than we should, and sometimes do. But it is our experience that corn planted in May, in this area at least, sulks and shivers and sometimes rots. If it sprouts, it usually huddles and waits for June. And the corn we plant in early June always seems to catch up with it.

In the flower garden the Shirley poppies amaze me day by day, growing like mad. We scatter seed in the Fall, some sprout and winter over, and the others come early. All of them bloom before we expect them, pleasant surprises. There are buds on some of them already, though they aren't six inches tall.

I SHOT A WOODCHUCK this morning, the first we have seen this year though they were out in early April. This one was on his way to the succulence of the vegetable garden when I interrupted him with a .22 bullet. I buried him unshriven, hoping Pat wouldn't find the spot. Pat considers himself the woodchuck policeman around here, but he is not above digging up one I have buried and making himself socially undesirable. He considers ripe woodchuck an entrancing odor.

Some years ago I wrote a lighthearted, good-natured essay on the woodchuck. I was most friendly. At that time we had had no woodchuck troubles. The essay appeared in print in February. Two months later the woodchucks began to converge. They cleaned out the beans. They ate the young peas. They made a salad of lettuce tops and beets, even depredated the cucumbers. I shot eleven woodchucks in the garden that Summer, and I haven't had a generous thought about woodchucks since.

No woodchuck is welcome within a hundred yards of our garden. There is provender aplenty up on the mountain, the kind of food woodchucks have been eating and thriving on for many generations. Let them stay where they belong and I shall not disturb them. But down here they are going to meet trouble, and I am a better-than-average shot. And much the same goes for the rabbits, who have the pastures and the woodland for their own range.

Spring

WE ALL HAVE OUR SUMMATION DAYS, when we draw a figurative line and tot up both the year and the years. Today happens to be mine, my anniversary, the day of my birth.

I am not summarizing, however. I am thinking how fortunate I am. And I am thinking how much any child of mid-May has to be thankful for. When he is young he can say: "The robin sings for me, and the oriole, and the lilacs bloom today. The trout are eager in the brook. Summer is not yet here, but close at hand. My years begin with song."

When he comes to be middle-aged he can say: "Another Winter is over and gone, and the earth resumes its vigor. My years are like the season, at their flowering, new growth on old stems and the strength of maturity in the trunk."

And when the years amount to age he can say: "I have seen the season turn with the sun, all my days, and each year I feel the growing warmth as my world turns green. My years are Spring, all of them, Spring returning like a promise and a fragrant fulfillment."

TIME IS A STRANGE COMMODITY, repeating and repeating itself. Mid-May was here last year, and ten years ago, and ten centuries ago, and here it is again. I wasn't here, but someone else was, ten centuries ago. Two hundred years ago Indians were here, on this particular land where now I live. An Indian of my age stood here and looked across the river on this day and saw the sun rise at the same moment that it rose this morning. And now those who speculate on such matters say that probably still earlier men were here before the last Ice Age, perhaps as long as 100,000 years ago. Whether this is true or not, this day 100,000 years ago was just as long as it is today. If man was here he just happened to partake of that particular fragment of time. He experienced it without altering it in the slightest. It slid over him with even less effect than on the hills around him, except that when that day ended he was one day older, one day nearer extinction.

We try to measure time, build machines to tick it off in seconds, as though thus to gain possession of it, feeling that we

can better grasp it in little bits. And all we do is harness ourselves to machines which tick, tick, tick.

We live in the midst of time, and the more we try to possess it, the more it possesses us. The real need is not for
possession of time but for possession of ourselves. Yesterday
was not so much a gauge of time, of my years, as it was a gauge
of me, of what I have done with the fragment of time that I
have known.

I HAVE PLANNED FOR YEARS to keep an ac-
curate and orderly journal of first bloom among the early
flowers, but I never quite achieved it. I go poking around in
early March and come home and make my notes. A few days
later I look again and forget to make the entries. April comes
and I make a list, knowing that I have missed a dozen entries.
Then May is here and I have missed the premieres of half the
blossoms, so I merely note that I have now seen them in full
bloom.

Today I have leafed back through the daily journals of half a dozen years and I find that one year I said on May 16: "Saw the first buttercup today. Columbines about to open." Another May 16 I wrote, "Dogwood is superb." Still another year the entry was: "Anemones out in clouds. Jack-in-the-pulpit everywhere. Trilliums (small) out, and yellow violets." And another year my May 16 comment was: "A very nasty hailstorm brought down most of the apple blossoms and ruined most of the lilacs, which were full out."

These entries are less an index of blossom time than an index of my own preoccupations. Elsewhere I found a record, for instance, of rue anemone in bloom on March 20, of lilacs full out on May 5, of buttercups in April.

No two years' seasons are alike, and no flower ever grew which came to blossom by the clock or calendar. The Time of First Bloom is a movable feast, not quite as movable as Easter but certainly one that has scant relation to man-made dates.

PAT HAS BEEN GONE ALL DAY. I wonder if he is on a binge. This is the season. But now we understand.

One Spring he took off up the road and was gone all day and night. The next day Charley phoned to say that Pat was up there, with a nondescript little bitch that had strayed in from somewhere. I went up and got Pat and tied him up here at home. Normally I can tie Pat with a length of twine and he stays, observing even a token tether. This day I used a rope, and within five minutes he bit it through and was gone. That afternoon I fetched him home again and tied him with a heavier rope. It balked him fifteen minutes. Once more I went and got him, and that time I put him on a chain. He moaned all night, and the next morning he pleaded bitterly for freedom. I let him go. He went back to Charley's.

Meanwhile, Charley had called the dog warden and got rid of the stray bitch. But Pat wouldn't accept her absence as permanent. He made a nuisance of himself for two more days, howling for his lost love at Charley's and howling for his freedom when confined here. So I phoned the dog warden.

Dave, the warden, said he thought he knew the solution. There was a farmer twenty-odd miles from here, a man who liked dogs, who would like to have such a dog as Pat. Pat should be happy there. So we bade Pat good-by and Dave took him in his pickup, and we told each other that it had been nice knowing Pat, that he had never done a mean or sneaky thing, and he was going to have a good home. We would miss him, but obviously he didn't want to live here any longer.

For two days we missed him everywhere we turned. Charley stopped past and we talked for ten minutes, about everything except dogs, both of us knowing we were avoiding the one topic we wanted to talk about. Then, as Charley left, he said, "I hope that fellow treats old Pat right. Hope he takes him hunting." He got in his car and hurried off.

That evening Charley phoned. His voice was full of pleased but controlled emotion. "Want a dog?" he asked.

"What's his name?" I asked, sensing the answer.

Charley laughed. "Pat's here! Just got here. Footsore and tired out. Ate like he hadn't had a full meal in a week."

"I'll come get him," I said.

"Let him sleep," Charley said. "Just thought you'd like to know he's back."

The next morning when I got up Pat was asleep on the front porch. I let him in and he greeted me with a quick lick at my hands, then looked away, shamefaced, and went to his place in the living room and lay down, as though renewing his claim. And that was that. I phoned Dave, the warden, and he said the farmer where he took Pat had reported that Pat left there the first evening.

The next Spring Pat was gone for two days, we never knew where, and came home tired and repentant. Now he is gone again. But he'll be back. If he doesn't come back we shall just remember what a gentleman he was, and we shall know that he had to go wherever he has gone.

I WENT UP THE MOUNTAIN ALONE TODAY, trying not to think of Pat or listen for his voice. And on a rocky slope which catches the full warmth of the sun I found a mass of columbine in bloom, a great spread of crimson and gold and silvery blue-green foliage. After looking at my records a couple of days ago I judge that they are blooming about on schedule.

These eastern columbines have small petals and long spurs, petals yellow as buttercups, of which they are botanical cousins. Evolution somehow not only made the columbine quite different from the buttercup but all but did away with the columbine's petals in achieving the flower's long, scarlet spurs, which are ingenious nectar pouches to lure the bees.

I can marvel at the results of evolution, but in the case of the columbine I am also baffled. In our flower garden we have Colorado columbines which just now are opening bud. Their flowers at their most magnificent are four inches across, with big petals and long spurs, beautiful things of a blue like the May sky in Colorado. You could almost hide an eastern wild columbine beneath one petal of those Colorado columbines.

Here is the puzzler: Our Colorado columbines are also wildlings, the result of undisturbed natural selection and evolution. They were grown from wild columbine seed gathered in Colorado. Why did evolution, from the same base stalk, produce the little red and yellow columbines native to my mountainside here and the huge blue ones on a Colorado mountain two thousand miles from here?

We have baltimore orioles all over the place. Two pairs of them are nesting in the big maples just across the road from the house, weaving their pouch nests far out at the tips of swaying branches. Oriole nests are always woven, an in-and-out weaving of hairs, strings and plant fibers that forms a kind of rough fabric. Looking at such a nest—I gathered several of them last Fall, to examine their texture and materials —I can see the far-back origins of the shirt I am wearing; for I have no doubt that ancient man—more likely, woman— learned weaving from the nest-building of birds. There is nothing else in nature that could have set a similar example.

Weaving and the knot, fundamentally allied, seem to me among the most remarkable of man's early inventions. They called for an unusual combination of imagination and manual dexterity. The wheel was there all the time, in any rolling log. But the discoverer of weaving had to see in his mind's eye what would happen if a certain crossing of fibers were continued, to envisage a length of fabric as the result.

There is always the temptation to minimize the quality of the primitive mind. Within the field of its own necessities, I suspect that the primitive mind was of very high quality indeed. Certainly the early stone tools and instruments were splendidly conceived and executed. The invention of the bow and arrow was not a result of second-rate thinking; and the atl-atl, or spear thrower, was more than a display of ingenuity. But these were inventions to project weapons and missiles beyond normal manual reach, to catch food or repel enemies. Weaving, if one excepts fish nets, was essentially a domestic achievement, for personal comfort and adornment. The weaver was a peaceful person, and I pay him homage. His was one of the basic arts.

PAT CAME HOME. He was on the front porch, sound asleep, when I got up this morning. He heard me and asked to come in, and went to his own place in the living room. He has spent a rugged two days somewhere. We welcomed him, but without the eagerness we felt inside. He is penitent, and we aren't going to ease his penitence too much or too soon. No fatted calf for him. All he got was a big bowl of corn flakes and milk, followed by a big can of mixed dog food when he was still hungry.

He is asleep here in my study as I write, so sound and weary a sleep he doesn't even twitch as he so often does, or utter those muffled little yips which persuade me that dogs dream as certainly as humans do. He is sleeping the utterly worn-out sleep of a tired dog, and I won't disturb him. I believe in letting lying dogs sleep.

TURN OF SPEECH, as we call it, is a strange and personal matter. It sums up the personal approach to an idea.

By tradition, we expect a tart economy of words from New Englanders, for example, as though they spent long Summer days and Winter evenings mulling ideas and shaping them to a few pungent phrases, whittling away every sliver of excess. Actually, some of the most talkative people I know are New Englanders and some of the most laconic are Westerners. Pungency of speech is an individual matter, not one of regions.

Today we saw, for the first time in months, an elderly woman who has had troubles, as we say. Her most recent trouble was the death of a son in an accident. She said, "I'm glad it was a sudden death. A dying death is hard." And, speaking of the trials and difficulties of her life, she said, "I guess you've got to know the low to know the high."

The strange thing to me is that this woman is the widow of a college professor, well read, traveled, long a city person. But she came from a Midwestern state, from a farm family. She seemed today to revert to her childhood background, perhaps unconsciously quoting phrases she heard from a pioneer grandmother. I suspect that we all, at one time or another, speak in such echoes out of our own past.

Spring

THERE WAS A violent electrical storm today, followed by a slashing rain that lasted only a quarter of an hour.

Thunderstorms fascinate me, perhaps because they are such in-the-raw manifestations of natural forces. The meteorologists say that the energy released in one medium-sized electrical storm is considerably greater than that expended in one ordinary atomic bomb explosion. Most of that energy, of course, is expended in the air, in sheer noise; but when one small sliver of lightning touches a tree, that tree often explodes, a more complete explosion than any charge of dynamite ever generated. If the whole potential of today's thunderstorm had been concentrated in one flash directed at Tom's Mountain, it probably would have left us, if at all, living on the verge of a chasm. And Tom's Mountain is no mean hill.

Our storm today, as usual, boomed and echoed and shot its bolts from cloud to cloud, and there was the sweet ozone smell just ahead of the rain smell, the exhilarating ozone created by electrical discharges through the atmosphere. Then the clean, cool rain smell, with a wind ahead of it, and after the

smell came the rain, charging down the river on a million pattering feet. It rained like mad for a few minutes, then the clouds broke, the sun shone and the road steamed. But the river was littered with river-bank debris for an hour.

As far as I can see, of all that tremendous bombardment not one bolt struck a tree within half a mile of here. Only God knows how many million or billion volts of energy were shot off harmlessly in the air. There is still, an hour later, a hint of ozone, and the air is sweet and dustless and fresh and clean.

THE FIRST OF THE SWEET CORN IS UP, and we hope for an early crop. More will be planted this week, for a succession to keep us in corn until frost.

We have tried a dozen varieties of sweet corn, and we have tried to simplify by planting what are advertised as successions, different varieties which you plant in one burst of energy on the same day and which come to ear and ripeness at different times. Sometimes they work, sometimes they don't. One year we planted a succession of eight varieties, which were to be ready at one-week intervals. They came along beautifully and we thought we had the whole problem in hand. Then came a spell of hot, dry weather, and every ear of that corn was ready to pick within less than two weeks.

So now we plant only a few varieties, variants of Marcross and Golden Bantam, mostly, but a few rows of Lincoln too. But we plant them in series, a few rows every two weeks, from mid-May till the latter part of June. This nearly always gives us corn when we want it. Our heaviest planting is the one in June's second week. That is for the freezer. We have found that corn is one of the most satisfying of all things we put in the freezer from the garden. We are always pleased with the strawberries we freeze, and with the small wild black-cap raspberries, and with the asparagus and the sweet corn.

Some freeze their corn on the cob. We cut it off, for economy of space. We think it tastes better, too. We have kept our frozen corn a year and a half, on occasion, and found it as good then as it was two months after freezing.

WHOEVER FIRST USED THE EXPRESSION "getting your feet on the ground" had a pretty good idea of the relative importance of things. The job of tilling the soil doesn't automatically confer wisdom or rectitude on the tiller, but anyone who deals with the earth and the seasons, even in the way of a back-yard garden, has a better sense of time and a better sense of proportion. You can't talk a weed out of existence or arbitrate with a bean beetle. And you can't pass a law that will compel a tomato to mature in sixty days.

The soil isn't temperamental, and it isn't given to ideological argument. You plant and cultivate, and you take precautions against bugs and blight, and usually you harvest. You do your share, and the soil does its share, and the job gets done.

The primary requisite is that one not be afraid to get his hands in the soil and that he keep his feet on the ground.

DECORATION DAY, and May at its close, and June and Summer are here at hand. May, which came in with daffodils and goes out with peonies ready to burst bud and lilacs fading, and in between almost all the flowers of Spring. That's May for you, and you can count on it as on few months in the year. It may start cold or it may start late, but before it comes to its end May has fulfilled its promises. It is no welsher's month.

Regardless of calendars and solstices, May is the height of Spring and when it ends Summer begins. With roses, true, and often with a few fine Spring days. Those wondrous pastel greens that were new leaves, different for every tree in the woodland, have now merged into Summer greens, so like each other that the eye can scarcely tell a maple from a birch on a still day and on a hillside across the valley. The meadow grass that was not yet ready for pasturing when April ended is now almost ready for the first mowing; and what rural chore is more completely Summer work than haying? The orchards that were leafing out a month ago have shed their bloom and set fruit.

There is a cold certainty about January, and August is ripe as sweet corn. But May is all growth and flowering, from the last of the bloodroot to the first of the daisies and buttercups. May is new as a baby radish, prime as a scallion, sweet as a swamp violet. May is full of bird song, bee hum, flowing brooks. Here it is, and almost gone; and having lived with it again, having felt its pulse and exaltation, I know that any year with May in it is a year worth living.

THERE IS A SWEETNESS at May's end that no other time of the year can equal. And by sweetness I mean more than flower fragrance or honey taste; this is the greater sweetness of understanding and emotion, the glow of pleasure in being.

This is the sensory season. Trees are in leaf and it is a

green world full of elusive fragrances. Walk through an orchard and you can smell as well as feel the strength of grass underfoot, new grass reaching toward the sun. Boughs naked only a little while ago, then bright and heady with blossom, now rustle with leaf and tingle with the strength of fruition. When I pause to listen I can almost hear the flow of sap and the mysterious workings of chlorophyll.

The hills are rounded with their own green growth, the soft hills of lush and friendly land. The valleys sing with running water, valleys that have not yet felt the thirst of Summer. Even the rocks are alive with vine, the creeping tendrils of life that would root in granite and suck faint sustenance from sandstone.

We walked up to the shoulder of the mountain today and looked far across the valley, to the green fields and the green of woodlands and the shadow of valleys. The air vibrated with bird song, which is the great rhythm made palpable to the ear. All the senses tingled, alive with the season as the world itself is alive. Nothing was impossible. High achievement was all around us, beating on every one of our senses for recognition.

JUNE

I NEVER REMEMBER IN APRIL how tall the grass will be in the pastures and hay fields by June. Or that daisies will frost the fence row and buttercups gild the meadow. I forget that choke-cherries will be in bloom with their sharp-tanged fragrance, and that June is other things than roses and honeysuckle.

June is really a time of relative quiet, serenity after the rush of sprouting and leafing and flowering and before the fierce heat that drives toward maturity and seed. June's air can be as sweet as the wild strawberries that will grace its middle weeks, sweet as clover, a sweetness that might be cloying if it weren't still so new.

Birds are still singing at their best, not only morning and evening but all through the day. The oriole, the tanager and the robin can make an early day vibrate with song, and a part of the song seemed this morning to be in the air even when I couldn't hear a bird note. The rasping that is July and August, the scraping of cicadas and all their kin, is yet in abeyance. June doesn't assault the ears. It flatters them and softens the call of the frog and the whippoorwill and is a joy.

These things I seem to have to learn all over again each June, and I wonder how I could have forgotten. I shall forget them again, and next March I shall think of June and roses and wonder what else it was that made last June so wonderful. Then June will come again and I shall find it a happy memory rediscovered and ready to live again.

ROBERT BRIDGES SAID, "Beauty is the best of all we know." I wonder if beauty doesn't also bring out the best of all we are. That takes me over into the verge of aesthetics, where the study of the beautiful always follows the practice. Man made and worked in the materials of beauty before he tried to explain what beauty is. Theory followed the thing itself, and at some distance. The beauty itself came from inside, instinctive; analysis was imposed upon it from outside. The created beauty was a sum of certain elements, and when the analysis took it apart, to study it piece by piece, all that remained was the pieces. The analysts never could put it back together quite the same way they found it. It lacked some mysterious quality; it was only the sum of its parts, not a whole any longer.

I am thinking of today, a June day that had its particular beauty. If I try to analyze it, it was considerably less than perfect. It had fifteen hours of sunlight. The temperature reached the high 80s, too warm for seedlings in the garden. There were occasional clouds, but no shower, although we need rain. Even the morning was hot, and this evening has a touch of sultriness. When I take it apart it wasn't a beautiful day at all. But as long as I left it alone, a day complete, it was beautiful, a part of the best of all I know.

THERE ARE ALL KINDS OF FISHERMEN, as well as persons who do not fish at all. Probably the most baffling of the cult are the still-fishermen, those who spend hours in a small boat or on the bank with a bamboo pole or a bait rod, apparently sitting in the sun with no pressing purpose, no worries, no energy. Nonfishermen shake their heads in bafflement. Fly fishermen smile condescendingly. But the still-fishermen go right on fishing, for perch and bluegills, bullheads, even the lowly rock bass. Pan-fishing, some call it; they fish not only to catch fish, but to eat them. And usually they fish with worms for bait.

Still-fishermen are generally quiet, patient folk with a touch of poetry in their souls. They seldom talk about it, but they find something soothing and reassuring in a river bank or a pond, at dawn, at dusk, even at midday when the fish seldom bite. They know the quiet waters, these fishermen, and the look of a mud turtle on a log, the quick beat of a kingfisher's wings, the flash of a dragonfly. They know sunrise and sunset. They know where a man can have an hour's meditation between bites as well as where he can be kept so busy he has no time for thought or worry.

Fishing is not all catching fish, by any means; but I think it is well to come home with your supper. And what better supper for any fisherman than a couple of fat, 12-inch yellow perch? Some may argue the point, but few of the dissenters will be still-fishermen; most of them agree that any man's choice is his own catch. Worm-fishing breeds individualism and tolerance in about equal proportions. I don't recall ever hearing of a bait rod or a bamboo pole being used to pound an opinion into a dissenter's head.

FLAX, plain old-fashioned blue flax, comes to bloom in a corner of the flower garden, and if there is a more beautiful floral blue than that of a flax flower one hour after sunrise I have yet to see it. Forget-me-nots, bluets, even spider-wort, cannot match it. Blue-eyed grass, out in the pasture, comes closest; but the flax so outsizes the blue-eyed grass that comparison is difficult. Flax flowers are an inch and a half across and a hundred to the clump. Each flower lasts only a day, but new ones keep coming from buds that look, under my ten-power glass, amazingly like rosebuds with their tightly rolled petals. Blue roses!

Historically my flax plants speak of the pyramids and the flood plain of the Nile, and of far migration, and of northern Europe where men had flax-blue eyes and women wore flax-yellow hair in long braids called flahta, one of the lingual ancestors of our word *flax*. But this morning, seeing those blue flowers, I think of Dakota, where I once saw two hundred acres of flax in one field, and all in bloom.

"TO EVERY THING THERE IS A SEASON," said the moody author of Ecclesiastes, ". . . a time to plant, and a time to pluck up that which is planted."

No gardener or farmer could quibble with that, but I do ask why, at this particular time, the seasons so conspicuously overlap. This is a time to plant and tend the seedlings. It is also a time to pluck up the weeds which planted themselves. This is a time to mow the grass and rake it, a time to hoe and spray and till and dust and nip off dead lilac blooms and tie up the rambler roses. This is a time!

Why does grass grow two inches overnight, now, when it has all Summer ahead? Certainly there is an answer, simple and based on the solid facts of botany. But why, then, does that answer not apply to beans, say, or sweet corn? Of course I am not asking for simple answers, or logical ones. I am pleading for time, time to get all the jobs done and go fishing.

The grapes should be sprayed again. So should the pears. The raspberries are in bloom. Buttercups are everywhere. Hawkweed runs wild. Chickweed flourishes in the lettuce bed, and so does purslane. Clover spreads among the flowers. Iris are in flower.

"To everything there is a season." This season seems to be it, the season for everything at once.

IT IS SURPRISING what a good day's work does for the garden. After my complaint of yesterday I went at the weeding, finished it soon after noon, unlimbered the power mower and had the lawn in hand by four o'clock, tied up the rambler roses, snipped off the most offending of the dead lilac heads, and hoed the tallest corn. And I still had time to catch a small mess of perch. Had someone laid out such a schedule of work for me I would have said flatly that it couldn't be done.

It is also surprising what a good day's work in the garden does for me. I feel fine and fit this morning, and very virtuous indeed. Virtuous enough to last for another week.

Albert has started mowing the second pasture, which he saved for hay. I can't stay at my desk with all that activity going on. Besides, the smell of the new-cut hay, combined with the fragrance of the new-cut lawn, comes billowing in my study window. It's like a sniff of salt air to an old sailor.

ALBERT WASN'T MAKING HAY. He was cutting grass and chopping it and putting it into his silo. Charley was there helping, with his hired man, and they were running the mower with one tractor, the chopper with another, and hauling the grass away with two high-sided trucks. It was virtually a production line, and they had that pasture sheared and in the silo by noon. For the man who runs in bad weather luck, as they say, the chopper and the silo are priceless. A man doesn't have a whole field of hay down and curing when an unpredicted thunderstorm hits. He doesn't have hay, either, but he has good ensilage.

After the noon meal they all moved up to Charley's place, and I went along. Charley cut his alfalfa yesterday, turned it this morning before he came down to help Albert, and it was now ready to bale, thanks to a sizzling sun. I rode the baler for a round or two, then helped wrestle bales onto the trucks. Charley stopped the baler twice while I was with him, to shoo pheasants out of the hay. Otherwise they would have just crouched there and been caught up and killed by the baler. Charley doesn't hunt pheasants, and neither does Albert, and they hate to see anything killed needlessly. I once saw Albert stop his mower to allow a mother cottontail to get out of the way, then get off and move her young ones out of the nest and over onto the mowed grass, safe.

Charley had about ten acres of alfalfa in that field, and we got it all baled and under cover this afternoon. A good thing, for it is muttering and flashing lightning tonight. We'll have a shower before morning.

THE SHOWER CAME, and it was too wet to hoe the beans this morning, so I went up the mountain to the springhouse, Pat and I, and got drenched by the water on the trees and underbrush. Going up there I thought of the wild gardens I have tried to make, one place or another, moving woods plants into a corner of the cultivated garden and dosing them with lime and leaf mold and pine needles and gravel. Only one of those wild gardens was worth half the work that went into it. That was the one into which I moved a dozen wild strawberry plants. Most of the other wildlings paled and gave up in a year or two, and the strawberries took over. Each June for three years I picked a quart of wild berries, little nuggets of June sweetness.

Some people have beautiful wild gardens, and I know the work that went into them. But I now have a whole mountainside for my wild garden, and I don't have to turn a hand to keep it going. It thrives mightily, and it constantly surprises me. Late last Summer, on my way to the springhouse, I found two purple-flowering raspberries, *Rubus odoratus*, in full bloom. It isn't a rare wildling, but there are few on my mountain and I had never seen one beside the path. But there these were with their big crimson-pink flowers, big as wild roses.

Today I found cranesbill, buttercups, wild strawberries, a dozen varieties of fern, jack-in-the-pulpit, trillium, Dutchman's-breeches (now in seed pod), evening primroses still in bud, pyrola, the one-flowered variety, and dwarf ginseng with its little puff of white blossom. These I saw without even searching, close beside the path. Had I gone where Pat went, into every thicket and gully and over every ledge and stump, I should have found fifty others, I am sure. Pat didn't flush a rabbit, but among the pines near the springhouse he put up a couple of grouse, which startled him even more than they did me.

I was out in the thinnest light of dawn this morning, looking for deer. The deer have been feeding in a small opening on the mountain, where the pines stand tall beyond and a seep spring waters the grass; I have seen their tracks there often. So this morning I was up before daylight and, leaving Pat safely housed, went there to watch. I took my stand in a thicket of saplings ten feet high, ash and sumac mostly, where I had a clear view of the glade, and I waited.

The birds were there before me, of course. A blue jay announced my coming. Then two song sparrows asked my business. As quietly as possible, I made my way into the undergrowth and waited, hoping I looked something like a stump in khaki pants and an old brown coat. Apparently I looked enough like a stump to get by, for within five minutes the birds quieted down. A chickadee came and perched on a twig within three feet of my face. A fox sparrow scratched his way into the leaves within an arm's length, pausing only once or twice to look at me curiously.

No deer came, but within twenty minutes after I took my stand a cottontail rabbit hopped across the clearing toward my stand and sat watching me. He shook his head and flapped his ears as though bewildered, as though thinking, "There wasn't a stump there yesterday." Then he approached me, aimless. He nibbled at the grass, he scratched one ear with a long hind foot, he went twice around a clump of violets. Then he wriggled his nose at me, looked me in the eye, and hopped directly to me. He sniffed at my boot toe, nosed the cuff of my khaki pants; then he turned and hopped away, only to come back, quite unable to make up his mind, and sniff again. He was the most completely aimless rabbit I ever saw.

The rabbit went away, still undecided where he was going, still diverted by a dozen things, and the fox sparrow scratched dead leaves onto one of my boots. I was of no consequence to him, none at all. The chickadee perched on my shoulder for a moment. Two field mice, their white bellies gleaming, came out of the grass and stood on their hind feet beside a tiny maple seedling, sniffing the air.

Then the sun rose and the mists began to rise from the seep spring. The bird chorus in the woods began to swell. Another blue jay flew over, squawked a time or two at me, and settled in a pine to watch.

Still no sign of the deer.

I waited till an hour after sunrise, and then the mosquitoes got after me. Why they didn't attack sooner, I can't imagine. But when they went to work on me I had to give up. I came home without having seen my deer, but I had a splendid hour and a half with the other folk who live there.

THINKING OF SOMETHING ELSE, I closed the garage door all the way last night, and this morning there was a to-do out there. The barn swallows demanded entry. So I let them in. Two families of them are nesting there, and I usually leave the door a few inches open so they can get in and out.

The garage is the former milk barn, an old structure with hewn beams and wide boards and a loft overhead that once was used for straw. Until I battened it to keep out the snow it was open to birds as well as wind, and a couple of broken windowpanes made it virtually a flyway. Now I have it so tight that the birds can't get in except through the doorway. The swallows should know this, but if they do they believe they have property rights which include an obligation on my part to leave the sliding door part way open. They have nested there for years, in their unwieldy mud structures stuck on the old beams, and apparently they continued to find enough insects to make it worth their while even after the cows and the flies departed.

We welcome the swallows. They are generally quiet, orderly folk, and they must eat tremendous numbers of insects. Of an evening they gather in flocks, both my barn swallows and the purple martins and now and then a few white-breasted tree swallows, and course the river. We sometimes go out in the boat just to sit and watch their amazing flight. To me there is no

more graceful bird in the air than a swallow. And they seem to have a sense of fun, for often two of them appear to play tag, competing in aerial acrobatics.

We seldom think of barn swallows as companionable birds, such as robins or catbirds, for instance, who choose to nest close to human habitations. Yet the barn swallows prefer to nest inside a building, and if there is any choice they seem to pick one which is used constantly by human beings. My big old barn, for instance, offers a hundred good places for barn swallows to nest, and it has enough gaps and cracks to admit a whole flock of birds. But not one pair of barn swallows nests there. The barn is a little distance from the house and I go there only once a week or so. The swallows choose, instead, the

garage, despite its disadvantages. I go to the garage every day.

And at evening if we sit on the front porch the swallows come and perch on the electric line between the house and the garage, choosing a place near the porch. Until we go outside there is seldom a bird on that line; five minutes after we go out and sit down there are half a dozen of them.

YARROW BEGINS TO OPEN its gray-white heads along the fences, and when I walk there I stir the pungent odor of its crushed foliage, faint but with a sharp tang. The foliage itself is surprisingly delicate, finer cut than that of the daintiest fern and a silvery green unlike anything around it.

This yarrow migrated here from Europe long ago and found American soil and climate to its liking. There is only one species, a western one, that is native to America; but this imported yarrow now grows almost everywhere. It is often mistaken for the wild carrot, Queen Anne's lace, though they are not even remotely related. Yarrow is a composite and Queen Anne's lace is a member of the parsley family.

Tradition says that Achilles discovered yarrow and brewed a tonic from it. The doubtful legend is preserved in its botanical name, *Achillea millefolium*, and the reputed medicinal qualities were respected by the "yarb" doctors, who gathered and dried it, leaf, stem and bud. The customary infusion was a handful of dried yarrow to a pint of boiling water. The tea thus produced was used as a general tonic and for digestive ills. It has a pungent taste, much like the odor of the crushed green leaves, and is not my idea of a good beverage. Probably, like so many of the old herbal remedies, it was as potent as a threat as it was as a medicine, particularly among children.

BOTANICALLY, an herb is a plant with a certain minimum of woody structure, usually one which dies down each year and sends up new shoots, if it is a perennial, each Spring. The classification, herbs, shrubs, and trees, roughly indicates the distinction.

The medicinal study of herbs, though surrounded by superstition, led directly to botany. Some of the first printed books were herbals, among the earliest and most famous those of Leonard Fuchs and Otto Brunfels, in German, and of William Turner and John Gerard, in English. The medicinal use of herbs, of course, goes far back into the misty past, to the Romans, the Greeks, the Egyptians, and still beyond. And it comes all the way down to the present day, for we still use countless herbal derivatives in our modern pharmacopoeia. Rhubarb and soda is an example, and it was prescribed for me not long ago by a doctor who said his doctor father prescribed it and he hasn't found anything better for its particular purpose.

A chemist friend of mine who dug lightly into the subject has a theory that many present-day discoveries are really rediscoveries of old, old remedies, and that much folk medicine of the past was based on a kind of vestigial knowledge filtered down from long-vanished civilizations.

IT RAINED TODAY and didn't begin to clear until near sunset. After dinner we went out to walk in the gathering darkness, and Barbara exclaimed how good it was to see the stars in their accustomed places after such a day. And we spoke of how a sky that clears by daylight may be full of radiance, but one that clears in darkness has glittering promise and reassurance in every ray of starlight.

We walked by starlight, and we remembered a time when we had no daylight leisure to walk. We spoke of how daylight is worktime, but that the great dreams are dreamed by starlight. There is warmth and life in the day's sunshine, but it is the stars that lure man's mind to the endless immensity of the universe.

Anaximander, back in the sixth century B.C., made what were probably the earliest known discoveries about the earth's movements, and the sun's, by watching the moon, definitely a nighttime occupation. He watched the moon and drew up his theories, then turned to daylight to apply them by making a sundial. So far as I can learn, nobody ever made a moondial; which may, or may not, indicate that the ancients didn't want to limit their nighttime speculation on the great mysteries by tying themselves to a clock.

A GARDEN IS COMPOUNDED, in roughly equal parts, of soil, industry and patience. The facts of garden life are based primarily on cause and effect. And no garden I have ever known was the accomplishment of one season. True, one can achieve a harvest of sorts in one season; but it is the repeated tillage, the compost and organic matter well worked in, the stones removed, the sour soil sweetened and the heavy soil lightened, that make a garden. And none of these things is accomplished overnight.

Weather is the great determinant in any garden, and there is little anyone can do about the weather except to live with it and make the best of it. We are fortunate here, being close beside the river, which reaches out with its mist even in time of drought to encourage our planting. And the soil is flood-plain soil, the wash from the mountain over the centuries leavened by the silt from ancient floods. It is almost without stones, a rarity in Connecticut and most of New England, and it is rich with care. But Barbara's peas thrive because she allows the weeds to shade and cool the roots. The carrots grow big because we plant them where the soil is light and deep. Some things we have learned; but perhaps the most important thing is that we shall go on learning, year after year.

EVEN ADAM MUST HAVE KNOWN in June that banishment from Eden was not an undiluted punishment, for surely Eden spilled its fields and gardens, its meadows and woodlands, out beyond the boundaries. As we walked through the June countryside today I knew in my heart that Eden endures, even today. I knew that faith endures, and reasons for it, and that with faith and hope all things are possible.

Daisies now whiten the meadows, and the oriole sings, and the slow turning of the earth is a part of the great current of time, which flows everywhere and forever. Change is like the leaf that spreads to catch the sun. The leaves clothe the earth while time flows, here and in Maine and Dakota and the Carolinas and even in the mesa country of New Mexico. The season we call June comes, and comes again and again, in all its fullness. I have seen June on the mountain tops and in the steaming lower valleys, and nowhere that I know of in this hemisphere is it less than a touch of perfection.

My theology is flexible, and to me Eden may be a memory or a legend; but I know that the Eden of June is very real and is mine for the knowing and the taking. It will be here, waiting, as long as there are men here to enjoy it, and probably long after.

A FINE, WARM, LAZY JUNE DAY. We went to the village to do some marketing, and the middle-aged woman behind the counter said, "This is a day to make one forget the Winter. I aged fifty years last Winter."

"You'll get them all back," I said, "before Summer is over."

She shook her head and smiled. "Only forty-nine of them," she said a little sadly.

I WENT FISHING ALONE, not caring much whether I caught fish or not, and I caught more than I have any day this season. Not quite alone, either, for Pat went along, to explore the river banks and to swim the river half a dozen times. What breeze there was came from the south, which I have heard some fishermen call "a fishing wind." It happens to be an upstream breeze here, and it comes most afternoons. I doubt that the fish even know it blows, but by sundown we are grateful for it on any hot day. It eases through the house, clearing out the day's warm accumulation, and it is a soft and soothing comfort on the porch or down on the grass.

I fileted the fish, all of them, since we were eating salad and cold meat, and we wrapped the filets and stowed them in the freezer. They freeze well, and in December and January they cook well. That is when that south wind, if it blows at all, is edged like a knife. If I admit that this south wind is now a fishing wind, in January it is a fish-chowder wind, so I am winner either way.

WE ARE HERBIVOROUS PEOPLE in the Summer and we have an idea that vegetables lose flavor, and probably vitamins, with every minute they spend between the garden and the pot. We like our green beans, for example, plucked at 11:45 and eaten promptly at noon. And preferably very small beans, beans so small they haven't yet shed their dried blossoms. Fancy fare indeed, and no doubt profligate, for if we let them grow another week we would have twice or three times the bulk. But half the flavor.

Corn, too, should be hurried to the pot. Barbara says she likes to have the water boiling before we go out to pluck the ears. Something of an exaggeration, but basically sound. But I shall say no more about corn, for mention of it tantalizes me, with the earliest of ours now only knee high. There is sweet corn in the market, but it comes from Delaware and South Jersey and it has been away from the field twenty-four hours or more. It makes poor fare for those who know how sweet corn should taste.

First of the cucumbers are in bloom. So is Summer squash and zucchini. And so are the big white delphiniums, which are giant and so spectacular that strangers stop and ask about them. There are twenty-two blossom spikes on one clump and only one has opened flower, so we shall have delphiniums for several weeks to come. And another flowering late in the Summer.

FOLKLORE AND FABLE hold up the ant and the bee as classic examples of industry, but I can't see why the fable-makers overlooked the wasps. Particularly the thread-waisted wasps, the *Sphecidae*. Their industry, ingenuity and ruthlessness are something to behold.

I sat and watched one of the *Sphecidae*, a burrowing wasp, for an hour this morning. She had dug an egg cell beside the driveway to the garage, and she was stocking it with caterpillars. I found her near the end of her job, apparently, for she added only two more, then went inside and stayed long enough to lay eggs in the caterpillars which she had already paralyzed with her poison sting. Then she came out and closed the nest entrance, pushing soil into it and finally grasping a small pebble in her jaws and using it as a tamp to pack down the earth. That done, she flew away. Her eggs will hatch into larva in that well-provisioned cupboard and eat their fill of caterpillar.

Other members of the burrowing wasp tribe stock their egg cells with spiders, beetles, common flies, and even cicadas. And the mud-daubers, technically *Sceliphrons*, build multiple-celled mud nests for their larvas. There are several such nests in the garage, and I occasionally see one of those wasps stuffing a spider into one of the cells.

The wasp known as *Chalybion* also likes mud nests but has no notion of building one. It carries water to a mud-dauber's nest, softens its wall, tears it open, lays its eggs in a spider-filled cell already occupied by mud-dauber eggs, and closes the cell again. Presumably there is trouble in that cell when both kinds of eggs hatch.

SOLSTICE, WE CALL IT, the Summer solstice, when the earth begins to swing back on its trunnions and the longest daylight of the year is at hand and the creeping abbreviation sets in once more. Solstice, and Summer, and beedrone in the clover field. First fledglings out of the nest, corn almost knee high, brooks dwindling, rivers slowed down as if in pace with the green along their banks, settling into Summer's tempo.

Thus always in any land of changing seasons. The leaf, the spread of chlorophyll, has hastened to reach its maximum for the time of maximum sunlight. Now it settles down to work, its function for the year, to use the sunlight and promote growth. In the year's plan there is relatively little time for such work, only a few months; and into that span must be compressed the whole year's growth. There is little lagging. Once the earth has come to the solstice, Spring's preparations must be consolidated in a Summer of completion. The solstice is the year's meridian, not its resting place.

Call it what you will, order or plan or mere succession, there is an unmistakable clarity in the process. And meaning, even if only the meaning that comes from the orderly procession of events. Budding, and blossoming, and fruiting; sprouting, and growth, and seed; beginning, and continuation, and conclusion, over and over and over, so that it becomes continuity. It is on so grand a scale, so universal, that we miss the larger meaning in seeing only the detail. But there it is, a rhythm greater than that of the day or the season, greater even than the year. It is a rhythm of ages, of an eternity of past and future, all compressed into any Summer.

THE NUMBER OF BIRDS seems to vary from year to year, but I am sure this is an illusion. Their total number probably doesn't vary more than a few per cent, for the balance of nature as far as they are concerned is fairly stable. Richard H. Pough, of the Audubon Society, estimates the number of birds that regularly spend a part of the year in the United States and Canada at twelve to fifteen billion. That would be almost two thousand to the square mile, or three birds to the acre.

The average human population in the United States is about fifty to the square mile, so there are at least forty times as many birds as people. The people, however, are concentrated in the towns and cities, and the birds are concentrated in the open country. Even so, I should guess offhand that New York City stands very well up in its total bird population which, on the basis of the national average, should be around 750,000. Central Park, on that basis, would have around 3,000 birds, and I will venture that there are more than 3,000 English sparrows alone in that island of urban greenery.

Our place here, with its woodland, its pastures and its river banks, is an ideal place for birds. I am sure that we have, even in the depth of Winter, at least three birds to the acre. Last January I counted one flock of thirty-seven juncos which regularly fed here, and with that flock were a dozen or fifteen tree sparrows, four or five song sparrows and a dozen chickadees. I hesitate to estimate the total number of our chickadees, for every time I go up to the pine woods on the mountain I see them by the dozen. How many birds we have, of all species, I cannot even guess. The national average entitles us to around 300, and I am sure I heard half that many robins this morning.

IN ALL, ABOUT 1200 SPECIES and subspecies of birds are known in the United States. I have just turned up a list of species seen by qualified observers in the various states. This list is from some years back and it seems that no similar census has been taken since. No such list is all-inclusive, and to an extent it represents the activity of the observers as well as the number of birds, but it does give some index to the distribution of the species.

Almost half the total number known in the country, 546 of them, have been seen in Texas, which is not surprising if one considers the size of the state, the variety of climate and the length of Gulf Coast in Texas. California comes next, with 541, also understandable with California's long coast and varied climate and terrain. But number three surprises me. It is Nebraska, with 418 species reported. Nebraska, of course, extends from the Missouri River well onto the High Plains.

Number four is New York, with 412. Number five is another surprise, Colorado, with 403 species; but again there is a wide variety of climate and terrain, from High Plains to the Continental Divide, from grasslands to pine and spruce forests.

Illinois comes sixth with 390, Missouri seventh with 383; then Kansas, 379, just ahead of Washington with 372. And following come Arizona with 371, Massachusetts with 369, Florida with 362, and New Jersey with 358. I am disappointed to find that Connecticut, with 334, stands sixteenth, behind North Dakota with 338.

The remainder of the list tapers off to Idaho with 210 species. But the thing that surprises me in the list is the placing of the "desert" states, Arizona ahead of Massachusetts and Florida, New Mexico just behind Louisiana. I would have expected Louisiana to be near the top, not halfway down the list. And I certainly didn't expect to find Nebraska, Colorado, and Kansas in the first eight.

IN THE NEXT FEW WEEKS I can drive down any road and see which gardeners are really gardeners and which are only planters. I will know who can tend as well as harvest, who can take sunburn and backache, mosquitoes and deer flies, who is a weeder, who is a duster.

The first good crop of weeds now either has its foothold or has been mastered. The first of the corn is threatening to tassel. Green beans are setting on. Chard is ready to cut. Early lettuce is threatening to bolt. Beets need thinning. So do carrots. The beetles are threatening squash and cucumbers. I don't have to budge from home to know that. But whenever I go anywhere I can use such matters as a gauge of character.

The first flush of pride in harvest is over. The asparagus is all cut. The first crop of strawberries is picked and eaten, by the gardener or the birds. The early lettuce and radishes were bountiful, as always, and so were the scallions. But now comes the work for the real harvest, and most of it must be done either on the knees or with a bent back. Why, I can spot a gardener now, even at the supermarket in the village, by the bow in his back and the stains on his weeding-hand!

If the gardener can keep up the pace till the middle of July he probably can carry on through the Summer. Fortunately, lawn grass slows up somewhat by now, demanding fewer mowings. The flower gardens, except for weeding, should be pretty well in hand. But the vegetable garden—huh! Did you ever see a hammock slung beside a vegetable garden? Or a vegetable gardener in one? No. If he rests, it's leaning on a hoe. Particularly now.

A LETTER CAME TODAY from a friend in Bermuda, a man who worked for years as an editor in New York and retired a few years ago to return to the island of his birth and upbringing. He had been planting trees. In recent years a blight struck Bermuda's trees and Walter has undertaken a reforestation job. "I hope," he writes, "to have a thousand trees in the ground by the end of the year."

Walter is a gardener, a lover of growing things. The trees he is planting will not come to maturity in his lifetime. It will be another ten or twenty years before they provide benevolent shade and make a cool, green pleasure for the human eye. But in time there will be birds nesting in them and the whole land will be a pleasanter place. That is his hope and purpose.

This seems important to me, more important than much of the day-to-day news. The man who plants a tree, or even a perennial flower, has his eye on tomorrow. He believes that tomorrow there will still be men and women who look for beauty and tranquillity. His hopes exceed his own survival. He expects a future that will include the major satisfactions of today, and he is aware of such satisfactions here and now. It is quite possible that foreign ministers and national leaders the world over should be reminded, from time to time, that there are quiet tree-planters at work all over this world.

Summer

THERE WAS A HEAVY DEW LAST NIGHT and I suspect that I wakened at five this morning simply to see the world all a-glint and a-gleam. I wakened and got up and pulled on a shirt and khaki pants and went downstairs barefoot, and out to see the world. The world was on the verge of sunrise—we have daylight saving time—and it was that breathless moment when the sky is bursting with the sun's brilliance though the sun is still below the horizon.

I walked out onto the lawn. The grass was drenched and the droplets shimmered like frost. The whole lawn was white, and the pasture behind the house was a vast white pool. The air was warm, but the dew was icy on my feet; it was like standing ankle deep in a pool of Millstone Brook in April.

Pat heard me and came bounding from his house, the old brooder house with the climbing roses, leaving a trail as clear as if he had dashed through a light fall of snow. Every blade of grass he touched turned from white to green. Pat sniffed the air, then plunged headlong and rolled in the dewy grass, shivering sensuously and leaving a green wallow, then leaped up and shook himself and showered me.

We walked out toward the barn, and suddenly the sun came up and the gleaming world shimmered. A spider web between two boards on the fence was a web of silver and diamonds. The maples along the river bank shivered in a breeze and the dew showered from their leaves, and just for a few flashes there was a rainbow. A sunrise rainbow. That's why I got up at five, to see that sunrise rainbow among the trees!

I WATCHED A KINGBIRD go after a crow today and marveled, as always, at the kingbird's skill a-wing and his tremendous audacity. He will attack a crow or a hawk without hesitation, and he is almost as adept in the air as a swallow. Let a crow come near and the kingbird is off like a black-and-white jet fighter, screaming for reinforcements. Other kingbirds join him and the crow takes off for far places, the kingbirds harrying him. I have never seen it done, but some say a kingbird can kill a crow.

A friend in Florida tells me that one Summer he watched a pair of kingbirds kill seven buzzards near Tampa. The attack, as he described it, was much like that on a crow, but because the buzzard is less agile than a crow the battle was briefer. In several of the battles, he says, little Southern shrikes, "butcher birds," joined the kingbirds. My friend says he examined two of the buzzards when they fell and found that the kingbirds had pierced their skulls with blows of their beaks at the base of the brain.

A member of an ornithological group insists to me that this couldn't have happened. The kingbird, he says, has neither the beak nor the strength to pierce a buzzard's skull. Who is right in this matter, I do not know. I do know that the kingbird is a truculent and hard-hitting fighter. Until last Summer I would have said the kingbird has more courage per ounce than any other bird alive. Then I saw a ruby-throated hummingbird take after a kingbird and put him completely to rout. He swarmed all over that kingbird, like a swarm of angry bumblebees, and the kingbird didn't stay to argue.

THE BIG SUGAR MAPLES, typical of all maples, now begin their second phase of the season's growth. In late April they put forth blossoms in an amber glow. The blossoms passed through their cycle, first showering down their bud scales, then stretching their stamens and luring the bees, then fading to a yellowish green, finally maturing into tiny winged seeds that hung in clusters of pairs as the first green leaves unfolded. The leaves opened and spread and the trees took color, the deep leaf-green displacing the filmy yellow-green of the seed vanes.

Now the seeds begin to spiral down, one-bladed miniature helicopters that spin away from the parent tree. And at the twig-ends another set of new leaves appears. These are the growth leaves. With them comes the season's extension of new twig, still soft and green. It thrusts out from last year's twig-ends, widening the tree and heightening it. At the tip of this new growth are small new leaves, a younger, fresher green, so the whole tree is now mottled as with dancing sunlight.

Thus the outer growth. Meanwhile, unseen in the trunk, other processes are at work fashioning a new layer of fiber beneath the bark, a new season's growth ring that I shall never see unless the trunk itself is felled by ax or saw or storm.

The growth of the conifer is much the same, but in its own precise manner. The white pine puts forth its tufts of needles, soft as kitten fur at first as they burst the bud-sheath. Five needles in a tuft, five branches in each year's whorl, for the white pines count as the old Romans did, by fives.

THE DAISIES ARE AT THEIR PEAK along the roadsides and at the edge of my pastures. I've heard some people call them Farmer's Curse, but I like them, in their place; which is, of course, not in a corn field or a garden. I came back from the fence row a little while ago with a handful of them, common field daisies, *Chrysanthemum leucanthemum*. Some people call them oxeye daisies, though that is a redundancy, for daisy is nothing more than day's eye, in the Old English.

The English daisy, however, is different from these, having a fleshy stem and colored petals. We sometimes grow English daisies in the flower garden, a pretty but unpretentious flower.

It is always worth five minutes or so to study a daisy with a magnifying glass. I carry a ten-power pocket glass, which is about the right size. Through the glass one can see that the center of a daisy, like a sunflower, is made up of a mass of tiny florets, each one a flower and perfect in itself, with petals and stamens and pistils. None of them is much bigger in diameter than the head of a common pin. Yet each of these tiny florets, when the daisy matures, produces its own seed. The fringe of white petals around this composite center apparently was put there only to attract the bees, though each of those white petals is itself a pistillate flower and, if properly fertilized, will produce a seed. Tansy, a close relative, has in the process of evolution eliminated the border petals completely.

Each of these daisies here on my desk is not a white and yellow flower at all; each one is a massed bouquet of miniature yellow blossoms, the whole bouquet edged with white blooms.

THE DAY LILIES, the common *Hemerocallis fulva*, are in full bloom along the roadside fence of my pastures, and in the big bed on the river bank where they are fighting for possession with the scouring rushes. That river-bank lily bed, I suspect, was started when someone dug up a clump of unwanted day lilies and tossed them there to die, for I have seen discarded clumps take root on an ash heap and in a gravel bed. It is amazing the way they spread and persist. They are al-

most as tough as chicory, another immigrant, which now begins to spread its blue at the roadside.

Another immigrant of the lily family, and also one which came here first from Europe as a garden flower, is the star-of-Bethlehem, with its six-petaled white flowers striped with green on the outside. Star-of-Bethlehem also runs wild in many places, though I find little around here. It is established in our flower garden, probably brought there long ago as a gift from some farm wife.

And over in the corner of the vegetable garden where we tried to segregate the rhubarb are yellow meadow lilies and Canada wood lilies, wildlings and native. The wood lily holds its orange-red blossoms upward, one of the few wild lilies to do so, and its petals are not joined at the base as are those of the pendant meadow lily.

Still another lily, though seldom thought of as such, is the Solomon's seal which grows with the day lilies at the roadside. It is almost through blooming, and green berries are beginning to form, berries that will be blue-black as a fox grape by October.

JULY

I suspect that it wasn't wholly coincidence that the Declaration was proclaimed in early July, for in that day everyone lived much closer to the land than now. And man with his footing in the soil has little patience with outside interference in July. He's too busy with natural problems to be very tolerant with man-made ones.

Corn has to be laid by, cultivated the last time, cleaned of weeds before it begins to "tawsel" out and shoot up eight feet high. Hay, the second cutting, has to be taken care of, and if rain comes while it's drying there's more trouble than a whole political convention can think up. Wheat has to be harvested when it's ripe. Oats demand attention. A harvest too early finds the grain not properly filled; a few days too late and the grain shatters and is lost. Harvest time happens also to be hail time, thunderstorm time; and even a high wind can level a ripe field of small grain.

Meanwhile, silos must be filled, and there are the daily chores. There's the kitchen garden to tend—a farmer can't leave all the gardening to his wife, no matter how willing; she, too, has other things to do, what with young chickens and canning and freezing for next Winter and daily cooking and the farmhouse routine. But the garden, too, is a part of the independence.

The Declaration is a document well remembered. But there is another declaration, unwritten except on sweaty faces, to be read by anyone who looks, in July. It says the same thing as the written one, and it says it year after year, on farm after farm. I see it every day, now.

"FLOWERS," HELENE SAID, "say their own thanks."

That was some years ago, but we remember each time we look at our flower garden. We had driven up to see Helene and Frank, in another state, and when we admired their flowers Frank got a spade and began digging. They would have given us a truckload of plants if we hadn't called a halt. Finally, with the car loaded to the gunwales, we tried to say our thanks, but Helene said, "Please, no thanks. When we moved here a dear old lady gave us loads, and when I tried to thank her she said, 'You never say thanks for flowers. You plant them and care for them and when the time comes you share them with others. Flowers say their own thanks.' "

So we brought them home and planted them and gave them care, and we, too, have shared them. Others gave us flowers, many others, since gardeners are by nature generous. Thus our garden has grown and spread to other gardens all over the countryside. And the primroses, the primula, the iris, the tulips, the anthemus, the many-colored violets, the clematis, the grape hyacinths—the whole garden, which is so full of beauty today and so spilling over with fragrance, says thanks over and over again to our friends.

THERE IS A BREEZE and the bees are very busy. Lorus and Margery, who are imaginative biologists as well as husband and wife, first pointed out to me that bees are always busiest on windy days, and why.

Investigating insect vision, they did a series of experiments with honeybees. The bee's eye is large and many-faceted. Each facet is a kind of individual eye, and each of those facets seems to be acutely sensitive to light, shade and motion. Investigating that sensitivity, my biologist friends prepared cards of plain white and checkered black and white and held them in front of captive bees. The bees responded to the plain white card with a normal motion of the feelers and seemed to follow the card's movement. When a checkered card was held in front of the bees, the feelers waved in a frenzy; apparently the checks affected one eye facet after another, giving a series of exciting stimuli. When the checkered card was moved from side to side the bees were so excited they could scarcely contain themselves.

These experiments seemed to indicate that bees were more interested in clusters of small flowers than in one large flower. Field experiments proved that theory. They also showed that on a windy day, when many small flowers were in motion, the bees were out in great numbers and busy all day long.

If I kept a hive of bees I should specialize in small flowers, such as candytuft and phlox and clover, and on still, quiet days I should be tempted to set an electric fan going among the blossoms. Then I should quickly get a hiveful of honey!

INDEPENDENCE SEEMS TO ME to be a very personal quality, a matter of the mind and the emotions and the whole approach to life. It is a positive matter, rather than a refusal to knuckle down to some outside force. And it involves many of the broad, indefinable generalities—liberty, justice, honor, integrity. It is more than a matter of politics or even of social organization.

Independence means to me the right to make what I can of myself, to think as clearly as my brain will allow, to be as much of an individual, an entity, as I can. It means my right to make a place for myself in human society, but it doesn't mean that society is somehow obliged to make a place for me. It means that I shall face the consequences of my own folly and not that some town or state or nation shall shield me from them. This is somewhat old-fashioned; I know that. But the pendulum of fashion, in human behavior as well as dress, has its swings, and it returns again and again to the point where individual responsibility is again in good repute.

Independence means obligations as well as rights. The right to work, and the obligation to work at my full capacity. The right to earn, the obligation to save. The right to worship as I please, and the obligation to abide by my best beliefs and instincts. The right to justice, and the obligation to recognize right and truth. The right to hope, to dream, to plan, and the obligation to serve my own kind.

These are not new ideas. They are so old they are worn smooth with repetitions. They stem from ancient tribal days. They happen also to be embedded in the Declaration of Independence, which most of us remember, one way or another, today.

OUR TOMATOES ARE DOING SPLENDIDLY. We shall have the first ripe one within another two weeks. And speaking of tomatoes, I grow weary of that old nonsense about their being so long considered poisonous. The tale has been knocked down many times, most effectively by Lewis Gannett in his book, *Cream Hill*, published in 1949, but it persists. Only the other day I heard a man on the radio say tomatoes were considered poisonous "only fifty or sixty years ago." And one of my encyclopedias says they weren't considered edible until "within the last century." Nonsense! Tomatoes were being canned and sold commercially on Long Island, in Baltimore, in Cincinnati, and probably elsewhere, as early as 1855. Nobody cans and sells a food product generally considered poisonous.

The tomato is a native American. Aztecs and Incas grew and ate tomatoes in prehistoric times. The name comes from the Aztec word *tomatl*. Spaniards took tomato seeds from Mexico to Spain early in the sixteenth century and they were grown, eaten, and improved uninterruptedly there for two hundred years. From Spain they went to England, and from England and Spain they came to America. Thomas Jefferson's own records speak of growing tomatoes, both the Spanish tomato and others. The Spanish variety was "much larger than the common kind," so there was a "common kind" grown at that time. And they were considered a vegetable, not a garden decoration.

So let's be through with at least a little of this "poisonous tomato" nonsense.

THE ELDERBERRIES ARE IN BLOOM, the big clumps at the river bank, the bushes beside the barn, the big one just across the brook from the garden. For several years I tried to grub out the one by the garden, then gave up. Besides, when it's in bloom that bush is as pretty as any shrub on the lawn.

Time was when the elderberry was highly respected. The white flower heads which now cover the bushes and are a lure for bees by the hundred mature into lush pannicles of purplish black berries, and these berries are full of juice so sweet it will not turn into jelly without the help of alien pectin. But that juice, properly handled, makes elderberry wine; and there was a time when most rural cellars had at least a jug and often a keg of elderberry wine. Elderberry wine had certain medicinal qualities, and it was surprising how many countrymen felt a bit puny as long as the elderberry wine lasted, puny enough to need a glass of it every day.

Elderberries also made many a tasty pie in country kitchens. Professor Jim, an upstate New Yorker who became a city man and a teacher, tells me that in his boyhood they gathered elderberries and dried them so they might have elderberry pies all Winter. Jim gave Barbara a recipe for elderberry pie just the other day, the one his mother used many years ago.

But most of the pleasures of the elderberry are past and forgotten. Most farmers hereabout grub them out, though they do leave a few along the fence rows for the birds. The birds love the berries, and the bees love the blossoms. And as I said, the bushes just now are pretty as any shrub on the lawn.

ON THIS DAY A FEW YEARS AGO we drove west from Denver to Mesa Verde, with California our ultimate objective. It was one of those superb mountain days, a wondrous deep blue sky with a few cumulus clouds sailing high and far away. We drove up Wolf Creek Pass and topped the Continental Divide at an elevation of 10,850 feet, more than two miles above sea level. We parked at the crest and went on foot among the rocks and dwarfed trees, looking for wild flowers. Walking only a few hundred yards, I found the trickling waters of two tiny brooks, one of which ran west, toward the San Juan and the Colorado River, the other east, toward the Platte, the Missouri and the Mississippi.

Within fifteen minutes there we found yellow rocket in bloom, a personal delight for it is sometimes known as Barbara's Cress; and Indian Paintbrush, and a dwarf milkweed, and a very sweet wild rose, and *Elephantella groenlandica*, commonly called Little Red Elephant because its small flowers are like miniature elephant heads. Cinquefoil was also in yellow bloom, and of all things there was a dwarf purple aster, an Alpine version of the familiar purple aster of New England's Autumn.

Time is telescoped in all mountains, and so are the seasons. Those were not only Spring flowers, but Summer flowers and the flowers of early Autumn. The mild seasons come close together, crammed into a few weeks, at that altitude. We got into the car again and went on, dropping swiftly from early May on the divide into July again in the valley twenty miles farther on.

I AM BEING DIFFICULT TODAY. I am an old bear with a sore paw and a growl. A carload of strangers came up the road in midmorning and parked on the river bank only fifty yards from the house. I went outdoors a few minutes later and an assertive young man from the party announced, "We

are going to have a picnic here." I said, "There's more shade on down the river." He said, "This is all right." I said nothing more. I came back in and tried to work.

They picnicked. But before they picnicked they prowled up and down the river bank, got into my boat, inspected my garage and barn, leaving doors open to the wind, got a drink at the trough and left the water running, all with whoops and hollering and loud laughter. Pat barked and tried to warn them off, and I finally brought him indoors to stop his noise. But there was no working for me. The picnickers tried the echoes, and my patience. They broke branches from a tree, they tried unsuccessfully to build a fire where there should be no fires. Finally they left, without so much as a thank-you, and I went out and picked up their paper bags and paper plates and paper napkins.

I shall say no more about this now, for my sore paw is very sore.

MY ANNOYANCE HAS EASED somewhat with a night's sleep, but this morning I am wondering why yesterday's incidents happened. There probably will not be a repetition all Summer, but something of the kind happens every year. Unless they are faced by a sign saying, NO TRESPASSING, POSITIVELY !!! there are those who invade a man's privacy with the utmost callousness, to act like fools and vandals.

Most people are friendly and courteous and considerate. They know how to act when away from home. But for the sins of the few, the loud and boorish minority, all roaming strangers are suspect. I know that for a few days my hackles will rise a little when any strange car stops along my road, even though its people only want to watch a bird or look at the mountain.

And even more than the intruders, I shall resent my own reaction. A man should not feel that way toward anybody. A man should live at peace with himself and those around him. I resent having to fight for that privilege.

THERE IS AN AWESOME MAJESTY about a July thunderstorm such as came this afternoon. It has been a hot day, almost sultry, with one of those steely blue skies that seems to have no clouds yet refuses to be honest blue. At about three o'clock the sky darkened, though with only a hint of cloud. Ten minutes more and the clouds were here, rising like a mist over the hills. The hush was so deep that even a bird call seemed overloud. The trees waited in the breathless air, leaves unrustled.

The clouds spread to cover half the sky. There was a swish, far off, a sudden wind in distant trees. Lightning flashed, back near the eastern horizon, and the cloud banks were black in its glow. Another flash, closer. Thunder rolled back from Tom's Mountain, bumping, echoing. A gust of wind swept down the river, dancing water advancing like a wave. A hush, a pause, and the birds all were silent. Another flash, so close I winced, and thunder rattled the panes.

The darkness turned to gray on the woods up the mountain. The gray marched down the slope and we could hear the rush of rain, the pelt and swish and lesser roar. Still not a breath of wind here, but we could see the trees swaying, hear the wind-roar.

Then the rain came down the river too, a gray curtain. The whole valley quivered, the trees trembling. Then it was here, in a rush, and the whole river leaped to meet it in answering spatters. The maples roared, rain on leaf, and began to stream, silver trunks blackening. The apple trees behind the house were roaring too. The darkness was gone. It was a silvery, soft-glowing world, the rain sheeting down. The lightning had passed, the thunder was ended. It rained a torrent for twenty minutes.

And now we must go out and straighten up the corn.

THUNDERSTORMS AND HURRICANES do strange things to Barbara and to Pat. Not the storms themselves, but the air pressures or the atmospheric charges, we don't know which. All we know is that when, in Summer, Barbara frowns at the sky and gets uneasy, and when Pat comes and asks to be let in the house and is restless and uneasy, something is going to happen. Barbara talks to Pat, and Pat talks to Barbara, and they both look at me as though asking, "Don't you know it's going to storm? How can you be so calm about it?" And as the storm approaches they simply can't be still; they have to prowl. Barbara sometimes gets a headache, and maybe Pat does too.

Then the storm comes, with lightning and rain, and they look at me as though to say, "We told you so!" As though I didn't know it. And they begin to relax. Five minutes of rain out of such a storm and either of them can sit down again. Barbara's headache vanishes. Pat looks out the open doorway a few minutes, sighs, and lies down and goes to sleep.

Come late Summer and Fall, hurricane season, and the same thing happens. They feel it coming. They talk about it to each other, not needing words. They say, "There's a hurricane down off Georgia or the Carolinas," and I say, "Weather report says we may get a blow tomorrow." But they don't need the radio to know it. They are tuned in direct. And they stay tuned in till the storm passes or vanishes a thousand miles out to sea.

OUR HOUSE USED TO BE GREEN, a green-shingled farmhouse. We didn't like it green, and it needed paint. We thought of painting it white, though it would be difficult to cover the green with white. Then Alice, who is an artist at many things, visited us and said, "Wait and see what the house wants." That was good advice and in no sense fey. Too many houses never had a chance to indicate the color they should have; too many owners impose their own whims. A house can be made uneasy, not only to look at but to live with, when the basic needs of house and setting are ignored.

We waited. At last we knew, or thought we did. The house should be red. A quiet, weathered red, mellow. So we told Layton, who is painter and carpenter and machinist and many other things as well, and Layton came. We bought paint and started work, spraying the weathered green shingles with a warm, red paint. We painted every building on the place red except the beautiful old silvery gray barn which has never had a pint of paint on it and never shall. And the green-shingled house became a mellowed, weathered red house.

It was the color the house wanted all the time. It looks the way it should look, at ease in its setting. And a farmer friend who shook his head skeptically when we started with the red paint stopped past this morning and asked, "Just what was that paint you used? What make, and what's the name of the color?" I told him and asked where he was going to use it. "Well," he said, "I thought I'd start with the barn. But the house needs painting too, and it's cheaper to use all the same kind." Which was his way of saying he liked this color.

I HAVE NO OBJECTION WHATEVER to what the plant culturists have done to and for domestic raspberries. I have a patch of them that are both beautiful and full of flavor, and so big that a dozen of them make a handful. But when I go fishing now or just walking down the valley or up the mountain I find it a prime satisfaction to find unreconstructed wild raspberries.

I think my favorite is the little black-cap. It doesn't grow any bigger than the end of my little finger, and unless it is ripe, almost to the hour, it isn't worth picking and throwing away. But when I find a bush festooned with terminal berries at that prime moment, ready to drop off at a touch, I pick a handful of honey-sweetness that is wonderful. Now and then we pick a few quarts of them—a tedious business, I admit—for a very special jelly, one served only to connoisseurs. But usually we just pick a handful and eat them and walk on.

Up on the mountain there is also the little cloudberry, which grows scarcely ankle high and has a pale, winy, delicate-flavored little berry. I could pick cloudberries half a day and not gather two quarts. But when I am walking the hills they come at proper intervals for picking, and eating, and resting.

The beauty of the lot, of course, is the purple-flowered raspberry, which has a crimson-pink blossom big as a wild rose. The fruit hasn't much flavor, but one can't have everything. And a man out walking or fishing can look at one bush and eat from another, can't he? That's why wild raspberries are still wild.

HAWKWEED BLOOMS BEAUTIFULLY, but it is a pest in the hay fields and pastures, where it proliferates mightily. It is another example of an import which adapted itself too well. Originally it came from England as a garden flower, but it escaped and began to wander. A few years ago I saw it yellowing one hay field after another in Maine, and it is a nuisance through much of New England.

There are two common varieties, the bright yellow one called Canada hawkweed, *Hieracium Canadense*, and the orange one called tawny hawkweed, *H. aurantiacum*. The yellow one has flowers the color of dandelions, borne on a tall, smooth stem rising from a cluster of dark green, notched leaves. The flowers are in small clusters, each individual bloom like a scant-petaled dandelion about an inch in diameter. The orange one has a shorter flower stem rising from a ground clump of untoothed leaves, and the flowers are a deep, rusty orange, a warm Van Gogh color. The stems and flower cups of the orange variety are covered with brown hairs like a beard stubble. In England it is called Grim the Collier, for this stubble-bearded reason. Some here call it Devil's Paintbrush.

The yellow variety is common through southern New England and seems to be making its way south and west. The orange hawkweed is a hardier plant, flourishing in Vermont, New Hampshire and Maine, but it, too, is working southward. We have it here. The common name, hawkweed, springs from a legend that hawks drink its juice to sharpen their eyesight. Barbara picked a handful of the orange kind yesterday and put it in a vase in the living room, where its color is warm and faintly exotic.

THIS HAS BEEN ONE OF THOSE RARE, dazzling, blue days, without a cloud. Not skim-milk blue, which is a sky full of moisture that neither goes up nor comes down; but the blue of flax flowers fresh at dawn, which marks a sky to be lived with and enjoyed.

We have a good many such days here, far more than in the coastal area, and that is one reason this feels like home; for the blue sky is typical of the High Country where I grew up. I lived too long, in later years, where such blue skies came only after the violence of a thunderstorm, when it seemed that the smothering gauze of humidity had been ripped by the lightning and washed away by the rain.

Today there has been the blue of infinity; and there is no illusion about that. Blue light is there, my physicist friends assure me, the blue end of the spectrum filtered out of the sun's rays by dust particles that float high in the upper atmosphere. Above that layer, in the upper atmosphere itself, the sky is a deep purplish gray. And the murk that masks the blue sky lies below, earthward, in layers of smoke or mist or scud clouds gathering for a storm. Clear the sky, as with a rain or a gentle wind, and it is as it was today, healing to the heart and easing to the senses.

THE BOTANICAL NAME is *Asclepias,* honoring Aesculapius, the Greek god of healing. The everyday name is milkweed, and the two best known members of the family, butterfly weed and common milkweed, are now in bloom. Butterfly weed lifts its showy orange flower head only in favored places, but the common milkweed is everywhere with its tassely tufts of lavender and white florets which are full of sweetness, a subtle mixture of tuberose and honeysuckle fragrance.

Roadside weed though it is, the milkweed has virtues beyond a pretty flower and a sweet scent. Its milky sap contains caoutchouc, the raw material of rubber, which periodically attracts rubber researchers. Fibers of its stem have been used for cordage. Fluff from the pod has been used to stuff pillows; the silky fibers lack the natural twist, however, that would make them valuable for thread or yarn. Both roots and juice have been used by generations of herbalists, particularly for respiratory ills. And the young shoots make excellent cooked greens; we eat them like asparagus and call them a delicacy.

The common milkweed's florets are fertilized chiefly by the bees. The florets occur in tufts of seventy or more, each less than a quarter of an inch in diameter; and each, by one of those quirks of nature, is an insect trap. One misstep and the ant or bee fertilizing the flower is caught by a leg and doomed to a starving death. Yet for untold centuries ants and bees have fertilized the milkweed bloom, never learning. Insects never learn, it seems, perhaps because their lives are too short to do more than obey simple compulsion and instinct. And so the milkweed survives and multiplies, and the world is a somewhat sweeter place.

THE HOLLYHOCKS ARE IN BLOOM, and they seem very New England to me. That is simply because my first trip through New England was in July, and I saw hollyhocks in every dooryard. They belong, in my mind, with stock and candytuft and stone walls and Seth Thomas clocks and white church spires and elms. All those things are found elsewhere— I have seen them in Ohio, and in Illinois, and even in Kansas, in villages that might have been lifted bodily out of Connecticut or Massachusetts—but to me they are native here.

The hollyhocks are as old in this country as New England itself. They bloomed in dooryards here when settlers were tending maize in the Indian way and still living in wigwams they patterned on those of the Indians. The name goes back to medieval English: holihoc, the *holi* for holy, the *hoc* for either leaf or mallow, more likely the latter since they belong to the mallow family, the altheas. They are said to have been native to India and the Near East, and the Crusaders probably brought them back to northern Europe, as they brought other beautiful things.

They have botanical kin in the New World, however. In the marshes just back of the dunes along our Middle Atlantic coast grow the giant mallows, shrubby plants with flowers big as the span of a man's hand. I have seen great patches of them along the New Jersey shore.

These domesticated mallows, our hollyhocks, persist beside old cellar holes, abandoned and forgotten for at least one generation. But in a garden, tended and cared for, they have the crisp beauty of tulle and lawn and bright, cool China silk.

SOMETIMES THEY ARE CALLED "escapes," sometimes "volunteers." The name doesn't matter. They are tough, hardy independents which have adapted themselves to a hard way of life and which thrive and reproduce not only without the help of the gardener or farmer but often in the face of his opposition. Most of them are flowers—petunias, phlox, balsam, flowering tobacco, day lilies, an occasional hollyhock; but some are vegetables and shrubs—stray lilacs, barberry, even asparagus lifting its plumes beside a country road. They are many, and they are persistent, and I admire them for their vigor and independence.

To the neat gardener and the methodical farmer they are weeds. They don't belong where they are and they don't reproduce true to type or color, the type imposed upon them by the hybridists. They revert, as phlox does to magenta. But they develop a hardiness, a resistance to drought and insects and disease, that the plant breeder sometimes finds useful; and on occasion they produce sports, new variants, and back to the gardens they come. Thus they have occasional value even in the eyes of those who disdain them.

To me they are welcome symbols in a world of insistent conformity. They go their own way, meet conditions as they are, and survive by sheer persistence and root-strength. They need no coddling. They choose their own soil and climate. They fight their own battle of survival. It does my heart good to see a rejected phlox or hollyhock or even a petunia blooming in a place where all the odds seem to be against success.

CHARLEY STOPPED IN TODAY to see how the muskmelons are doing. They are doing all right, and if the season doesn't get frosted too early we shall have all the melons we can eat.

Charley gave us the seed, and in a way it is a homecoming for those melons. Twenty years or so ago a friend from up in Massachusetts gave a handful of muskmelon seeds to the farmer who lived here. Our season is short for melons, but these seeds were of an unnamed variety the Massachusetts man had devel-

110

oped. They were grown locally, handed about from gardener to gardener, and he suggested that they be tried here. My predecessor tried them and they flourished. He gave some of the seed to Charley. Charley and Elitha have grown them ever since; and after a proper time of watching, to see that we were really gardeners, Charley gave us some of the seed.

As I say, they are doing fine. Charley inspected them and nodded approval. "They still like this soil," he said. Not a word about the care they get; that is taken for granted.

WHENEVER WE GO OUT IN THE BOAT now we smell the basswood blossoms. And we hear the bees, which swarm to them.

The basswood is a linden and our native basswood is close kin to the famous European shade tree. The name "bass" comes from "bast," or fiber, the reference being to the tough inner bark of the tree, which was long used in making cordage and nets. The wood itself is soft, fine grained and easily worked into wooden ware, occasionally into furniture. Indians once made dugout canoes from large basswood trunks, and now many chopping bowls are turned from basswood.

The strangest thing about the basswood is its flower and the eventual fruit. The flower is small and creamy white and so full of nectar that it literally drips. If we anchor the boat under an overhanging basswood now we are soon dewed with little specks of nectar, colorless and sticky and fragrant. The flowers grow from a pendant stem that springs from the center of a leaflike wing. This wing, which is long and slender and a slightly lighter green than the tree's big cottonwood-like leaves, eventually provides a glider for the seed. When the seed has ripened the seed wing loosens like any leaf and is borne away by the wind. Thus are new groves of basswood started.

Our river, like most streams hereabout, is intermittently lined with basswoods. They hug the stream bank, liking the wet footing, and they make deep, cool shade. They are good neighbors, especially on a July afternoon full of blazing sun.

ONE OF THE MOST DIFFICULT of all sounds to put down on paper is the song of a bird. The reason is that vocal music is primarily a matter of vowel sounds with their consonants giving a familiar form rather than a sound of their own. Try to translate bird songs into words and you run into all kinds of stumbling blocks. For instance, even the familiar song of the chickadee is nearly always transcribed as chick-a-dee-dee-dee, but it might as accurately be set down as sip-o'-tea-tea-tea.

The whippoorwills are calling every night now. It is generally conceded that although individual whippoorwills have a sharp variation in voice quality they all make sounds that translate as "whip poor Will." An allowable variant is "whup-poo-ree." But I can with equal plausibility say that those on our mountainside are serenading my wife, saying over and over, "Bar-bar-ree, Bar-bar-ree!"

It was Thoreau, I believe, who translated the call of the Baltimore oriole as, "Eat it, Potter, eat it!" A change of consonants makes that, "Beat it, rotter, beat it!" Another of the local orioles' songs is quite obviously, "I'm an oriole, suh!" uttered with a fine Eastern Shore of Maryland accent.

When I was a boy I was quite sure that the meadow larks of the Colorado plains said, most melodically, in mid-June, "This is the time of the equinox." In April they said, "Now is the time to build a nest." And in September it was, "Summer is gone and now it's Fall."

THE NIGHT SKIES OF MIDSUMMER get little attention, unless there is a full moon and a cool breeze. Besides, full-leafed trees and mosquitoes get in the way. But the stars are still there, though at first sight it may be difficult to find familiar groups.

Last night we had a brilliant, clean-washed sky and the Little Dipper, which pivots on the Pole Star, stuck straight up, in the early evening, its bowl turned earthward and obviously empty. To the left the Big Dipper hung straight down, for all the world like the old tin dipper that hung on its nail beside the water pail in my grandmother's Summer kitchen. Cassiopeia was far to the east and near the horizon, the irregular *W* which outlines the lady's chair and which was high in the sky a few months ago.

Other familiar groups lay near the southern horizon. Aquila, the Eagle, flew rather high, in the southeast. Below it was Sagittarius, the Archer. But last night it wasn't an archer at all; it was a teapot sitting on some hot spot on the horizon, its handle to the left, its spout to the right. And directly to the south, equally near the horizon, was Scorpius, with the train of stars in its hooked tail particularly bright.

Overhead the stars have now thinned out. What has happened, of course, is that the major constellations are in other parts of the sky. Hercules and Boötes ride high, but they are the only ones that make me crane my neck. That's one virtue of the Summer star pattern, and one reason there seem to be fewer stars in the evening sky of July than of December.

I DON'T LIKE CROWS. A man is entitled to some biases. Particularly, I don't like those crows who have chosen the trees just behind the barn for their dawn conventions. I don't mind getting up at five, but four-thirty is too early.

Those who have looked into the matter professionally insist that crows eat beetles, bugs and worms. That's all right, and I'll go along a certain distance. But must they eat the *early* beetle, bug and worm? Crows get up much too early and much too full of noise. How a crow can eat anything and still make all the noise he does is beyond me. He doesn't pause long enough, at sunrise, to swallow a gnat. Squawk, squawk, squawk, squawk, squawk! Three crows can keep anyone awake within half a mile. Four crows can rouse the countryside. We have at least a dozen crows.

It wouldn't be so bad if a crow could sing. All birds have a vested right in song at any hour. But the crow is simply the loudmouth of birddom, the antithesis of song. If his diet were keyed to his voice he would subsist on coarse gravel, cockleburs, rusty nails and broken glass. Instead he eats sprouting corn and ripening fruit and little birds and small chickens and eggs —and a few beetles, bugs and worms. On such a diet he manages the roughest, toughest sound on wings.

I am thankful for one thing. Nature saw to it that crows can't crossbreed with owls or whippoorwills, or any other night birds.

SUMMER SQUASH, the little yellow crookneck variety, is now at its prime, and the green zucchini will be ready in a few days.

Barbara grows her squashes thus: I start a pit as though I were going to transplant a tree, a good thirty inches in diameter. But I go down only six or eight inches. In the bottom we put a layer of well-rotted manure and a handful of chemical fertilizer, 5-10-5 or its equivalent. On top of that goes three or four inches of soil. In the soil Barbara plants the squash seed, fifteen or so. The seed sprouts and grows, and we fill the pit to deepen the roots. A side dressing of phosphate goes on. When the plants are six inches high she thins out all but the strongest four or five. Those left grow like mad, making a cluster of squash plants five feet in diameter and, on occasion, five feet high. I never saw such plants. They bloom, they set fruit, and we begin to eat.

We take our Summer squash all ways. Sometimes we pick very small ones, four inches long, and eat them raw with mayonnaise or oil and vinegar. Sometimes we let them get ten inches long and slice and boil them in a minimum of water and eat them with a maximum of butter and salt and pepper to taste. Sometimes we slice and fry them, dusted with meal. Zucchini we either boil in bits or fry with peppers, Italian style. But always we pick them young, all Summer squashes, for we have a theory that they achieve all the flavor they are going to have in their first few days. Picked small, that flavor is concentrated.

EVERY TIME WE GO ANYWHERE at this time of year I look at the gardens, for one of America's unheralded sights is its back-yard or kitchen gardens. Not flowers, but vegetables. I have seen them in the little towns and all through the farmlands, coast to coast, but I remember them particularly in the Midwest, green and fresh and neatly weeded, often bordered with poppies or petunias. Many of them are as pretty as the pictures in the January seed catalogues, for this is a country of practical gardeners.

There are the morning garden and the evening garden. The morning garden belongs to the women. I see them, in house-dresses or dungarees, in straw hats, in sunbonnets, bareheaded, doing the fine weeding in the rows or picking beans or cutting lettuce for the day's salad. The evening garden belongs to the men. You see the men there after their day's work is done, with a wheel hoe or a hand hoe, or with nothing but a pipe and an air of pride and contentment.

It was Thomas Jefferson who wrote, in a letter to the painter, Charles Wilson Peale: "No' occupation is so delightful as the culture of the earth, and no culture comparable to that of the garden. Such a variety of subjects, some one always coming to perfection, the failure of one thing repaired by the success of another, and instead of one harvest a continuing one through the year."

Jefferson wrote that in 1811, at the age of 68.

THE GREAT MULLEINS stand majestic at the edge of the pasture and along the roadside, gray-green in lonely grandeur. They are of no consequence as flowering plants, not half as pretty in bloom as a Canada thistle, which also grows in the pasture, or even a wild sunflower along the road. But there is a classic beauty in the mullein's symmetry and its tall, straight stem and carefully graduated leaves. There is a smaller cousin, the moth mullein, with very different leaves, smooth and glossy green, and with pretty yellow or white flowers in a loose head. But the moth mullein is only a flower; the great mullein is a kind of apotheosis of simple plant perfection.

Last January I was walking on the mountain a few days after one of our lesser snowstorms, and I came to an opening in the woods and found the broad rosette of a great mullein standing in the open and clear of snow. It was as though the plant had generated warmth to melt the snow around it for a foot in all directions. The broad, rounded, hairy leaves were green, though frost-crisped and withered at the edges. Its central stalk was gone, but it looked ready to start growing the next day. It waited, however, until May.

I saw that plant again today, and it had sent up a stalk as tall as I am and two inches through at the base. The rosette of base leaves was almost the same color it was in January, and up the stem, regular as though calibrated, were acute-pointed leaves clasping the stem and graduated from a foot long at the base to only about an inch at the top, where the flower head grew, a dusty green mass of buds of which only one or two at a time will open into yellow florets. It has no flowering beauty, except for moths, butterflies and bees, which pollenize it. It is simply a plant grown to the kind of perfection a sculptor might have dreamed.

When we went fishing this afternoon four dragonflies followed the boat and supervised my line. They seemed as interested as though they were fishermen themselves; which they are, in a way, for they are seiners of the air. They

live on small flying insects which they catch on the wing by forming a seinelike net of their legs and swooping after gnats or whatever quarry. These were big fellows with clear, dark wings and dark, striped bodies, the kind that boys used to call snake-feeders, or devil's darning needles, or horse-stingers, though they never stung a horse or anything else.

We see them every time we go out on the water, for they find all kinds of insect food there. And, of course, water is their natal element. The females, when they are ready to lay eggs, swoop low over the water, skimming it and occasionally dipping the tips of their bodies into it. At each dip they eject eggs,

gelatin-covered with a protective coating. The gelatin dissolves in the water and the eggs sink to the bottom. There in the silt they hatch into nymphs a good deal like the damsel flies treasured by trout fishermen. The nymphs climb onto grass and sedge at the edge of the water and there slowly grow their wings.

Dragonflies are among the strongest-winged of all insects, and on occasion they migrate long distances, though even entomologists don't know why. And they are among the earth's venerable creatures—fossil dragonflies, millions of years old, are much like those of today except that some of the fossil ones had two-foot wingspreads.

Those which accompanied us today were males, simply out for a good time. They darted and spiraled and played tag over the boat for an hour, and we caught some very nice perch.

THERE ARE LAWS OF NATURE that I doubt we shall ever understand. Take such a simple matter as the twining of vines, bindweed or bittersweet, for example. They climb by twisting their limber stems around a stronger support, even as our pole beans climb the poles we set for them. In this northern hemisphere they twist, with few exceptions, from right to left, clockwise. Why is this so?

There are other examples. Smoke rising from a chimney also twists, when it rises in still air and has any twist to it, from right to left. Cyclonic storms, such as hurricanes, move in the same direction as they come whirling up the coast from Florida and the Caribbean. And water whirlpooling down a kitchen sink or through an outlet at the bottom of a dam usually makes the same clockwise motion.

It is all very well to say that it is a result of the turning of the earth, and to find other parallels; and it even lends a kind of reasonable air to say that in the southern hemisphere the twist is in the opposite direction. These are facts, not ultimate answers. That is the way things happen, not why they happen.

Is a bindweed, a wild morning-glory, aware of the turning of the earth? Is a pole bean so endowed with this knowledge that I cannot force it to twist the other way? Is such knowledge embedded in the seed itself? Winds I can understand, and their inevitable direction. Vines are something else. Vines are living things, not air forced this way or that by outside forces. No, there is some law beyond, some way of life, some necessity in nature that I can recognize but not wholly understand.

A SWEET SERENITY now possesses the land. The struggle is now the measured reach toward growth and maturity. The green world is now fully green. The early rush for a place in the sun is over. Grapes fatten on my vine. Earliest apples show reddening cheeks. The pasture which Albert cut for ensilage is lush and green again. Wild blackberries ripen.

The frantic frog chorus that was so loud a little while ago has relaxed and now only the slow roll of the frog grandfathers echoes drowsily in the night. The brook, so loud in May, now whispers. On ponds and backwaters are large patches of green algae, and cattails lift green bayoneted ranks from the mucky margins.

The heat of midday brings the cicada's shrill drone, one of the drowsiest of all Summer sounds. When the cicadas rasp I know that the insect horde is out of the egg and the pupa and moving toward that stage again. Beetles swarm the grass, ants are on the march, grasshoppers launch from the grass before me as I walk the pasture. Green hornworms gnaw at the tomatoes, strange creatures that in turn become broad-winged sphinx moths and haunt the flower beds at dusk.

The struggle for life goes on, but the great haste of the green world is past. Even in the insect world a balance is struck. It is as though I were being bidden to watch and listen and understand, to relax the little worries and know the big ones for what they are. It is as though I, too, were bidden to strike a balance of serenity.

AUGUST

CHICORY BLOOMS along almost every roadside, and if it were less of a weed, less common and persistent, it would be considered a beautiful, hardy blue flower. But it is a weed and unwelcome in field and garden, even though it has its virtues. It came from Europe originally, quickly naturalized itself, and now has spread well over the country. I have seen it at the roadside in Kansas, on the Continental Divide, even on the Pacific Coast. It may yet rival the sunflower in distribution.

I am sure I have drunk plenty of chicory masquerading as coffee. The brew is made by drying the roots, roasting them, and grinding them into a powder, then steeping the powder. Pure chicory makes an acceptable drink, but it is no good when mixed with guileless coffee. If one must go to the point of substitution, one of the cereal beverages is better, to my taste.

But chicory, even the wild variety, has its virtues as a salad or a cooked green. We have tried the young, tender shoots in early Spring, both raw and cooked, and I prefer dandelions, which are available at about the same time. We grow the cultivated variety of chicory and like it in a salad, particularly when it is well blanched; unbleached, it is bitter to my palate. But it does belong with romaine and endive and crisp lettuce and a precise amount of oil and vinegar in any Summer salad.

Just now, though, I can forget the taste of wild chicory. Its flowers are such a wondrous blue that I can forgive the plant almost anything. Just as long as it doesn't invade the garden.

A HOE IS A SIMPLE TOOL. What is it but a blade set across the end of a handle? The size of the blade may vary, and the length of the handle, but there it is, a sharpened blade on one end of a stout handle—and you on the other end.

The hoe has been used repeatedly to symbolize drudging labor and serfdom, but to me it stands for man's communion with the soil. Certainly there is no disgrace nor any deep degradation inherent in the hoe. It is the stand-by of the gardener, and you can usually tell the quality of the gardener by looking at his hoe. Is it sharp? Is its blade bright with use? Is its handle polished by its owner's palm and calloused fingers?

You plant with a hoe, if you are a gardener, and you ply it all Summer long. Between weedings you loosen the soil and give encouragement to the plants themselves. Even the name comes from a race of gardeners, from the old French. But the tool is older than the French. Primitive people used a hoe, in one form or another, before there were towns or cities. The first Europeans to reach America found the natives here hoeing their maize with such an instrument, bladed often with the shoulder blade of a deer. It goes back to the Stone Age.

It is embedded in the common speech. The independent person hoes his own row, tends to his own business and gets the job done. The good worker hoes a clean row, does the job well. Old-fashioned, to be sure, but clear in its meaning. And, so far as I can find, it was the theorists, not the doers, who made the hoe the symbol of drudgery and oppression.

WE HAVE HAD A MINOR DROUGHT and the field corn is firing, sere at the base. Unless the rain which threatens today comes and settles down for a day or two we shall have short crops. The pastures, except those close along the river, are dry and turning yellow. The woods are tindery. The river itself is low.

In terms of water, drought is relative, but not in its effect. On the plains country of the West a total annual rainfall of twenty inches is considered generous. That much moisture will raise a crop and keep grasslands grazable. It is possible to get by with fifteen inches if it is well distributed. But let the year's total fall below fifteen inches and there is trouble.

Drought, which means no crop and little grass, also means dust storms on the plains. Five inches of rain can mean the difference between desert and farmland.

Here in my corner of New England the annual rainfall averages forty-seven inches. On the western plains that much moisture would mean flood and disaster, ruining the dry-land crops. But if you take ten inches off that total here, we are in trouble. Up to now we are running about four inches short, and we are fearful. Should August continue as rainless as July was, the situation would be acute. We could have a year with thirty inches of moisture, twice the allowable minimum for the plains, and still suffer from a distressing and costly drought.

I am fortunate—as I have said before—being so close beside the river. The night mist from the river waters my pastures and the garden, thus relieving both. But we need rain; the whole countryside needs rain.

We had a shower today; not enough, but a kind of promise of what may yet happen. The rain ceased

around noon, but the clouds still hang low, a thick overcast without thunderheads, so we probably shall get more tonight or tomorrow.

We were on our way home from the village this morning when the rain began. We were passing a corn field when it started pelting down, and it was one of the few times I ever saw a rainstorm raise a cloud of dust. The rain, huge drops which spattered big as silver dollars on the windshield, struck the dry soil of that corn field and each drop was like a blow on the powder-dry soil. The dust leaped. I could see it rising, even as the rain fell. It rose in a cloud and hung there, in the rain, for fully a minute before the rain brought it back down. There was so much dust in the air that we could smell it, and for a time the rain on the car was muddy brown. Then we had passed that field and the rain washed the car clean.

Not much water ran at the roadside, and the brooks didn't seem to rise half an inch. The rain went right into the soil. And this evening the pastures look fresh and green again. But we need more rain. What we need is several days of it, slow and easy, to fill the soil again and soak down to the roots of things.

It is now dusk, and even as I write the rain has started to fall again. The birds are singing happily. They, too, like the rain. This isn't a shower; it is going to continue into the night.

IT RAINED ALL NIGHT, the slow rain that is good to sleep with, and it continues unabated today. We went out this morning and picked cucumbers, and got soaked, and brought the cukes indoors and have been busy at the pickling kettle. A good occupation for a rainy day, one that pays dividends for next Winter—pickle in the rain, relish them in the snow.

Each time I smell the pickling kettle I am glad that man did not invent refrigeration too early. If he had he might have neglected the art of using spices. The great demand for spices, which was a prime factor in much early trade and exploration, rose from the difficulty of preserving meat. Meat could be dried or pickled or smoked or salted, but it lost much of its savor. Then it was discovered that spices helped to preserve meat and to make it palatable even if it were somewhat less than fresh. I am sure that many an aging joint of beef was gagged down only because pepper and other stout condiments had dulled the taste buds into acquiescence.

Spices were more than delicate flavorings when Marco Polo was a lad. Had there been such a thing as mechanical refrigeration, Europe's traffic with the East would have been of much less consequence, and it is quite possible that the voyages of Columbus would never have been undertaken. Kings and their courts were less interested in the shape of the earth than in the taste of their meat.

But out of that fugitive phase of history has come the savor of my pickling kettle, with its dill and mace and allspice and pepper and cinnamon. And out of that kettle will come, next Winter, dills and spiced sours and bread-and-butters and relish.

The house smells wonderful tonight.

THE RAIN LET UP LAST NIGHT, but it began again soon after dawn. The river runs high, though not in flood; but I took down the Bible a little while ago and have just read Noah's story again. It's a wonderful story, and the majesty of the language always thrills me.

Someone once asked William Allen White who had been the most powerful influence on his writing style. Mr. White looked at his questioner in surprise and said that the Bible had been the basic influence on most of the writers of his generation. He might have gone further, for the Bible has been the strongest direct influence on writing in the English language ever since the sixteenth century. Shakespeare probably is the one great writer we have who was not directly influenced by the King James Bible. It wasn't published until 1611, five years before Shakespeare's death. But the same influences which shaped the King James Bible must have influenced Shakespeare. And the Tyndale Bible, from which much of the King James version came, was published twenty-two years before Shakespeare was born; so even Shakespeare's language and wonderful sonority cannot be said to be Bible-free.

It wasn't until I read John Selden, a contemporary of Shakespeare who long outlived him, that I understood some of the amazing sentence structure of the Bible. Selden, who knew many of the men who helped compile the King James translation, pointed out that it is in many parts essentially a translation, almost literal, of ancient Hebraisms. Thus we have such sentences as: "It is my mouth that speaketh to you . . . His bowels did yearn for his brother . . . God ended the work which he had done." The language is long familiar, though the idiom remains strange even after all these years.

THE RAIN HAS ENDED and we have a new world, clean and bright and almost as fresh as it was in early May. The river runs high, but we haven't been flooded. It was precisely the kind of rain we needed, slow, steady, gentle, so there was a minimum of washing in fields and gardens and a maximum of penetration. The weary look is gone from the pastures and the corn fields look as they should, fresh and green and properly revived.

The way the lively green returns even during two or three days of overcast—rainy days, this time—convinces me that those actinic rays of the sun cut right through even heavy clouds and supply the chlorophyll with energy. Dust is more of a mask than clouds, more difficult for the sunlight to penetrate. That is one reason that even a light Summer shower is so helpful. It supplies little moisture, but it washes away the dust from the leaves and allows them to get to work again. It helps the plants to breathe.

I notice that the professional gardeners urge that the ornamental evergreens be sprayed with water, on the foliage, during the hot weather. It's the same idea, and it obviously works for the deciduous shrubs too.

THE SMELL OF CORN POLLEN is like no other fragrance in the world, and here in America it is as typical of August as the crunch of tooth on the roasting ear. It is a fragrance, however, that predates European settlement here by untold centuries. It hangs heavy now over the land, but it was here when Rome was young.

Despite research and exploration, the origins of our corn are still misted in the remote past. The most we can say is that the American Indians must have developed it, in one of the great botanical achievements of all time. It undoubtedly stems from a wild grass, but even that grass has been only tentatively identified as Central American teosinte. Indians of both Americas were growing sweet corn, pop corn and meal corn of various strains when the first Europeans arrived. Long before that it had passed that stage where it would revert to the wild type if left untended. Botanists can make only very rough estimates of its age.

The developments of corn since Europeans came here

have been notable, but in comparison to the original development even they remain minor. We have altered its appearance somewhat, greatly increased its yield, changed its milling qualities. But nubbins found in ancient cliff dwellings of the Southwest can be matched, feature by feature, by nubbins from almost any back-yard patch of today.

The pollen smell I smell here in my valley today is at least as old in this area as the occasional flint arrowheads we find. Now it is an odor known almost all over the world, in Australia, the Argentine, Asiatic Russia, most of Europe's flatlands, for Indian maize has become a staple foodstuff for the whole world. But its history is as elusive as the pollen smell itself.

THE SUMAC CATCHES MY EYE each time I drive down the road, for at a certain bend there is a big clump, the humble smooth sumac intermingled with the tall, airy staghorn. Just now their leaves form sworls and star patterns that delight the eye, and I wonder why no photographer has caught the beauty of their soft lines and the elusive play of light on their leaf and stem.

About a third of the way up my mountain, on a bench-like plateau, there is a gnarly stand of sumac, too, which I have thought from time to time to cut and burn, since it has no real purpose and only takes up room that pines might better use. But I walked up that way last evening as the full moon was rising, and I knew that I shall never lay an ax to it. In the moonlight it was like a grove of white-blossomed shrubs, dazzling in its beauty. All it was, of course, was the moonlight reflected from the shimmery underside of the pendant sumac leaves, but the effect was pure magic. It was silvery white moonlight multiplied and magnified.

I shall leave those sumacs for Fall, too. When Fall begins to creep across the land the sumac is the first to know it. Some impatient stems will take on a touch of scarlet before this month is out, but the full color will not come until the birches turn to tarnished gold. Then that benchland will be pure magnificence with its slow turn from faint scarlet to red orange and deepest crimson.

And when Winter comes again it will be dark and beautiful against the snow, with its grotesque stems and its fat candle-flame heads of deep red berries for the birds. Even in Winter nakedness it is a lovely thing to see.

LOOKING AT THE SQUASH PLANTS this morning I thought that the Indians of the Southwest had an eye for beauty as well as meaning when they chose the squash blossom as a symbol of fertility and plenty. It has a generous grace of form as well as a richness of color ranging from golden orange to sun yellow. On one of our Hubbard plants the bloom is a hand's breadth across, so big it is almost rank, yet the petal texture is tissue thin, easily crushed by a careless finger.

The modern botanist speaks of the family as *Cucurbita* and includes in it the pumpkin, the muskmelon, the cucumber and the squashes of all sizes and shapes. The Indians called it askutasquash and contributed the syllable we apply to one branch of the family. The Indians' askutasquash were primarily the tough-shelled pumpkins and the tough-skinned squash that mature late and keep well into Winter. Squash and corn were usually grown in the same field, and squash blossoms and corn tassels were twin symbols of fertility in Indian ceremonies over much of this land.

Look at a classic Navaho silver necklace and you will find the squash blossom, stylized in the white metal with open petals and round fertile ovary beneath, for it is the female flower. In silver it is conventionalized to a fine simplicity, but there it is, the August blossom of the squash vine which crept along the sandy soil and opened its petals to the sun, the rain and the four-winged bee. And there it is in our garden, askutasquash or *Cucurbita*, as you will, symbol of the soil's fertility, live in color and open to the sun, the rain and the bees.

THE URGENCY THAT WAS MIDSUMMER now begins to relax and September comes in sight over the land. I see it in

the trees, at the roadside where uncut weeds begin to reach maturity, and in the fields and pastures. Oat fields are stubble now, the golden grain harvested. Corn stands taller than I do, the ears in silk and filling day by day. The first goldenrod begins to gleam in the fence rows where wild asters will be taking the place of daisy and black-eyed Susan before long.

Spring is sprouting, and early Summer is the rush of growth and the competition of blooming. But late Summer is more sedate; it is fulfillment of time and purpose, the seed, the fruit, for which growth itself was destined. The time of haste is past, the pod, the capsule, the nut, the seed-head already formed and coming to completion. The egg is hatched, the fledgling now on the wing. Even the bees are less urgent in their rounds. Small rabbits scurry at the roadside, well past the nursling stage; and woodchucks, full of sun and succulence, begin to lay on the fat for hibernation.

Hot days are still upon us, but the sun's nooning is from a different angle; and nights lengthen, dusk to dawn. I heard the owl last night, and today the crows are restless and full of noise. All a part of the pattern, the maturing change that has its own calendar. For who can stay the wind or hasten the apple? Time flows with the season, not the other way around, and the season flows like a river, from its own springs. Summer ripens and matures, even as the fox grapes on my river bank, and August leans toward September and equinox and Autumn.

I WALKED DOWN TO THE BOGLAND at the bend in the road today, where stagnant backwaters from the river form a pond and a swamp. It is largely scummed over, full of algae, and I had the feeling that anything could happen in such waters, any kind of life arise from them. Here in the dead heat of August was the marshy margin and the primordial ooze, black and mucky, with cattails standing rank. I felt, in approaching it, as if I were walking backward in time toward remote beginnings.

Even the pond creatures and those along its margin belong to another age. Of the reptiles, the snapping turtle that lay on a rotting log and glared at me was one of the ancients, armored like a creature of the Silurian age and eying the world as from the midst of a tree-fern jungle. The frogs, too, are primitives, tadpoles which have shed gills and tails and crept up onto the land in the venerable cycle of living things from the ooze to the rocks. The water snakes were still slithering through the vanished age when pterodactyls had not yet grown wings.

The birds, too, had an other-worldly air, the gaunt herons with their beady eyes and darting beaks, the bobtailed kingfishers which have little grace or actual beauty for all their quick, spectacular efficiency. They, too, might be creatures from that ancient in-between time when the dry land was still rising from the swamps.

The water was green with algae, tepid with mud warmth, a kind of protoplasmic soup full of strange and struggling uncertainties. But the hills looked down, and the hills were certainty itself, land risen from the muck, the maturity of an ancient age.

THE SENTIMENTAL VIEW of nature is strangely twisted. It gives to birds and beasts, even to the elements themselves, attributes which they not only lack but are totally unaware of; and it sees morality lessons in the birds, the bees, the trees and the flowers. The fact is that nature has no morality and draws no morals. Nature rests on a solid basis of cause and effect, but neither the causes nor the effects are moral or immoral in the human sense. Spring is in no sense a reward for those who have endured Winter. The gorgeous spectacle of Autumn has a botanical and a chemical reason, but not an aesthetic one.

When I hear someone talk about the happy little birds and the delightful little animals I wince. Animals do play, or seem to, at times, and there seems to be a sense of happiness in birds sometimes; but I am not sure even of that. Birds and animals are not noticeably tolerant and life in the woods and fields is a constant round of attack and competition. When I see the way the birds squabble at our feeding station, gluttonous and ill tempered, I wish some of the sentimentalists would pause and look. Life among the birds is a grim matter of survival, and those who get pushed around too much do not survive.

Even in the plant world the same basic truth exists. Competition is constant, for root space, for sun, for moisture, for attention from the agents of pollination, for the means of survival. And the wars are even more pronounced and evident among the insects.

Man is really the only creature, probably the only living thing, which tempers the competition and possesses compassion to any degree. Examples of it elsewhere are extremely rare.

WE WERE EATING DINNER on the porch this evening when we heard a large splash in the river. I looked up, but the long shadows made dusk on the water. I saw something moving there, something the color of a tan Great Dane, and I wondered for an instant whose dog was coming to visit us. Pat, lying on the grass, looked up but without the alert interest he would have shown for an intruder. Then Barbara exclaimed, "A deer!"

It was a large doe. She came up the steep bank and looked at us, not fifty yards away, and crossed the road and went around the garage, unhurried, quite without fear. She paused inquisitively at the old horse trough, then leaped the barnyard fence, light as thistledown, and walked with dainty, unhurried steps to the next fence and leaped it with ridiculous ease. Her big ears funneled for alarming sounds, and twice she turned to look at us; but she was still unhurried as she crossed the pasture, so confident she stopped to pluck a few mouthfuls of clover. Then she sailed over the far fence as easily as I would have stepped over a log, and went into the woods and up the mountainside.

There had been no yelping of dogs on the other side of the river, no sign or sound of a chase. She wasn't frightened. She merely came down to the river, crossed for her own reasons, and went on about her business, which obviously was up on the mountain. And Pat, who bristles and raises an alarm at the sight of a heifer outside the pasture, gave her but that one look, then lay back content and dozed again. He knew, and she knew, that she was no intruder. She lives here, though we seldom see her; this is her land even more literally than it is mine.

DAWN COMES MISTY NOW, as with a foretaste of the chill ahead. Over the river the mist is like smoke, curling and wreathing in the sunrise air as the mysterious little currents of breeze play tag. White smoke, the incense of fading Summer, which vanishes as the sun reaches an hour above the horizon.

This is not the haze of high humidity which clouds the hills on a sultry midsummer morning; this is the shimmery gauze of the changing season, the dew which washes the dust from the Summer-weary leaves along the river and keeps my valley green beyond the season's prime. This is the blown breath of Autumn long before there is even a hint of frost in the air.

It was here this morning, though the sky was clear and the horizon clean, a brilliant morning full of blue and green and the long shadows of sunrise. It was not a gray mist; it was white, white as daisy petals, whiter than cumulus clouds, shimmery white and so thin it shimmered of silver as the sun struck through it. It was like a spider web jeweled with dew, and even less tangible. I could wave a hand and see a swirl and a quick gleam of sun in the momentarily mistless air.

Indian Summer will come, and the thin, far haze on the hilltops; but this is even less substantial. The haze of Indian Summer will be day-long; this is morning mist, sunrise magic that vanished even as I watched. It is a curl of shimmer, the very essence of impermanence, a swift glimpse of Autumn already around the bend of the river and waiting there beyond the hills.

WE SPEAK OF NIGHT as being black, and in a sense we are right, for at night we are all but color-blind. That part of our eye which gives us night vision, such as it is, lacks the ability to distinguish red from green. But the night sky is not black. It is blue, a deep, deep blue, much more like that color which was once known as midnight blue than any other color in the spectrum. For proof, if you care to have it, take a camera loaded with color film and expose it to the night sky when there is no moon. When the negative is developed it will show you this intense blue, seen through the impartial eye of the camera and recorded on the color-sensitive film.

We think of night as black because it lacks the distinguishing colors of daylight. Go into a flower garden on a moonless night and you can't distinguish a blue petunia from a maroon dahlia. You can make out the white flowers, which pick up enough light from the stars or even from the remote glow in any night sky to become obvious. But yellow loses its identity in the darkness almost as completely as does red. Only in strong starlight can yellow be distinguished as such.

We walked this evening under a moonless sky and in an all but colorless world. The maples were gray, trunk and branch and leaf. So was the big popple, though some of its leaves turned a shimmery side which caught the faint starlight. The white birches were stark and ghostly. Queen Anne's lace at the roadside was a drift of puffy white, smoky. Black-eyed Susans were invisible. And Pat was a most peculiar shape, only part dog, the white part.

THE WINDS OF AUGUST are particularly painful to some people, not because they are winds but because they are laden with pollen. To those susceptible to hay fever such winds are poisonous. They carry pollen of ragweed, plantain, certain grasses and certain trees, and that pollen is in a minor way as poisonous as a snake's venom. Wind-blown pollen con-

tains proteins that are poisonous to the human system, particularly those pollens which can penetrate the mucous membranes. Some persons are more susceptible than others, and some are almost critically susceptible.

The likeness to snake venom is no mere figure of speech. Venom is a concentrated form of lethal proteins, with other ingredients. All pollen has a large amount of protein, too. But the pollen of most plants contains a type of protein not readily absorbed by human membranes, and therefore not so poisonous. And a good deal of pollen is not wind-borne, being either too heavy or designed, in the peculiar scheme of plant life, for more direct transportation, such as that provided by bees.

Generally speaking, no plant with conspicuous flowers or strong fragrance will cause trouble for hay fever sufferers. Such plants have pollen designed to be carried by insects. The petals of showy flowers, or their fragrance, is usually proof of this, for both petals and fragrance are the flower's means of attracting insects. It is the lesser flowers or grasses and weeds that do the damage, for they are wind-pollinated.

WHAT A DULL PLACE the flower garden would be from now until deep frost if all the petunias were still in Brazil! These descendants of a native South American flower come to bloom at just the right time to fill those gaps where earlier blossoms finished their season's work and departed. Given any kind of encouragement, the petunias bloom like mad, to the delight of the hummingbirds, the moths, and me, until only the chrysanthemums remain to defy the frost.

The petunia's name comes from the Brazilian word for tobacco and is a cousin of nicotiana and other variants in the tobacco family. It comes in too many colors to list, and self-sown seed is seldom true to its parenthood. Petunias are among our most persistent self-seeders, and we do little to discourage this trait. We let them grow unless they interfere with other flowers, and every night and on damp, cool mornings we are surrounded by sweet, faintly spiced fragrance, so powerful it pervades the whole garden side of the house.

Plant breeders have done strange and surprising things with petunia blossoms, adding frills and flounces and even furbelows to the original trumpet. They have varied and variegated the colors. The results do not always please me, but they must please someone. When I want to transform a bare corner of the garden in a hurry, I scatter a light peppering of run-

135

of-the-mill petunia seeds and they flourish mightily. But that is seldom necessary. We restrain the idealistic impulse in June and let enough volunteers grow to have plenty to move around later. Meticulous gardeners frown on such practice, but I'm just a country boy who likes flowers.

I HEARD A MAN CALLED BIASED TODAY, as though bias were a sin. To be sure the man was biased, and will be all his life. Show me an unbiased man and I will show you a man not only without character but without convictions or beliefs. I suspect that the most biased of men we know are those generally regarded as admirable members of society—preachers, and judges, and even teachers. The preacher is biased in favor of the good and moral life, the judge is biased in the direction of justice, and the teacher's bias is in the direction of knowledge and its intelligent use.

It's the direction of the bias that is important, not the fact of a bias itself. We all have our likes and dislikes, in food, in dress, in books, in ideas, in people, and that is as it should be. Take away those and you take away the individuality and the inherent right of all of us to think and believe. A bias is a positive thing as well as a negative. How can you go through life without taking a stand? If you are against something, you must be for its opposite, and you can't be in favor of one proposition without finding its reverse distasteful or objectionable.

I am biased in many ways, and there are times when there is no alternative to taking a stand. I register my bias every time I cast my ballot. Each day I live some bias or other. And every time I write a letter or a piece for the public prints I must reveal some of my biases. Otherwise I would have nothing to say. God preserve the bias in us; but God also give us the wisdom to know bias, including our own, when we see it. Give me an honest bias any time in preference to a dishonest impartiality.

THE SHRILL SOUND OF THE CICADA rises to a crescendo on the quiet air this afternoon, then dies away in a diminuendo that is the voice of the season itself, a little tired, a little satisfied, slowly coming to the inevitable end.

It was for this that the year turned, the ice melted, the seed sprouted, the new shoot opened bud and the blossom opened petal. This is the sequence, certain as sunrise, and there is a quiet triumph about it, a feeling of completion.

THERE IS A SMALL PATCH of horse balm or rich weed, as some call it, in the thin woods at the edge of the middle pasture. It is a member of the mint family and one of the few mints with a yellow flower, a small flower that blooms at the tip and has a strong lemon scent. As a flower it is inconsequential, but its botanical name, *Collinsonia Canadensis,* is a reminder of Peter Collinson, an English amateur botanist and naturalist of the eighteenth century.

Peter Collinson was one of the group of inquiring minds which poked into all kinds of natural phenomena and, by the very act of inquiry, helped lay the groundwork for natural science. He had a number of American correspondents and exchanged not only ideas but plants with them. He had a part in introducing into this country the culture of hemp and flax and silkworms, and he introduced many American plants into England.

I find no ready reference to correspondence between Collinson and Jefferson, though they were of kindred minds. But in another part of the broad field of natural science Collinson had an eager ally in Benjamin Franklin. It was Collinson who gave Franklin his first information about electrical experiments being made in Europe. Collinson, the man for whom the horse weed in my woodland was named, thus had a hand in Franklin's experiments. Indirectly, it was Peter Collinson who helped put electric lights and electric power into my house. I should thank him every day.

I WONDER WHAT HAPPENS to highway engineers when they get a commission to build a road. Something happens, because one of them lays a ruler on a map and draws a line, another one gets behind a transit and runs that line through whatever is in the way, and still another gets on a bulldozer and rips out a gash across the countryside. Trees fall, houses are torn down, villages are bisected, landmarks are obliterated. And they call it "Highway Improvement."

Last year a comfortable old road up in Massachusetts was doomed to "improvement." True, it was a somewhat winding road, but a driver with any prudence could drive there in safety, shaded by twin rows of fine old maples. When the "improvers" were through, those trees, which had been seventy-five years growing, were gone in smoke. Now one can lunge across the devastated countryside there at sixty or seventy miles an hour on a long concrete slab. To what end?

Today we drove on a broad strip of new highway just fifteen miles from here which extends only ten miles or so, between two villages, and is not in any sense a main traffic artery. It was completed only a few months ago. Before the engineers went to work on it, for whatever their mysterious reasons, it was a pleasant, tree-lined road. Today it was a barren strip of new highway, without a tree, a scar on the landscape.

It happens all the time and everywhere. Devastation is wrought in the name of The Highway, and the devastation is excused as a necessity of progress. Progress whither? I have yet to drive along one of these stark new highways without seeing a crew at work planting grass and trees and bushes. First the devastation, then the repairs, the strange apology for the stupidity of those who drew a line on a map, ran that line with a transit, gouged it out with a bulldozer, none of them able to avoid an irreplaceable grove or a fine old house or even a quiet, peaceful village.

Now comes the time of rich purple in the fields and meadows, denoting not only a time but a maturity. It is as though the whole Summer had been building toward this deep, strong color to match the gold of late sunlight and early goldenrod. And this is, in a sense, what has been happening. Flower colors are mysterious in origin. It is generally accepted that the full, hot sun of the tropics produces the strong colors, the brilliant golden yellows, the deep oranges, the full-bodied scarlets. And it is also understood that the lesser sun of the temperate zones produces lesser colors, for the most part. Cultivated flowers, of course, are excepted in this theorizing.

Our early Spring brings us, except in the violets, the weaker shades, the whites, the pinks, the thin yellows and the light blues. Early Summer warms the landscape with stronger yellows, deeper blues, some orange, and a variety of reds. But it takes late August and the accumulation of sun and warmth to give us the strength of purple in showy mass.

The thistles flaunt it. Burdock, troublesome weed that it is, reveals purple flower tufts that will ripen into hook-spined burs eager to hitch a ride to new fields. Ironweed, standing tall in the lowlands, lifts massed heads of deep purple to the sun. And the asters now approach their season, not only the white and lavender ones but the rich purple ones that carry New England's name.

Summer begins to fray away toward September, but it does so in purple majesty, strong, full-bodied, full of sunlight.

I WISH I KNEW THE MAN TO THANK for the magnificent Norway spruce which grows just outside my study window. It is more than three feet through at the butt and it towers a hundred feet into the air. I know its height, for I have measured it by triangulation. It has been kept trimmed twenty feet up from the ground, but its long, sweeping branches droop so low I have to stoop when I go beneath it. It shades a circle almost forty feet in diameter. In Summer it is a canopy in light showers, a vast, cool, green tepee where we lie or sit in comfort. In Winter it has a wind-murmur that is pleasant to sleep with. It provides me with bushels of resinous cones to tinder my fire.

A man in the village, a man in his eighties, remembers it as a big tree in his boyhood and says it must be two hundred years old. I see other such trees scattered through this region, but few of them as big and venerable. Someone must have passed this way, long, long ago, with a cartload of seedlings and swapped them for butter and eggs. The pioneer farmers planted them and no doubt disease and storm and thoughtless ax took a good many of them. But those that survived have thriven mightily, though I see no young groves of them.

I share my tree with the birds and squirrels, as we share all trees. House wrens nest in it, and an occasional robin, and the squirrels explore its heights. But it is the Winter birds which most love it, for it shelters chickadees from the storms and provides endless employment for nuthatches and brown creepers.

LOOKING AT THE TREETOPS now I begin to see again that no Summer lasts forever. Change sets in with the shifting sun. The brilliant green of active chlorophyll begins to fade, the bulk of its work done. True, the change comes slowly and it is essentially a difference that has been there since Spring opened the first leaf buds, but one does not see those differences earlier in the overwhelming greenness of a fresh, new world.

I went up the mountainside today and looked down, and the elms along the river looked weary, their leaves definitely rusty. The apple trees, always a yellower green than the maples, for instance, are now yellower still and a few completely yellow leaves have begun to fall. All shagbarks tend to an early sere, and their rust creeps across the leaves now, though they are still a deeper green than the white ash which grows plentifully among the hickories.

Maples still are lush green. They vary in leaf color all season long, and the row of sugar maples beside the river is a study in shades of green, some dark as oaks, some almost as light as birches. The giant poplar, the maverick in that row of maples, is the yellowest green of all, the green I knew best as a boy for it is almost identical with that of its close cousin, the cottonwood.

The brightest greens, it seems to me, are on those trees that will flaunt the most brilliant reds and yellows in another month or six weeks. The Autumn colors, of course, come from acids and sugars left in the leaves when their Summer's work is done; but it may be that those which face Fall in a blaze of color are those which have put in the busiest Summer. Certainly those which are greenest now will be brightest later, the maples, the oaks and the lesser dogwoods.

THE COWS HAVE CUT A PATH across the pasture with their cloven hoofs. It runs from the lower gate diagonally to the fence, then out toward a wild cherry tree, around the tree, back to the fence, across Millstone Brook and, by a winding route, to the far end of the upper pasture. They take this path going and coming, single-file, each time cutting the path a little deeper.

I have walked that path repeatedly, wondering why a cow should have chosen that particular route. It wanders, and for no reason that I can see. I think that if I had laid out that path I should have fixed my eye on the destination and gone straight to it. Then I look back on my own life, to where I started and where I went in my journey before I arrived where

I am now, and by contrast with mine this cowpath is ruler-straight.

My path was more like that of the river at my door, which loops upon itself. And yet, even the river made its way around major obstacles. I, stubbornly human, persisted in climbing over hill after hill even though, as I now can see, there were ways around. But each time I climbed a hill I told myself that I had strengthened my muscles and seen a new vista.

I suppose the whole matter turns upon the question whether the objective or the journey is more important. My theological friends insist upon the objectives, and yet I find that even they tend to the belief that theirs is the only true road, thus confounding their own argument. And I know that when I meet a man, either a temporal or a spiritual man, who has gone directly to his objective, I too often find him a narrow man with little range of experience. He has climbed too few hills, for my taste, seen too few unfamiliar vistas. He is a one-track man.

THE GOLDENROD is early September's flower, but it livens late August too, the golden spray that lines the fence rows and the pastures and meadows, yellow as the late Summer sun itself. Even its foliage partakes of the season, a dusty green rather than the pristine green of June when the world was new and shining; and its flowers are Autumn-generous, fulfillment in multiple, as becomes the season. Only the asters, which come to their full glory just a little later, are as beautiful now, stem by stem.

Solidago is the botanical name of the goldenrod, reminder of its herbal qualities. The name, from the Latin, means to strengthen, allusion to the general and generous healing qualities once attributed to it. So it is *Solidago*, the strengthener, goldenrod the strong and generous. We no longer deal much in infusions of goldenrod, but the plant is unchanged; and it certainly remains a symbol of strength and persistence in the face of all odds. Give it a roothold almost anywhere and it makes its own way, coming up to September with a spray of bloom.

Most of the goldenrods—they belong to the composites and are of a large family with an amazing number of variants —are natives of America. The distribution is broad, evidenced by the fact that such widely separated states as Alabama, Kentucky and Nebraska have chosen the goldenrod as their state flower. It grows at the seaside and in the Midlands and even in the mountains. But best of all it grows with the purple asters and the Joe Pye weed and the ironweed, gold for their blues and purples when the days themselves turn blue and gold.

I RESPECT THE CHEMISTS. They have accomplished some remarkable things, for my convenience and my comfort and for the public welfare. But now and then they and their allies and sales promoters reach right over into the field of vandalism. The latest example is the development of a spray to kill roadside weeds and shrubbery. It no doubt has its legitimate purpose, but when it is promoted as a boon to highway maintenance men it is time for someone to shout, "No!" The proposed plan is to spray all roadsides, particularly such secondary and country roads as I live on, which lace the whole nation with pleasant escapes from the roaring turnpikes.

If this should become a national project, every sprayed roadside will be as sterile and uninhabited as a city gutter. Birds will retreat to the remote woodland. Wildflowers will be found only on the inaccessible hilltops and in the trackless swamps. Rabbits and other small game will be robbed of their homes. We will all live in a land where the roads are as barren as the back alleys of Chicago.

But it may fail as a project, not because of the reasons I cite but because with the vegetation gone the roadsides will wash and erode with every rain and the roads themselves will be undermined. Even highway engineers should be able to understand that.

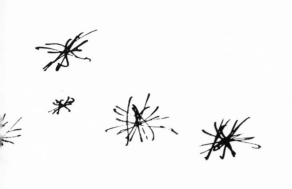

SEPTEMBER

I SPENT TWO HOURS this afternoon counting goldenrod blossoms. Probably someone else has done it, but I have never seen the figures. I took one spray of Sweet Goldenrod, *Solidago odora*, and counted the individual flowers. There were 3,023 on that one spray. But that is only a base count. Each of those flowers is made up of five to ten florets grouped in a head like the center of a sunflower. I needed a 10-power glass to see them clearly, but there they were, each floret with its own stamens and pollen, its own pistil and ovary. So on that one average goldenrod plume were a minium of 15,000 to 20,000 florets. When all the seed comes to ripeness, that one plume would seed half an acre with one seed for every square foot.

But seed casualties are high. Probably not more than ten seeds from one goldenrod plume will strike favorable soil and sprout. At least half of those will fail to survive. Nature is generous in her seeding, but also harsh in her conditions. Otherwise, my pastures would have nothing but goldenrod instead of grass and clover. Or thistles, or any one of a hundred non-forage plants.

Another item worth considering is that each of those thousands of goldenrod florets produces pollen. We now know that goldenrod pollen is not a common source of hay fever, but it is a source of honey. Each time I look at the goldenrod along the fence rows I see almost as many bees among the yellow blossoms as there were among the clover blooms two months ago. Goldenrod is the last big crop for the bees, and beekeepers tell me they depend on goldenrod for most of their late Summer and early Autumn honey. So the honey known commercially as "clover honey" probably has a good deal of essence of goldenrod in it.

THOSE WHO HAVE LIVED with a garden all Summer come now to the time when a sense of immediacy begins to close in. Days shorten. Growth slackens. The garden is still full and overflowing with plenty, but we know this may be the last full crop.

At planting time the season stretched ahead almost without limit. The first fruits were precious, garner from the fertile soil. Midsummer brought bounty. Then so much came at once that there was a surfeit. We wearied of green beans, wearied even of sweet corn, could eat only so much of Summer squash. But now, with the end in sight, when frost shall be creeping down our valley, the garden and its produce are precious again.

Late corn is at its peak. We have begun again to have it twice a day. But now we ask if the late lettuce will make its way to the salad bowl. It is just beginning to head. Will we be fortunate, as last year, and have it well into October? Will the scattered blossoms on the limas make more pods, or is this the final crop? And what of the string beans and the Summer squash, which we scorned a month ago? Will the blight now strike the tomato vines, or will we have still another canning of them? Should we pick green tomatoes and make piccalilli, or risk a frost? Will the Winter squash have another month of growth and maturity?

We eat, stuffing ourselves with vitamins against the dark days ahead, and the flavor, under the pressure of uncertainties, once more has the savor of the first garden peas. It was there all the time, but it palled on us until the end was in sight.

WE THINK OF FULL AUTUMN, sere leaf and hard frost, as the time for bird migration. But southbound singers who summered north of us have been with us since the first katydids saluted the August dark. They came so quietly that we were scarcely aware of them unless we heard some sweet, familiar fragment of song in the cool of early morning. I heard such fragments this morning and tentatively identified them as songs of a yellowthroat and a mourning warbler, though I am not sure and I never did catch sight of them.

Most of these migrants sing a little, but not much, for the mating season is past and gone. And we see few flashing, colorful wings, for the adults have passed the height of their colorful season and the youngsters haven't yet achieved it. The birds wear sober traveling clothes on their southward trip.

We speak of them as migrants and we think of them going south for the Winter, which is only partially true. We think of them from our own viewpoint, that of relatively static creatures. But the birds actually are only going from one part of their range to another, and their range or homeland is tremendous in extent. To use an exaggerated comparison, they are like farmers who go from the upland corn field at one end

of their farms to the river bottom meadow at the other end. The farmer doesn't "migrate" from one field to another. The birds happen to use "fields" that are hundreds, sometimes thousands, of miles apart.

We are harvesting a small crop of potatoes such as not half a dozen other people ever grew. They are a brand-new variety, developed by a friend of ours in the village, a gentleman of years who retired from business not long ago to work in his garden. He has been a gardener for perhaps seventy years, though we knew him first as a merchant, a quiet little man full of courtesy and reticence. Last Spring we heard that he grew the best tomato plants in the whole area, so we went to see him.

He had a big garden and an ample cold frame and a homemade greenhouse. His plants were unusually good. He and Barbara talked garden with that instinctive understanding of those who know garden soil intimately, and she provoked his admiration by saying she had bigger green beans than he had, and bigger corn, a fact he verified a few days later by a visit to us. Barbara chose her tomato plants and he gave her several more, his own favorites, and he recommended the earliest cabbage we ever grew. And finally he took us to his sanctum, his greenhouse. There he proudly showed us a flat of potato seedlings small as sprouting carrots. Potatoes growing from seed.

Potato seed is almost pepper-fine. It grows in those little ball-pods which appear where the potato plant has bloomed. Few people have the patience to gather it or to plant and tend it, but this man is patience personified. And before we left he gave us a double handful of seed potatoes he grew from such seedlings, on condition that we would plant them. We did, and they grew like mad, and now we are digging them. They are big, long and smooth and fine of flavor and texture. We shall save enough to plant a long row of them next year, that we may perpetuate the Beebe potato and give it a name, at least privately, which its originator is too modest to do. Like most of the deeply devoted gardeners I ever knew, he wants no credit. All he wants is time and soil in which to plant seeds, watch them sprout, see them grow, nurture them to fruition. But anyone with the skill and patience to see that a potato blossom is fertilized with the right pollen, to bring that blossom to seed, to gather the seed, to grow it and bring potato seedlings to maturity with a brand-new variety, has a touch of genius in my lexicon.

THE CARDINAL FLOWERS are in bloom on the mountain just above the middle pasture. They offer one of the most satisfying reds in the whole wildflower spectrum; the only one that can rival it, in this area at least, is the Oswego tea, the deep red variety of wild bergamot, now almost through blossoming.

The cardinal flower is one of the wild lobelias, a late-blooming member of the family. Its flowers grow in loose spikes and each flower is a kind of slender tube with long triple-lobed lips loose as tatters. The length of the tube makes the flower something of a rarity; it is too long for insect tongues, and even the long-tongued bumblebee can make little headway here. The hummingbird and the sphinx moth are the only creatures really equipped to get the cardinal flower's nectar and cross-fertilize it. In consequence, since hummingbirds are far less numerous than bees, the cardinal flower matures few seeds. The plant does most of its multiplying by perennial shoots and ranging roots.

The lobelias were named for Mattias de l'Obel, a Flemish physician and botanist who lived in Shakespeare's day. He wrote several works on plants, undoubtedly used herbs in his own medicines, and dedicated his most important botanical study to Queen Elizabeth I. One American lobelia, *Lobelia inflata*, or Indian tobacco, is still used somewhat in medicine. But the cardinal flower is the spectacular member of the family. It has an acrid, milky juice, possibly medicinal; but even its botanical name, *Lobelia cardinalis*, refers to its enduring glory, its color.

Fall

Last night was cool, the chilliest of the season, and when I went out this morning to look at the flowers I found the bumblebees in the zinnias. That is a good index to the season.

To a bumblebee, a zinnia is more than a flower. It is a bed with a coverlet, protection from the dew and the chill. As I went from one big zinnia flower to another I ruffled back the petals and found six bumblebees in the first ten flowers, all of them too sluggish and sleepy to resent my intrusion. They had crawled in last evening and let the petals curl back over them, snug as could be.

I left them alone and came in and made the breakfast coffee, watching from the kitchen window. Sure enough, before the sun was an hour high here came the birds. Three thrashers came and began to search the zinnias. They, too, know that the bumblebees sleep there. They worked down the row of zinnias, breakfasting on the bees. And I turned back to the stove and set the bacon to cook. I breakfasted on hogs that don't know a zinnia from a calla lily.

Looking up the mountain this morning I saw Autumn sitting on the first ledge, in a red and yellow shirt, with a jug of sweet cider in one hand, a bunch of purple asters in the other, a grin on his face and an unspoken hello in his eyes. He sat there for an hour or two, then went on up the mountainside and disappeared among the pines. The day became too warm for him. But he will be back.

After lunch I went fishing, or at least made that excuse for getting out on the river. I took the motor and went leisurely upstream a couple of miles, then drifted slowly back. The water is so slack and the current so slow that it took more than an hour to drift down. The sky was a magnificent blue, a few big cumulus clouds drifted far away to the west, and the sun was hot. In the sluggish backwaters beyond the island the blackbirds were noisy and when I passed close by they rose in a cloud and circled and came back and settled in the reeds again, chattering. A woodpecker hammered at a dead limb on a big popple and the rattling of his busy beak made a splendid echo; I suspect that he was less interested in the grubs he might find than in the sound he made.

Just above the house I drifted into a slow eddy on the far side of the river; I sat there, quiet, for ten minutes, and my eye caught a lithe movement on the bank. A half-grown fox came up the game path along the bank, not ten feet from me. He paused and watched me with beady eyes for perhaps half a minute, ears eager, nose wrinkling for my scent, then turned and went on, alert, unhurried.

WE SPEAK OF THE WIND and its voices, but most of the voices are in the trees. And even those voices vary from season to season, almost from month to month. They are speaking today, as the Fall winds rise—the winds, not the gales which have, beyond denial, voices all their own.

The oaks speak today with a heavy voice, crisp with the crispness of their leaves. The big maples have a strong voice, with their big leaves rustling and thousands of them. At first

listening one might think there was little difference between the voice of the oaks and that of the maples, but stand in an oak grove and listen, then move to a clump of maples. The difference is clear, a softer voice in the maples with their softer leaves and looser stems.

The whisperers, of course, are the members of the willow family, the poplars in particular. Aspens and cottonwoods whisper in anything but an absolute calm; give them a breeze and you can hear them afar, fairly chattering, their heart-shaped leaves on long, limber stems, each leaf dancing against a dozen others. The birches come a close second in their whispering, the small gray birches in particular; as their leaves crisp with September they, too, almost chatter.

The evergreens, the pines and spruces and hemlocks, hum rather than speak, and theirs is closest of all to music. The music of the pines is heard best at night, and best of all on a Winter night when their deciduous brothers of the woodland stand stark in the starlight. But the big Norway spruce outside my study is singing a September song today.

A RAINY DAY AND A DARK DAY, and although it is yet early September it had the feel of Fall. The house was warm enough, according to the thermometer, but it felt chill, and I put on a heavier shirt to work at my desk this morning. This afternoon we built a fire on the hearth and the heavy air made it smoke into the room until the flue had warmed up. We had the wood-smoke smell of Autumn, a tang that persisted long after the smoke went up the flue as it should.

The slow, chill wash of the rain and the metallic patter in the downspouts, together with the hearth fire, gave the feel of October, of full Autumn. How different are the rains of the four seasons! This was a cool rain, an end-of-Summer rain, quiet, persistent. It brought down the first leaves, the few that have rushed the season. Two months from now we shall have the early Winter rains of November, which can be as cold as sleet and carry the threat of ice and snow. Rainy November days eat into my spirit. I think of them as black rains.

April rains can be as cold as those of November, but they have a different feel. Still touched with March, they also have the hope of May in them. The earth seems to welcome them, and though they may drench me when I go outside I do not feel as wet as when I am drenched by November rain. Then comes July rain, full of passion and often full of violence. July rain has temper but no sullenness. July days seldom sulk, and sulkiness is twice as hard to live with as sharp outbursts of temper followed by clearing skies or emotions.

Today was a scowling day, but this evening the air begins to clear. September can't maintain a surly mood very long.

WE HAVE BEEN TOTALING UP ACCOUNTS of various kinds, and it occurs to me again that few people keep really honest records in the country. And from what I hear, the folk who come out from the city are the worst of all sinners in this respect. The city man who moves to the country spends his first few years underestimating the cost, then gradually achieves a complete about-face and shamelessly overestimates.

At first there is a pride in economy, but the time comes when he takes pride in extravagance.

Not long ago we visited folk who had moved from the city only a year or so ago, and the man showed me with great pride a fine stone wall in front of his house. "It didn't cost me a penny!" he said. "We just moved it from over behind the barn." Four workmen got fifteen dollars a day for three weeks to move that wall, but the proud new squire ignored that. The stones didn't cost him a penny. Five years from now, if I know that man, he will be telling everyone who asks that the wall cost him two thousand dollars.

Another relative newcomer calculated the cost of his garden. "Seed," he said, "came to six dollars and forty cents. Add a couple dollars for insecticides and that covers it. Eight dollars and a half. And look at the vegetables!" Another friend, who has reached the next stage, calculated differently. Interest on land investment, labor for plowing, seed, fertilizer, insecticide, wages of a man who works in that garden four days a week. On that basis he says his tomatoes cost twenty cents apiece, cabbage thirty cents a head, onions seven cents each, and so on. I think he overcharged himself about twenty per cent, but no more than that.

It is difficult to keep completely accurate accounts. For instance, Charley plows our garden and manures it. He does this in return for the use of the corn crib and storage space in the barn. How can I calculate that cost? Albert brought up a load of manure for the new asparagus bed last Spring. This was, I suppose, in return for the use of my chain saw a day or two. While he was rebuilding pasture fences last year, Albert said the garden fence needed replacing. I helped with labor, and the posts came from my timber land. Some of the posts for the pasture fence did too. How do you calculate the cost of the new garden fence?

We hire no outside help for the garden, so that item has no place on the bill. But if I take account of the time we spend gardening and charge for it at the going rate for such help— well, the lettuce and the beans and the squash and the corn and all the rest of that fine produce would cost aplenty. And the jars of tomatoes we can each year can't be written off for the cost of the gas under the pressure canner, either.

The fact is that we can't tally up an exact accounting for these things. It's useless to try. All I know is that whatever they cost, they are worth it.

THE DIPPER SWUNG LOW in the north, this evening, and Cassiopeia was off to the east of the Pole Star. To the east of Cassiopeia stood a moon that will soon be full and was already colored like the pumpkins in the garden. We couldn't stay indors. We went out and climbed to the shoulder of the mountain and sat on the big rock. An owl was hooting up on the hillside, but there was no other bird sound. Then Pat, who had gone along, delighted, sniffed off into the darkness and picked up a rabbit trail. He gave his trail yelp and vanished among the shadows.

We sat and listened to Pat trail that rabbit all over the mountainside, the echoes coming back from the birch hollow, then from the upper benchland, then from the big pines, so we could follow his course without moving an inch. And at last we came back to the house, Pat's voice still eager high up on the mountain.

We came back past the white birch clump twined with wild grape, and there was the winy smell, wild tanged. Closer to home we met the cidery smell of early apples on the ground. We get a hint of it by daylight, but it was strong on the cool night air. Then we came to the rank hay smell at the bar-way to the road. Not the sweet hay fragrance of June, but the mint-and-goldenrod smell of tall weeds recently mowed, with the tantalizing sweetness of sweet clover mingled in. Then, as we came up the road, the wet, cool, faintly muddy smell of the river.

Fall

We came up the road to the house, and Pat was still there high on the mountain, and the owl hooted near the rock where we had sat. And I wished I could hoot or bark.

LAST NIGHT, after we had been in the house about half an hour, I heard something at the back door and thought it was Pat, who had persisted in his own devices up on the mountain. It was late dusk. I flipped on the outside light. Pat wasn't there, but down the steps at Pat's food pan was a skunk, eating a few small scraps Pat had left. He saw the light, blinked beady black eyes, and solemnly came up the steps. He came up and onto the narrow back porch to the screen door. I was inside with no light in the kitchen. The skunk came up almost to the door and stood there, staring at me, not eighteen inches away.

There was nothing to do but brazen it out, hoping he took no offense. And make no move that would alarm him. He looked up, seeming to stare at me. His black was black as fresh stove polish, his white stripe and tail-tip were dazzling. And his moist black nose wriggled inquisitively. He stood there for what seemed ten minutes, but perhaps was one long minute. Then he turned, solemnly, and edged away, looking back. I still didn't dare make a move, or he would have gone into immediate action. I waited, and he crossed the porch and went down the steps, deliberate as a cat. And walked across the yard, unhurried, almost regal in his tail-high leisure.

Pat, fortunately, didn't return until fifteen minutes later. But I was glad to have met this black-and-white neighbor face to face. That, I may add, is the preferred way to meet a skunk. And I shall see to it that no more scraps are left in Pat's pan to lure skunks.

THE HARVEST MOON IS WITH US; and regardless of the calendar the harvest moon is as Autumnal as a corn shock. Given reasonably clear skies, we shall have four or five moonlit evenings in a row, for the harvest moon is not a hasty moon; it comes early and stays late.

157

There was a time when the harvest moon gave the busy farmer the equivalent of an extra day or two. He, could return to his fields after supper and evening milking and continue his harvest by moonlight. That was when corn was cut by hand and husked by hand, when shocks tepeed the fields and fodder was stacked in the barnyard, when the bangboard echoed and the huskin' peg was familiar to the hand. But times change, and schedules. Now most of the farmer's long days come at plowing time, or planting, or at hay time. Corn is cut by machine and chopped by machine and stowed in the silo, or it is left standing in the field till a few fine late Fall days, then picked by mechanical picker, a machine that can outstrip a dozen men.

There's harvesting to be done now, of course, but much of it centers in the kitchen rather than the barns. The last bountiful yield comes from the garden, the late sweet corn, the last of the tomatoes, the root vegetables, the dozen and one kinds of pickles and relishes. But even there the new machines help, the pressure cookers and canners, and the freezer.

It's still the harvest moon, though, and we all think it's rather wonderful. Charley stopped past today and said, "Next full moon should be good coon hunting time." The next full moon will be the hunter's moon.

MAN HAS LONG WISHED HE COULD FLY as a bird does, with no more effort and with no mechanical adjuncts. But the more I learn about birds and their ways, the more doubtful I am about the price I should have to pay for such an accomplishment. Flight requires more energy than the most strenuous of normal human activity. That energy calls for lots of fuel. If I had to eat as much as a bird eats I should consume fifty to eighty pounds of bread, meat and vegetables every day; most adult birds eat more than a quarter of their own weight daily, and some eat half their own weight. Birds still in the nest, growing and feathering out, often require food equal to or even exceeding their own weight each day. That's why the parent birds are so busy when they have a nestful of fledglings.

Fall

To convert all this food into energy, all birds have a very high rate of metabolism. That is one reason they also live with what we would consider a constant fever. The normal temperature of most birds ranges from 105 to 108 degrees. Some birds have a daily rhythm, up to around 108 degrees during the active, daylight hours, and down to 104 at night.

Since a bird has relatively little space in which to store energy in the form of fat, all birds have to be constantly in search of food. Starve a bird for two days and that bird is on the verge of death; every gram of fat has been used up and the energy demands have begun to consume essential flesh and muscle.

The life of a bird is not all carefree song and joyous flight. I'm content to do without wings and live as I do.

RAGWORT STILL SHOWS its rather dusty yellow flowers at the roadside, and soapwort makes a display of pink in the waste places. They are only two of the dozens of worts that thrive and bloom without particular notice or acclaim, since the old-time gatherers of wild herbs have largely disappeared. For the worts were among the prime items on the "yarb" list. The very fact that the syllable *wort* is incorporated in the common name is testimony to their past. "Wort" goes back to the Gothic word for root and to the Anglo-Saxon *wyrt*, meaning herb.

Any casual list of the worts will run to at least a hundred and fifty plants, running the alphabetical scale from adderwort to yellowwort. Go through such a list and you find the whole range of human ailments set forth, at least so much of the range as was known and denominated a hundred years ago. Take cankerwort. Go on down to gutwort, which may have lacked elegance but probably reduced many an ache. Nettlewort may have assuaged the sting of the nettle, and if so it was surely potent. Quinsywort certainly was used as a hot infusion for a very sore throat.

There was even a rupturewort. We still recognize soapwort, which is nothing more than Bouncing Bet, a pleasant flower with a root that can substitute for soap. And there is toothwort, there is navelwort, there is sneezewort, there is wart-wort. The worts, the persistent herbs in the old back-country apothecary, constitute a kind of lexicon of human aches and ills, of pain and hope and trust, and inevitably of occasional cure.

THIS MORNING two members of a road crew working nearby came to the door and said, "There's a sheep trapped on the island. Could you take your boat and maybe get it off?" So we went, the three of us.

The island is only a hundred yards long and a third that wide. It lies across thirty feet of shallow water from the far shore of the river. We beached the boat and the ewe bleated in fear. She must have been driven there by stray dogs, panicked enough to enter the shallow water. We finally drove her to one end of the island and I caught her, flipped her on her back, and hog-tied her sharp-hoofed feet. We put her in the boat and brought her down here and turned her loose in the big barn. I phoned around and found that she belonged to a farmer up the river, and his son-in-law came and got her in his car.

Before the road men went back to work they asked, "Where did you learn to handle sheep?" I told them I grew up on a ranch. That explained everything to them, everything that could be readily explained. Had they asked, "Where did you learn to handle a boat?" the answer would have been much more complicated. I never saw a boat until I was twenty years old. I capsized the first canoe I ever got into. That I should own a boat now and be able to maneuver it even passably is a marvel to me. But as for sheep, I heard sheep blatting by the thousand before I was ten years old.

THE FIRST FEW MAPLES have begun to turn. The turning of the maples particularly, among all the tree coloration, is individual and often spectacular, not alone in its color but in its variety and unpredictable piebald character.

Up at the edge of the middle pasture stands one young maple, not over fifteen feet high, which already is all a fiery red, every leaf. Not ten feet away is another maple, apparently the same age and kind, which hasn't yet turned so much as one leaf. Down the road last Fall I watched two maples side by side, big, towering trees; one turned a gorgeous red and remained in full color two weeks before its neighbor began to color. The reluctant one turned only at the last minute, so to speak, and both of them lost their leaves in the same rain.

We have a row of venerable maples beside the river, big trees three feet through at the butt. The two directly in front of the house turn brilliant yellow early, the two just beyond them are always a week or so later, and the two at the far end are still more deliberate. All turn yellow, with just a hint of pink in a couple of them. Just across the road, in the upper pasture beside the old barn, is another maple, probably a seedling from them, that is now turning red at the top. It usually does that and the color seeps down, a flame working down from the tip.

Some maples turn one branch at a time, as though the branches were complete individualists. And I am always pleased to see the way the tiny maples on the mountain, seedlings no more than two feet high, take on color earlier than their big brothers, like children being put to bed several hours before the grownups.

THE GARDEN NEEDS A FROST. I wish we would have a good frost, though there are those who look at me in horror when I say so. I am expected to brag about tomatoes I still have ripening. Actually, we have ripened plenty of tomatoes for this year. I am willing to call it quits and wait for next May and brand-new tomato plants. By then I will be fed up with canned tomatoes and I know I would then pay a dollar apiece for those greenish-orange tomatoes now on the vines. Well, make it a quarter apiece; I have my Scottish blood. But right now I would gladly settle for one final clean-up job in the garden and a chance to put the hoe away, and the duster and the cultivator.

That's one of the best things about nature in a land of four seasons—frost comes to put an end to the growth of succulent and growing things. No garden should endure, with all its dividends and demands, more than about six months a year. The other six months one should be allowed to rest and dream and yearn and get rid of the calluses. Six months, as it were, to appreciate.

Albert and I were talking about this late last Spring, when the temperature had been in the low 70s for almost a week. We agreed that it was just about perfect, that we could take a lot of it. Then Albert said, "But not a whole year. I don't want to grow more than one garden a year or cultivate more than one crop of corn. And one season's haying a year is plenty."

So I speak for others too when I say hail to the frost! Let those who make green-tomato pickles have those green tomatoes! The sweet corn stands sere and stripped. The beans are rustling in the wind. The squash are ready to quit. So am I. I want to put away the hoe. Let it frost!

Fall

THE BRIGHTEST COLOR in the woods just now is not the leaf of a tree or shrub but that of a vine. It's that cousin of the fox grape which botanists know as *Psedera quinquefolia* and which is sometimes known as woodbine and sometimes as Virginia creeper. I prefer Virginia creeper, though Virginia is only one of thirty or more states where it grows wild and in profusion; woodbine is an English name applied, even in this country, also to various honeysuckles.

I see the Virginia creeper this morning on a tall dead popple just across the river. The scarlet leaves make that old tree a veritable pillar of fire. I shall be looking at it for days, every time I look across the river from here, and no matter how many times I see it I shall admire its beauty. And Virginia-creeper vine on the garden fence, which holds its own in competition with the grapes there, is beginning to turn scarlet. Give it a few more days and it will be an intricate wall of color woven on the wires.

Some outlanders mistake it for poison ivy, though identification is easy. As the Latin name indicates, its leaves generally occur in groups of five on a stem; poison ivy leaves grow in threes and are a different shape. And the ivy leaves often turn orange and yellow rather than scarlet. Also, the inconspicuous berries on the ivy are a dull gray, and the berries on the Virginia creeper are miniatures of the wild grape and a lively blue. Country folk never mistake the two.

IT WAS LOWELL WHO CELEBRATED the rarity of June days, and it was Holmes the elder who wrote of "chill September." Neither of them seems to have noticed that some of the rarest days of the year come in September, days by no means chill and in every way pulsing with life that is only hinted at in languid June. September always brings a few such days, and this is one. If we appreciate such days it is not wholly because they follow the days of August. Such contrast helps, but they would be magnificent at any time.

Today the sky is clear and clean, the air is crisp without being chill, the wind is free of dust and not yet full of leaves. Late cicadas buzz, crickets fiddle in the tall grass, and this evening the katydids will set up their clatter. Crows caw with less than usual raucousness. Bees still hum over nodding heads of goldenrod. Asters, the Fall wildlings, spangle the roadside.

In a properly ordered world we should all go out onto the hills on such days and know that life is innately good. Enough, perhaps, that we take time to see and feel and sense the fundamental strength and continuing hospitality of the natural world around us. This is man's environment, and ours is, in a broad sense, a way of life that cherishes it. It somehow sums up the things for which we stand, as a race. We find meanings in it that accommodate the best of our beliefs. So we stand in the open, on such a clean, clear September day, and see the bold horizons of our faith, the hills of our strength, the granite substance of our enduring purpose.

WE EXPECT FROST in this area any time after mid-September, and occasionally before then. It hasn't come this year, though we have held our breath several nights and it has got down to thirty-four a couple of times. I thought it surely had come this morning, for the lawn was white, but it turned out to be only one of those heavy dews which look frosty, even in July, before the sun has warmed up.

The stated averages assembled by the statisticians indicate that killing frosts will strike us about September 25. It sounds absurd, but it is my experience, not only here but elsewhere, that the weather averages compiled by the meteorologists are usually on the dark or pessimistic side. A year ago I discussed this when I was discussing weather with the Weather Bureau in Washington, and I got my answer. The charts, which is to say the averages, are based on a certain weather period covering about fifty years and ending, as I remember it, some fifteen years ago. I was told that new charts, which will include the major part of the recent fifteen years, are now being prepared.

Weather observers insist that the climate is not changing, yet they admit that the past ten or fifteen years, as a whole, have been warmer than "average." "Average," to them, means that base period, a series of years before the warm trend set in. I am not qualified to quibble, but it seems to me it would be more reasonable to say that temperatures now appear to be higher than they were in the past, rather than to say they are "above average." The whole matter can become technical and involved, but when I see, year after year, charts showing "accumulated excess" of temperature amounting to almost three degrees a day, I wonder why it is called "excess" year after year.

I KNOW IT'S A TRICK of the light and the eye but the leaves of the white ash seem to me to turn blue in the Fall. A strange, indefinable blue with just a touch of pink in it; perhaps violet comes closer to the color I am thinking of. I go along a road and I see an ash which has turned to just the precise point, and its leaves are blue-violet.

I have gone up to such a tree a dozen times—I did so today, down along the pasture fence—and the leaves close up are a mixture of green and yellow and a kind of dirty in-between. I tell myself I am seeing things. I walk away and look back, and they are blue again, that indefinable blue-violet. The wind touches them and they flutter in the light, and they are yellowish green. Then they come to rest and the sun strikes them just so, and I see blue.

I am not completely mad, for Barbara too sees it at times. But not as often as I do.

There is a blue ash, *Fraxinus quadrangulata,* of the Midwest, but its name comes from a dye extracted from the inner bark, not from the color of stem, twig or leaf. The tree I am speaking of is *Fraxinus americana,* plain American white ash, which grows all through the Northeast and East and Midwest and even into Texas. The tree books I know say its leaves turn yellow in Autumn, and I agree. They do turn yellow. But not until they have passed through this blue phase.

This Hill, This Valley

KILLING FROST has struck the low-lying gardens in the village. Tomato vines are blackened and so are peppers, and such garden flowers as dwarf dahlias and nasturtiums. But the frost passed us by. That is the way of first frost; it is spotty, nipping gardens in the open before it touches those hemmed in by hedges or trees, putting a cold finger on those in a hollow, leaving those on nearby knolls untouched. Cold air flows downhill, as water does, and gathers in the hollows. Our garden gains ten days or so of frost-free time by being close beside the river, which gives off warmth and night fog all Fall. A most munificent river. It deposited the garden soil in the first place, it warms the air in Spring, its mists ease the dry spells, and now it delays the frost.

We were out today surveying the last garden get, knowing we must soon bring in our final harvest. Chard and kale will go on and on, and most of the late carrots will remain in the ground, to be dug during occasional thaws all Winter for stews. Parsnips and leeks will also stay where they are. But green tomatoes must be gathered for piccalilli and the squash must be brought in soon. We are through with the corn—the late nubbins can stay where they are, for the raccoons and the mice. Onions are already in. We finished with the beans weeks ago, except the last crop of limas; they must come in tomorrow. One last short row of beets can come in now for beet pickles. But beyond that there isn't much garnering to be done. Only the clean-up, to remove weeds and drying stalks.

THE SUN ROSE CLEAR in the east this morning, and it will sink in the west, by the compass, this evening; there is only a few seconds' difference between the span of today's light and tonight's darkness. Thus ends the calendar Summer, with the scarlet feathers of the sumac thrusting from roadside thickets, symbols of the Indian Summer to come. Thus end all Summers, with the bronze of maturity rustling in the garden, the crispness of Autumn in the air.

I don't have to be an astronomer to recognize an Autumn equinox. The precise time, perhaps, the day and hour and

second beyond the minute, is a matter to be calculated by rules of celestial mechanics; but the season, the time of change, is written on every bough and punctuated by every blade of grass. The blind can hear it and the deaf must see it with their eyes half closed. It is there in the touch of a leaf, the texture of a twig, tangible to the most casually inquisitive finger.

The dumb things know it. Woodchucks and coons are raiding the corn fields, the woodchucks adding a final ounce of fat for hibernation, the coons simply feasting. Gray squirrels rattle the leaves in the hickories as they take their share of the crop. Chipmunks gather grass and thistledown to line their nests for Winter. Migrant birds have already moved south.

The precise moment is unimportant. It is only a matter of mathematics relating to the orbit and inclination of the earth. The obvious truth is that Summer is past. The season merges with Autumn. The winesap reddens on the bough. The cricket chirps in the corner. The equinox is only a confirmation.

THERE IS A PREJUDICE among weathermen about speaking of storms that come at this time of year as equinoctial storms. Their reasoning is simple. The equinox is a matter of astronomical movements, the relative positions of sun and earth. Storms are a result of atmospheric conditions, not of astronomical relationships. Therefore, there are no equinoctial storms.

That, to me, is hair-splitting. The same reasoning would rule out Spring rains and Winter blizzards. I don't see how one can rule out the adjectives. It just happens that weather disturbances are the rule rather than the exception at this time of year. Things are happening in the atmosphere. Summer is ending. Autumn is beginning. Long, hot days are ended in our northern hemisphere. The earth is beginning to cool off, up here. There is a new movement of the air. It also happens that these changes are related to the movement of the sun and the position of the earth, for if the sun were not moving southward, as we say, there would be no such profound changes in the atmosphere.

Those factors which make the equinox also breed the stormy conditions. It is a period of change, and often that change is violent and stormy. At the moment our weather is relatively mild and undisturbed. But hurricanes are breeding in the far reaches of the Atlantic, and a deep low-pressure area is moving in from the northwest. Something is going to happen, and if it's a storm I shall insist that it can be called an equinoctial storm. Today has been just a bit too calm and mild to last.

A SQUALLY, OVERCAST DAY, weather in the making. The river is restless; it has a freight of leaves shaken down by something more than a hurrying squirrel. But I shall not be kept from work by the weather. . . .

I am convinced that there are no new securities. But as the wheel of time turns we rediscover the old ones. And that reminds me that I planned to secure the loft door at the barn before we had a blow. I found it loose and flapping a week ago but hadn't time to do more than tie it shut with a strand of binder twine. . . .

Well, I fixed that door. I found an old latch and fastened it on. And high time. The gusts are strengthening and the rain comes down, now, in periodic sheets. Pat, of course, went with me and he, too, got drenched. I have changed into dry clothes, but he shook himself—indoors, of course—and now lies here on my study floor, oozing. . . .

To get back to what I was saying. The wheel of time turns and we . . .

It is four o'clock of a stormy afternoon. I left the typewriter at a little after ten this morning. A crash sent me out of doors. It was a four-inch limb from the big popple, brittle and unequal to the gusty wind. It came down in the road and I had to move it, or I thought I should. Then I was wet enough to enjoy the storm, so I stayed out, checking the downspouts on the house, making sure the roof at the old chicken house I use as a carpenter shop was not leaking, having a look at the boat and its cover.

It was one of those exciting days, great forces on the loose. Water from the pasture was angling down across the asparagus bed, so I got a spade and opened a trench toward the brook to take the water, banking the asparagus bed with sod to check the erosion there. Then it was lunch time.

We ate in the kitchen. I was too wet to venture anywhere else in the house. After lunch it abated somewhat and Barbara put on boots and a raincoat and came out with me to feel as well as see this weather. We walked in the pasture, avoiding the trees, for the wind is pruning all trees mercilessly today. We watched the pines up on the mountainside, bending low beneath the wind, and marveled at the white birches leaning with the storm. We watched the brook, swollen to great proportions and sweeping out across the pasture in a sheet of water. We watched the river, beaten to a surf and with waves two feet high, whitecaps.

It is now four o'clock and dark as though this were November and an early sunset. The wind still rises. The rain strikes the windows with the sound of sleet. Here is my equinoctial storm!

THE STORM MOANED AND SLASHED most of the night and I expected to waken this morning to a house without electricity. But the power is still on. And the winds have died down, though the rain continues, heavy gray rain from a heavy gray sky. The river has risen at least a foot and there are streams at the roadside. But the barometer, which was falling all yesterday, has begun to rise again. The storm center is past.

I had to go to the village this morning to mail a couple of letters, and the road was littered with debris. At two places large limbs had come down, but they had been hauled to the roadside and the way cleared. Charley must have done that; I saw him pass in his truck this morning, going toward the village. His was the only vehicle on the road.

We did Fall chores today, straightening the clutter in the attic for storage of Summer clothes, cleaning the cellar and putting last year's leftover canned goods in front on the shelves, to be used first. Then I took inventory of our office supplies and made a tentative list of replacements, paper, pencils, carbon paper, typewriter ribbons, filing folders, manuscript envelopes. Two things give me a sense of affluence—a full pantry and a well-stocked supply cabinet.

This evening the rain begins to slacken. The storm should be over by tomorrow.

A CLEAR SKY THIS MORNING, clean, washed and shining. But I distrust it. We could have frost tonight, brought by the cold air mass which followed the humid warm front that generated our storm. So we cleaned out the garden. In came the last of the peppers, the tiny eggplant, carrots to go into the refrigerator, heads of lettuce. Butternut and acorn squash were picked and stowed. When that was done there wasn't much else to do; we had harvested more closely than we realized in the past few weeks.

The garden looks bare this evening, only the strawberry leaves and the asparagus fern making much of a show. And the kale, of course, which is hardy and as green as in July. I wish we could have harvested the Summer flowers and stowed them for Winter use. But all we do about the flowers is take up the choice gladiola bulbs and a dozen roots of the dwarf dahlias whose colors most please us, and stow them in the attic. One Spring the dahlias, in a bushel basket with peat moss around them, became so impatient that two of them budded and bloomed right there in the attic in April. It didn't do them a bit of harm, either; when we put them in the ground they grew and blossomed as vigorously as ever.

No FROST LAST NIGHT, but it was down in the low 30s. And, for the first time since April, it was quiet. The katydids were silent, too cold to fiddle. The tree crickets didn't make a sound. The frogs kept their own counsel. The darkness that only a few weeks ago quivered and hummed and vibrated with a thousand insects was almost palpably silent. I could hear the whisper of leaves brushing against one another.

But it is only a temporary quiet. Warm days and temperate nights will follow this first chill, and even after the first hard frost there will be mild days that turn into Indian Summer. And the night singers will be out again, fiddling desperately. Now they have merely crawled into a crevice or under a leaf. But their energies wane.

I went out to the garden this morning and saw how low the insect fires of life burn. Black crickets barely moved, even when prodded. Ants made slow progress, their legs stiff as with rheumatism. I found a grasshopper that could crawl but couldn't manage one leap. By this afternoon the sun had warmed the insects and life surged again, leaping and flying and agile once more.

The sun itself is life to the insect world and the temperature is of less importance, fundamentally, than the duration of sunlight. Days shorten. The sun moves south, as we say. And with that movement, the insect clock begins to run down. Even a week of 80-degree temperature couldn't really revive it now. The insects near the end of their days.

WE HAVE HAD OUR KILLING FROST, which blackened the last leaves on the tomato vines, left the zinnias limp, and scorched the marigolds. I went out to cut the frosted flowers and clean the flower garden, and the late phlox and the petunias are more beautiful than ever. So is the late-blooming delphinium.

The leaves have all fallen from the slim young ash trees that border the middle pasture. The dogwoods are at their height of color, one of the finest reds in the spectrum; we have few dogwoods, but there is a scattering of them in the hills nearby. Our big maples along the river are all yellow and the dazzle of their leaves in the early sun is unbelievable. Pure gold. The giant poplar has turned gold, too, but a brassier gold, the gold of cottonwoods I used to know. The gray birches up at the edge of the pines are still another yellow, with a touch of bronze, a yellower yellow than the leaves of the white birch.

I went up to the big clump of white birch, the one with seven big boles, this afternoon to look at the fox grapes which twine there. They are dead ripe. I picked all I could reach, about a gallon, and we shall make a few glasses of fox-grape jelly. The grape leaves are falling from the stems and have a texture almost exactly like that of a paper napkin. The stems will remain on the vines a little longer; then they, too, will be shed.

AUTUMN IS FLOWING past my door just now, in the river. Red maple leaves are there, and crisp poplar leaves, and the slim yellow leaves from the willows. The poplar leaves are golden galleons, prows high, gusted across the current, beached by an eddy. Milkweed floss dances over the slow stream, bouncing from its surface, too light to be caught until it has traveled a mile or more on the slight breeze that flows close to the water's surface. Even thistledown, set loose by some energetic goldfinch somewhere upstream, floats in the light drift of air over the water, shimmery gauze that will be borne to some new seed ground. Pokeberries, ink-black, and purple viburnums and the gray berries of red-osier dogwood drift past on broken stems.

Autumn takes firmer hold on the higher hills upstream and comes floating down to where I wait. Autumn gathers strength to take over the whole long valley, and now I see its outriders, its advance guard, on the waters that flow past my door.

A sunny day, almost mild, and we have been patching roofs. A windstorm a month ago took a large patch of roofing paper off the corn crib and another off the big chicken house which I use for a workshop, and on mild days I have been too busy and on idle days it has been too cold to replace that roofing, which cracks unless it is laid under a warm sun. But repairs can't wait forever.

Charley, who is going to use the corn crib this year, came down with a roll of new roofing paper. I went out to help, since it's my crib. We laid the roofing, nailed it down, got the joints properly cemented, and paused for a smoke. Charley said, "I've got another hour or two. Why don't we get at that chicken house?"

So we did. And when we had both patches finished we sat in the sun and talked, the slow talk about weather and feed and prices and the year ahead. At last Charley looked at his watch and said, "The cows'll be expecting me," and he got up to go.

I said, "Thanks for helping with the chicken house."

"I didn't have anything pressing," he said. And I knew

he felt satisfied at having helped. He felt square with me and the world, which is an important feeling for any man. He had paid me back for helping with the crib, which is his responsibility in our simple arrangement. We call it friendship and neighborliness, in an offhand way of speaking, but down inside it amounts to keeping square with yourself.

THUS ENDS SEPTEMBER, in a perfect day. Tonight a few katydids are calling, and a few crickets. I have looked up a formula sent to me for calculating the temperature by timing cricket and katydid calls.

For crickets you count the number of chirps in one minute, divide by four, add forty to the quotient, and you have the temperature in degrees Fahrenheit. It is even simpler to count the number of chirps in fifteen seconds and add forty. That should be the temperature.

For katydids, count the number of complete stridulations in one minute. That is, when the insect has made a full "Katy did" call, that is one complete stridulation. Count the complete calls for one minute, subtract nineteen, divide the difference by three, and add the quotient to sixty. The result should be the temperature in degrees Fahrenheit. Again, one can get the same result, approximately, by counting the number of calls in twenty seconds and adding fifty-four. And because the katydid's day and night calls are quite different, this method of estimating temperature is good only for the rate of night calls.

I timed the loudest katydid this evening. The average of three separate timings was eight calls in twenty seconds. Eight added to fifty-four makes sixty-two. My thermometer showed the temperature to be sixty-four at the time. It probably was two or three degrees cooler where the katydid was sitting than it was on my porch.

OCTOBER

I F I WERE TO UNDERTAKE a new mythology, October would be my god of travel, for now come perfect days to get out and wander the hills and valleys of these latitudes. The scene changes day to day, as though all the colors of the spectrum were being spilled across the landscape—radiant blue of lakes and ponds, green in every tone of the conifers and even among the reluctant oaks, yellows verging from sun shimmer to moon orange in the elms, the beeches, the hard maples, and reds that range to purplish browns, sumac and dogwood and swamp maple and sassafras and viburnum.

October is colorful, exuberant, full of lively spirit. Spring fever can't hold a candle to October fever when it comes to inner restlessness. The birds are on the wing, the leaves are footloose and eager for a breeze, the horizon is a challenge that amounts to an insidious summons. If I listen closely I can hear October whistling a soft melody as old as Autumn on this earth, and as insistent in its call to go.

THINGS NOW COME TO FULFILLMENT. It must have been at this season that man first discovered the potentialities of a ripe grape, for grape juice and cider have begun to potentiate.

Spring was all eagerness. Summer was hot laziness or sweaty haste. But Autumn is achievement and a measure of contentment. Hills wait for climbing. Woods are full of wine and gold. Answers to half-asked questions lie in the thin mist on the horizon. In Spring the impulse is to lie and wait for the answers to come. Now one must go and find the answers.

A migrant farmhand to whom I once gave a hitchhike lift summed it up. "Every Summer," he said, "I decide to pick one place and settle down. Then it comes Fall, and I just can't seem to stay put. If Fall would just skip a year maybe I could make up my mind and keep it made. But Fall never skips."

THERE'S A SCIENTIFIC EXPLANATION of the coloring of the leaves which deals in terms of chemistry as well as botany. Frost has nothing to do with it, of course; it's a matter of oxidation, of pigmentation, of chemical change, not entirely unrelated to the way the human skin tans or freckles. That's all very well to know. But there's also a rule of tongue, as one might say, which may be worth knowing. This rule says that the most colorful leaves appear on trees and bushes with sugar in their sap or tannin in their make-up.

The maples, most vivid of all, are the sweetest when the sap is running. Sweet gum, which has a sweet juice in midsummer, runs the maple a close second. Sour gum, which some call tupelo, has a sweet tang to its sap and a rainbow of color in its leaves. Sassafras, which has sweetness as well as an old familiar flavor, splashes the woods with variegated Autumn finery. The oaks, traditional source of tannin, are the bearers of the strongest reds and the deepest purples. Sumac, also well endowed with tannin, has its own colorful glory. And fruit trees, which have a special sweetness of sap, run to colorful leaves.

Go down the list and test them with the tongue and eye, season by season. If the sap is sweet the leaves will tend to gold and crimson; if the sap is pungent and full of the taste of tannin the leaves will show deep red and purple.

EVERYBODY SHOULD OWN A TREE at this time of year. Or a valley full of trees, or a whole hillside. Not legally, in the formal "Know all men" way, written on a piece of paper, but in the way that one comes to own a tree by seeing it at the turn of the road, or down the street, or in a park, and watching it day after day and seeing color come to its leaves.

That way it is your tree forever, any time you choose to pass that way, and neither fence nor title can take it from you.

I once owned a red maple that way. It stood at the turn of a road I drove along every day, and it was a tree of wonder, for it turned red and gold each year in a different combination. And once I owned a clump of flowering dogwood at the roadside. I watched it bloom in the Spring and grow through the Summer and deck itself with lacquered berries in September and turn wonderfully crimson in October. I own a whole valley in the Rockies, a valley full of quaking aspens, which I have seen slim and white of bole in Winter, and laced with green in Spring, and like a flow of molten gold down the mountainside in October.

I have come to own a row of maples along the river here, where I have sat in their June shade and watched them shed their seed, and seen their stark reality in leafless Winter. Now I revel in their gold, which is like sunlight even on an overcast day, and before long I shall scuffle in their leaves and own them that way. My ownership is beyond legal title. Others may own them too. Trees are anyone's for the finding, to own forever.

I WAS OUT FISHING THIS AFTERNOON and caught few fish; but I did catch a song sparrow taking a bath. I was anchored near the bank and had sat quietly for perhaps ten minutes when I heard this sparrow in a clump of red osiers. It sang twice, then came down the steep bank and perched in the brush and sang again, not five feet from me.

At the water's edge was a branch of osier sagging from its root so that the water lapped over its tip. The sparrow hopped onto that branch, out near its swaying tip, and flirted its tail. The first movement was tentative. Then the tail whipped the water in what seemed almost a rotary motion. It threw up a spray, like a spinning propeller half out of water. Thoroughly wet, the sparrow ruffled its feathers and shook itself, for all the world like a wet hen in the barnyard. It preened, carefully laid a few feathers in place again with its beak, then started all over again, whisking water with its tail in a motion too fast for the eye to follow. This time it spread its wings before it shook itself.

Three times it did this, drying itself each time. Then it went back up the bank and sang again. It sang two songs and watched me, then it came back and bathed again, as though displaying its technique.

All this happened in the shadow, the sun already so low that the river bank hid it. The air temperature, when I came to the house a little later, was in the low 50s. The water temperature certainly was no higher. Clearly this was not a matter of cooling off. It was a bath.

SINCE THE FIRST DECIDUOUS TREE rose above the primeval ooze, since birds and beasts first peopled the woodland, there has been this season of leaf-fall and abundance. When man came along, in the slow sequence of evolution, here was October, his for the taking. And over the centuries and the ages, man has made Autumn his own as far as he can ever make any season his own. Then he invented a calendar, a clock, and a Summer vacation.

Summer really isn't the ideal time for a vacation. It's all right as a time to get away from the tribulations of a job, perhaps, but a vacation should be more than an escape. Every October I wonder why, if man is as wise as he thinks he is, he orders his life in this way, why he is content with a brief escape at a time when the most enduring thing he can acquire is a

sunburn and perhaps a case of ivy poisoning. Now, not in midsummer, is the time when good things abound for man's enjoyment. If ever there was a season for man to savor this earth and know it intimately, October is its peak and prime.

Winds forever blow, rivers forever run, birds forever fly. But one doesn't have to look to know that now ducks are on the wing, and grouse and pheasants. Bucks are in the thicket. Bears fatten. Fox stalks rabbit, and rabbit is free and whimsical as the wind. Harvests are in, the hasty time is at an end, the whine and bite of Winter are still in the distance, over the hill, beyond the horizon.

And man? Man, the ingenious, the adaptable, the industrious, the discoverer and perfector of the twelve-month calendar—man is at his desk, tied to his own clock, with only a few brief glimpses of what might be his outdoors if he only had time by the horns instead of duty by the tail.

THERE WAS A WHITE FROST last night, but when I got up this morning, before the sun touched it, there were unfrosted circles under all the bushes on the lawn. It was as though the frost had settled, like dew, from above, and each bush sheltered its own small area.

When the sun rose it was a sparkling world. The sun had been in the air only an hour when a shower began from the big poplar. Its leaves had all turned gold, but at least half of them still hung on the branches. This morning as I watched them come down they came in a veritable rain, though

there wasn't a breath of a breeze. At times their sound was like the patter of heavy rain.

I have seen this happen many times, and I have a theory about its cause. When the leaves are being shed, a corky layer forms at the base of their stems, like a tiny cork closing the sap channels through which the leaf juices have been withdrawn. This corky layer turns hard and brittle, and then the leaves are cast loose, usually in a wind or rain. But sometimes we come to that precise moment with several clear, calm days which lead to a night of frost.

During such a night, moisture seeps into that corky layer. Frost comes, the moisture freezes and becomes a kind of adhesive holding the leaf to the branch. Then the sun rises. The sun melts the frost crystals at the base of the leaf stem. The formation of the frost pried the leaf loose, but as long as the frost remained the leaf was still tied. The frost melts, and down come the leaves of their own weight, hundreds, thousands, pried loose by the frost and then cut loose by the melting sun.

GIVE A MAN A FREE HAND and he builds himself a house with running water, several bathrooms, a two-car garage, telephones both upstairs and down, automatic central heat—and a fireplace. He wants no stable, no carriage house, no dug well with old oaken bucket, no outdoor privy. But he insists upon a fireplace. And on October evenings he, personally, arranges the kindling and lights the fire before he settles down to watch television or read a book.

The hearth fire is as antiquated as the stone arrowhead, yet we cling to it, generation after generation. The further we get from the pains of primitive living, the more we cherish it. Not long ago I inspected a supermodern house with glass walls on all sides and no partitions—and a fireplace in the middle! Give a man from a hearthless apartment a whiff of wood smoke and he groans with envy. Show him a leaky-roofed cabin forty miles from nowhere and if it has a fireplace he will buy it, or try to.

Fall

The reasons are all twined with intangibles as thin as wood smoke. Man is a natural fire-tender, has been since ancient times. There is a race pride, something reaching back to the cave man who first tamed fire. There is the instinct to bask safely in front of a fire while a hunk of buffalo meat simmers and wolves howl outside.

That makes it complicated. But it certainly can't be explained by saying that the man who builds a hearth fire wants to warm his hands. He seldom does. What he wants is to see the flames leap, at his command, and feel the glow and hear the simmering log. Don't ask me why. I'm a prejudiced witness. My hearth fire is going right this minute.

WE WALKED UP THE ROAD this evening, Barbara and Pat and I, and I came back full of questions.

Why are so many barns painted red? Why do robins scold in October exactly as they scold in May, and what are they scolding now? Why are dandelions perennials? Why do house flies congregate at the windows at this time of year? To get out? Open the window and they retreat in panic, scared to death of the open air. How cold does it have to get to shut up a frog? Is there a cleaner yellow anywhere, after the goldenrod is through, than the last, lingering evening primroses? Doesn't the woodpecker ever get a headache? Is there a more friendly sound in the woods than the chirring of a flicker? Why do we forget, year after year, how beautiful an Autumn day can be? Or an Autumn night, with the stars practically within whispering distance?

WHO CAN ENUMERATE all the sweet and pungent smells of a country woodshed? Who, for that matter, can describe a woodshed? Woodsheds differ more widely than houses or barns; their chief similarity is that they shelter firewood, among other things. And their pungence varies with their homeland.

My woodshed is a snug structure just five steps from the back door, four walls, two windows, a roof, and a dirt floor.

When I moved here it contained a jumble of everything from firewood to chicken wire, old paint and broken garden tools. I brought order out of it, in an initial burst of energy, and the firewood still is stacked neatly enough. But it is something of a jumble again, my own jumble now. And it doubles as a garden house, at least in Winter.

When I first brought order out there I unearthed a fine old chopping block, which is still there and is still used. It is a section of a splendid old oak a good thirty inches in diameter, and it was used for years before I found it. It is hollowed out at the top from a million hatchet blows, and down one side is a deep brown stain where many a chicken must have met the guillotine. I cut kindling on it.

My woodshed smells of birch and oak and maple and ash and poplar, and somewhat of apple. It also smells of cedar, for in one corner is a great heap of old shingles stripped from the garage roof when I put asbestos shingles there. They make excellent kindling. From one rafter dangles a pail with rat poison in it, safe from dogs, cats and children, but accessible to rats. There are several bushel baskets full of spruce cones, also for kindling. My woodshed is savory with the timber smells of this farm. It is a way station, midway between the flourishing tree and the flourishing fire.

EVEN AS THE AUTUMN DAYS SHORTEN they increase in height and breadth. It is as though there were a constant ratio which keeps the days in balance. The leaves are thinning out. The eye can reach. New vistas open. The horizon is just there beyond the trees on the other side of my river, now that the leaves have fallen. The sun slants in a window where two weeks ago there was thick maple shade.

The hills are no longer remote, and at night I can look up from almost anywhere and see the constellations of Andromeda and Pegasus. Even in a land of trees, we are no longer canopied from the sky or walled in from the horizon. The earth's distances invite the eye. And as the eye reaches, so must the mind stretch to meet these new horizons.

True, they are not new horizons; they have been there always. But the very fact that they seem new now, if only because newly seen, is human reason enough for the seasonal succession. Men blind their lives and thoughts by too many walls and canopies, at best. It is good to have the walls and canopies thin away, from time to time, and reveal the broader

scope. It is good to be reminded that not only have the days changed, but life itself is a matter of more than two dimensions.

Autumn is an eternal corrective. It is ripeness and color and a time of completion; but it is also breadth and depth and distance. I challenge anyone to stand with Autumn on a hilltop and fail to see a new expanse not only around him, but in him, too.

BARBARA SAW TWO BLUEBIRDS TODAY, and within an hour she saw a flock of juncos. How the birds and the seasons overlap!

The peony leaves have turned purple with the first frosts. I moved the peonies three years ago, when I was trying to clear the lawn for ease of mowing; they had been in a double row along the walk from the road to the house, but I put them at the back of the flower garden, for a background, and they have loved the change. All the bushes I have moved have liked their new homes, too, including the barberry. Why anyone would put barberry bushes in the middle of a lawn is a mystery to me, but there they were; so I moved them out to the pasture gate, where they continue to provide spots of color—they are a wonderful crimson now, loaded with berries —and continue to grow and feed the birds.

I have neither love nor great respect for barberry—except respect for its thorns. This is a purely personal matter, without good reason, I suppose. But when I move barberry I give it no coddling. I dig it up, thrust it into a new hole, tramp down the soil, and forget it. And it seems to thrive. One year I left a barberry bush unplanted and with little soil on its roots for a week before I put it into the ground. It grew wonderfully. If I had tried that with any of the bushes I admire they probably would have curled leaves and died.

One cynical observer commented the other day that barberry bushes are like women—they like neglect. That man is a bachelor, an aging bachelor.

I FOUND A SMALL PATCH OF HONEYSUCKLE today by following my nose. A honey fragrance was in the air, sweet and haunting, for that honeysuckle was in bloom. The green bank was speckled with the little twin-lipped trumpets, quite a number of them, though it is now mid-October. And they seemed twice as fragrant as they did in June.

Honeysuckle in October always seems like an Autumn bonus, though it can be found in green leaf, if not in blossom, as late as December in most years if one knows where to look. There are other flowers, too, that persist well into the frosty season. Some of the mints, for instance, I have found in bloom in December. And bouncing Bet and chicory and some of the lesser bur-marigolds as well as Fall's own asters often bloom well into November. But they are weedy blooms, in any lexicon, and they have little fragrance. Honeysuckle is something else again. To find it now in bloom is like finding a sweet fragment of June four months late—or eight months early. It is almost as good as opening a fresh comb of honey on a dreary February morning and smelling June when Winter is full of slush.

WE ARE HAVING A FEW DAYS of Indian Summer, and I wonder who gave it that name. The Indians don't seem to have; the name appears not to have been used until after the Revolution. The first mention of it I can find was in 1794, and then it was used by a Caucasian New Englander.

There's no fixed date for Indian Summer. It comes in the Fall, and that's about as close as anyone can come. Sometimes, as now, it comes in October, sometimes in November; sometimes it waits for the first hard frost, the black frost, as some call it, and sometimes it just appears over the hilltop and settles down while October is young and innocent. Some partisans insist that it can never come this early, but even they cannot set an arbitrary date. It isn't a calendar season; it makes its own rules.

When Indian Summer comes early it coincides with the best color of the year, the magnificence of maple and oak. Then it is doubly wonderful, as now. When it comes late it relieves a dull and frosty November and makes us forget, for a little while, that Winter is close at hand. Now and then—and this will stir argument, no doubt—it comes twice in a season, both early and late. Such years are memorable. This could be such a year, but whether it is or not I shall take Indian Summer now and know it is wonderful.

THE WOOLLY BEARS, the caterpillar phase of that insect known as *Isia isabella,* are humping their way about the grounds, hurrying somewhere to curl up in semi-darkness for the Winter. They remind me of busy little women hurrying about in fur coats. When, in due time, they shed their coats, these creatures too will emerge as resplendent beauties, winged with yellow and pink and fragile as any lovely moth.

Last November I looked for a woolly bear to examine its coat, which is believed by some soothsayers to forecast the Winter by its proportion of dark fur to lighter. This superstition, I must add, is ill founded. In any case, I searched for two hours without finding a curled-up caterpillar anywhere. But that evening I opened the outside cellar door and there, on a cold concrete step, I found my woolly bear, curled into a sleeping ball. The temperature was 28 at the time.

I took my caterpillar indoors, put it in a jelly glass, and waited till it warmed up to room temperature. When that happened it uncurled, lifted its bare black snout and looked around for something green and succulent. Not to tantalize the creature, I put it, still in the glass, on the ledge outside my study window. It remained there until April, roused of its own accord, ate a few apple leaves I gave it, and transformed itself into a pupa. A few weeks later it emerged as a moth with a beautifully speckled orange body and yellow and pink wings and flew away. And now its children are back, fur-coated and cameling across the lawn, hurrying to some dark Winter bedroom.

Curious about the speed of caterpillars, I once timed a woolly bear as it made its way across the lawn. It had to go around a good many tall grasses and it detoured several times for reasons I could not understand, but it still traveled fifteen feet in five minutes. That was one yard a minute, or about one-thirtieth of a mile an hour. Then I estimated weights and decided that I weigh at least 5,000 times as much as such a caterpillar. And I found that if I could walk as fast as that caterpillar, ounce for ounce, I could walk 170 miles an hour. Which merely proves the absurdity of all such comparisons.

THIS MONTH'S FULL MOON is called the Hunter's Moon, as last month's was the Harvest Moon. In both instances we have a series of nights when the moon rises only a little later each night, soon after sunset, giving the feeling of a full moon several nights in a row.

There is a complex reason which, as I interpret my astronomer friends, simmers down to the fact that the moon's orbit is elliptical rather than a true circle. The earth's own motions are also involved. As a result of these factors, the moon's rate of retardation—the lag in time of moonrise from one day to the next—varies considerably. Where I live, this lag may be as little as 23 minutes or as much as an hour and 17 minutes. It is at its maximum in Winter and Summer, and at its minimum in Spring and Fall. The long full moons of

March and April, September and October, are no illusion. Nor are the brief full moons of December and January, July and August.

For example, during the current five-day period surrounding the full moon the time lag of moonrise amounts to only three hours and 15 minutes, an average of about 38 minutes a day. Last June's full moon had a lag during the five-day period of six hours and 26 minutes, one hour and 17 minutes a day.

So we have the Hunter's Moon, a time of full moonlight for several evenings in a row. It is a magnificent moon tonight, and if it should be clear tomorrow it will be almost as magnificent. All the rest of this week, in fact, should be a time of moonlit evenings.

WE WERE HUSKING CORN TODAY. The corn picker was supposed to do it, but the husking rolls were a little worn, so we helped out. Albert was driving the tractor and Charley and I were going along for a ride in the wagon into which the picker delivered the ears. We worked, after a fashion, stripping the occasional ear that the picker didn't husk. There were just enough to occupy our hands, not enough to stop our talk.

We discussed the old days, when corn picking was done afoot and by hand, with a huskin' peg and a bangboard wagon and a team of horses that knew their job. And Charley, who has been growing corn a good many years, agreed that he preferred today's methods, even though a mechanical picker isn't as picturesque as a team and wagon. "With today's yields," he said, "it would take you all Fall to pick your crop by hand."

He was right. Modern hybrid seed corn has raised yields to phenomenal levels. Ours isn't an outstandingly good corn area, but last year Charley had one field that produced 200 bushels to the acre. The corn we were picking today, on average soil and with an average season, was producing more than a hundred bushels to the acre. When I was a boy and had uncles growing corn in the best part of Nebraska, eighty bushels to the acre was a top yield.

But, as Charley pointed out, in those days a farm hand's wages were about twenty dollars a month and good corn land sold for no more than seventy-five dollars an acre. Production isn't the only thing that has changed.

Some things remain, though, much as they have always been. Before I left the corn field Charley asked if I'd like, to go coon hunting one of these nights.

THERE IS A DEEP SCUFFLING OF LEAVES in the woodland now, and I see Taurus and the Pleiades in the eastern sky at evening. Orchardists have all their apples in, somehow symbolic of the whole Summer's yield. The pressure is relaxed. Country folk can mend walls and tidy up fields and gardens and snug the place for Winter.

Fall

The pace changes. It is not exactly a time for leisure, but there is occasion now to look at the far hills and think thoughts not bounded by a cornstalk's height or a pasture's breadth. The big rhythms seep into the soul, the rhythms of the seasons and the years rather than the rhythms of long days and short nights.

I can look at a white oak now and see the beauty of a stout tree in late October. I can watch the early flight of teal and marvel at the instinct which compasses them north and south. I can watch a squirrel at his hoarding and hear the sweet whispering of the chickadees in the pines above the middle pasture. I can feel the world about me, and see it, and somewhat understand.

Autumn is for understanding, for the longer thoughts and the deeper comprehensions. How well it is that the year should bring such a time, to rest the muscles, yes, from the Summer's tensions, but even more important to relax the mind and give it time to span the valleys of belief. Now a man's mind can reach beyond himself.

October is the fallen leaf, but it is also the wider horizon more clearly seen. It is the distant hill once more in sight, and the enduring constellations above that hill once again.

THIS IS THE TIME TO FIND the lesser fruits of Autumn, the wild berries that are too full of seeds, too bitter, too insignificant, for man's fare. This is the time to seek out the blue-black fruit of the fragrant honeysuckle and the scarlet clusters that top the jack-in-the-pulpit's dying stem. Black alder, the brilliant winterberry, is at its prime, and bittersweet is beginning to burst its husk and reveal its red-orange fruit. Snowberry, white as milkweed floss, shines now on its slender branches, and gray-silvered bayberries cluster along the stems with their warm fragrance.

Witch-hazel fruits are ripening, even as the perverse Autumn blooms of the same shrub flaunt their yellow-ribbon petals. Benzoin, the spice bush, is dropping its yellow leaves and revealing its red, spicy berries. Seedy little apples, too tart for human taste, turn rusty on the hawthorn. The wild roses, second cousin to the hawthorn and the apple itself, offer their own little lacquered haws. And overhead are the brilliant dogwood berries and the slate-blue sassafras fruits on their crimson stems.

The viburnums fill the underbrush with their assorted berries, all of them purplish in color. The huckleberries, both high and low, are mostly stripped by now, but a few of the fruits, black and shriveled, will remain among the richly colored leaves until the sparrows have passed by. Like most of these berries, they are bird fare. They have their own surprising beauty, though, which is seldom seen until the maples cease demanding attention.

A CHILL, DRENCHING RAIN this morning brought leaves down in showers, but it stopped by about nine-thirty. We had an errand that we had been putting off because it would take most of the day, and the days have been filled with Fall chores. So when the rain stopped we got out the car and went, driving sixty-odd miles under a sullen sky, doing the errand, and heading for home again. We got halfway home and the rain began again, a slow, gray rain. We didn't like it.

Then we approached the ridge fifteen miles from home, a long, rugged upthrust with several high points close to 2,000 feet which is called Canaan Mountain. The highway crosses Canaan Mountain at Norfolk, and if there is bad weather anywhere around it is to be found there. As we climbed toward Norfolk snow began to fall, fine spitting snow that slanted at us and bounced off the windshield. It increased to quite a flurry. Until then our spirits had reflected the day, but when the snow began we felt our own spirits lighten. It was the season's first snow. It had its own glow. It offered a faint challenge. We laughed and began recalling trips through snowstorms and over icy roads, and for ten minutes we had a fine review of Winters past.

Then we topped the ridge and dropped swiftly down on the homeward side, and the snow turned to rain, then to mist, and finally ended completely. We came on home under the same gray sky we had known most of the day, but we felt uplifted and brightened. We built a hearth fire and had a hot drink and knew it had been an exciting day. We had seen the first snow! It still sparkles in our memory this evening.

IT CLEARED DURING THE NIGHT and today it was smiling Autumn again. We went out in the car and drove close to a hundred miles, and we saw how bountiful the season has been, how good the harvest. . . .

A few years ago, after I had been all across the country and seen the plenty of our land I wrote a magazine article about the bounty of the American harvest. When the article was published I received a handful of letters criticizing me for my "satisfaction" in American plenty. Why, they asked, should we be smug or complacent in our plenty when so many other places were in need?

It seemed to me then, and it still seems so, that these dissenters were basically wrong. One need not be smug or complacent to be thankful for abundance. Nor can I see why one should regret abundance or feel guilty about it. Surely there is neither comfort nor sustenance for any hungry man in the knowledge that others are also in straitened circumstance. Want must be relieved from the plenty somewhere else. Hunger is never relieved by scarcity.

The notion that plenty is a sin stems back to a philosophy to which I cannot subscribe. It is essentially the philosophy of universal sin and punishment. It puts a moral value, somehow, on matters quite outside the scope of morality. Morality is a matter of mind, not of things, and especially not of the earth. There is neither morality nor immorality in a harvest; the moral factor enters, if at all, only when the harvest is distributed. The earth has again been bountiful, and

I am thankful. I may not be proud of what some men do with
that bounty, but that is another matter.

THERE IS ANOTHER PHASE of that morality
which for a long time baffled me. I come from pioneer stock
and am not far removed from pioneer life. Those I knew best
in my childhood had undergone pioneer privations, and out
of that experience often came an assumption that ease was
sinful and comfort was a device of the devil. There was even
something immoral about spending money for anything but
the bare necessities of life. Money took on a kind of moral
value, all by itself.

Only a few years ago I visited and had a meal at the
home of such a person, the widow of a pioneer who had sweated
for every penny he earned. She lived in a comfortable home,
but the food was skimped, even makeshift. At the dinner table

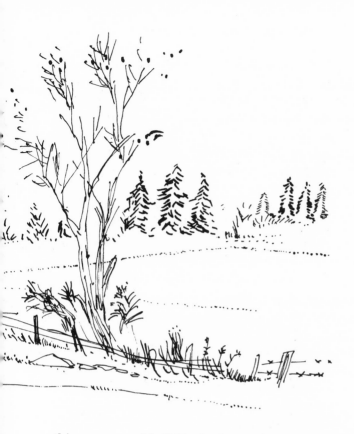

this woman said, "We don't eat fancy. Meat is so high I say
it's sinful to buy it. Why, I can remember when you could
buy a whole panful of steak for fifty cents!" There was both
indignation and unction in her voice. She was saying that she
was a righteous person, spiritually right, morally rectitudi-
nous, in not buying meat, although I knew she had an ample
income.

There is a peculiar echo of monasticism here, and as-
ceticism, which I recognize but which I cannot quite understand. I can see no moral satisfaction or spiritual virtue in
privation. To me, virtue lies in the middle road between asceti-
cism and sybaritism. Virtue, but not morality.

THE WITCH HAZEL is one of the few shrubs on
which one can find leaves, flowers and ripening seed pods all
together. The leaves are now a rusty gold and ready to drift

193

away, their year's work done. The seed pods are the result of last Fall's flowers, and in the weeks to come they will pop open with uncanny force and fling the seeds twenty or thirty feet. The flowers are October bloomers and their tufted yellow petals straggle like the unkempt hair of some blonde young witch. Among the shrub's eccentricities is the fact that staminate, pistillate and bisexual flowers appear at the same time and even on the same twig.

Botanically the witch hazel is *Hamamelis virginiana*, kin of the sweet gum tree. The popular name goes far back and its origin is uncertain. Some say it comes from "wych" or "wythe," and some say it comes from "witch." But there is some agreement that it has a relation to the use of a forked branch of Hamamelis as a divining rod, or dowser, to locate underground water. Many a good back-country well still offers its sweet plenty as proof that a witch-hazel branch, properly held in the right hands, could show a man where to dig. This peculiar form of searching for water was often called witching, but even there the source is uncertain, whether it referred to supernatural powers or merely to a wythe or branch from the bush of the strange name.

Where the "hazel" comes from is anybody's guess, since witch hazel is no kin to the hazelnut or filbert, which belongs to the birch family. There is some similarity in the leaves, however. Witch-hazel extract, made from bark and twigs, has long been used to ease sprains and bruises, but that explains nothing except the commercial value of the shrub.

CHARLEY PHONED THIS AFTERNOON and said, "It's going to be a nice night for a coon hunt. I'll stop by." And at early dark he stopped and picked me up in his car. There were Charley and Bill, the boy who works for him, and myself, and Poochie, Charley's dog, who was a cat-killing mongrel condemned to death in a pound before Charley heard about him and saved his life. "Any dog that kills cats," Charley says, "will make a coon dog." Poochie is getting old, but he was a notable coon dog in his prime.

We drove a mile down the road, to one of Albert's corn fields, and parked the car. We started through the corn under a half-moon. Poochie sniffed the air and vanished in the shadows. Charley began recounting Poochie's past triumphs. We walked across the field in the crisp night, and Poochie yelped twice. Charley listened, shook his head and said, "Rabbit," and we moved over to another corn row. Twice Poochie came back, looked at Charley questioningly, and was sent out again. We came back across the field. No coons.

We drove on to another corn field. Poochie put up two rabbits, but no coons. Bill went to the far corner of the field alone and Charley and I sat and waited, talking little, smoking quietly, feeling the night. Poochie came and looked at us once and went away again. No coons.

I spoke of the old buck coon I'd seen several times last Winter at the bend of the road just below the swamp. "I know that old boy," Charley said. "I've run him half a dozen times. He always gives a dog a good run." So we called in Poochie and Bill came back and we moved again, back to the big bend in the road.

Poochie took off once more. We trailed him across a little corn field, and just as we reached the far side Poochie began to talk. Charley said, "Coon!" and all the excitement of remembered boyhood was in his voice.

We sat down and waited. The coon ran all over that corn field, then out across the alfalfa field beyond, then back toward us, and Poochie's voice was music in the night. Then Poochie's cry changed and Charley said, "He's treed him!"

It was a towering maple in a clump that grew at the corner of a fence row of smaller trees. Poochie danced at the foot of the big maple, trying his best to climb it. Charley called him good dog and turned on his big flashlight and swung the beam upward. Bill held the .410 ready. Up near the top Charley found a dark shadowy mass about the size of the big buck coon. Charley said, "There he is!" And Bill said, "Shall I shoot him?" Charley hesitated. Poochie was more frantic than ever. "Can't disappoint the dog," Charley said.

Bill fired a shot. Small bits of leaf and twig pattered down. Poochie yelped frantically, but Charley's flashlight showed the shadow still there. Bill fired another shot. That time he brought down almost half the litter of a big crow's nest and I remembered that the crows had nested there, with great to-do, last Summer.

Charley said, "Damn!" Bill laughed. Poochie stopped yipping. "Guess he got away," Charley said. "Must have gone down the fence row." So we went back to the car, and it was one of those beautiful Fall nights when it's a privilege just to be alive. Charley talked about three years ago, when Poochie treed four coons in one night. Then we stopped at my place, and as I got out Charley said, "I'm kind of glad it wasn't that old boy. Aren't you?" And I was.

THE TEMPERATURE was down to 20 when I got up this morning and there was a thick scum of ice on the watering trough. But deep frost has delayed long this year. Normally we would have had it three weeks ago.

When I look up the mountainside now I see the pines and the hemlocks standing in vivid green above the ranks of naked boles of maple and birch and ash. As I look at them I think that Fall is the evergreens' season too. They come into their own in less colorful fashion than their broad-leafed companions, but they are like patient patriarchs whose virtues are best seen when more spectacular citizens have spent their energies. The deciduous leaves fall, and there the conifers stand, a stout phalanx against the mountainside, ready for Winter.

Fall

Below the pines and the hemlocks, reaching out into the pasture, are the cedars. We call them pasture cedars, for they creep into the open at every opportunity. They seldom grow much beyond good fence-post size, but where they are left undisturbed they form minor thickets. The cedars are colorful, but nothing like the other evergreens; they are rusty, not a clear green at all after September. Their scale-leaves begin to wither, not all of them but enough to take the brightness off the green. Those scale-leaves have a life of three or four years, after which they wither and shed, some of them every year. And in April and May the new leaves appear, bright and shining. But by late Fall they are always a bit drab, to me, dull green and often with a purplish tinge from the berries which are such a treasure for the Winter birds.

A FLOCK OF GEESE went over today, flying south and flying high. I don't know how high a goose can fly, but I am sure he can go much higher than most observers believe, and do it without distress. Any bird can.

During World War II I spent some time at the Air Force Tactical Center in Florida. One day I stopped in at the high-altitude laboratory where they were running tests on the effect of decompression on pilots. One young pilot turned to a flight surgeon and asked why carrier pigeons don't need oxygen or pressure at high altitudes. The surgeon gave a snap answer, "They do." The pilot laughed. "No," he said. "I took a pair of message pigeons up to 35,000 and they just fluffed up and went to sleep. I put them in paper bags and dropped 'em overboard, and when the bags opened the birds just spiraled down and lit out for home. Got there all right, too."

The surgeon was unconvinced. He sent for a pair of message pigeons and put them in the decompression chamber. He watched as pressure and temperature dropped to the levels of 30,000, 35,000 and finally 40,000 feet. Nothing happened. The birds showed no discomfort. They dozed. He took them up to a simulated altitude where their bones should have exploded. Still they didn't seem to mind. He brought the pressure back to that of sea level and the birds wakened and hopped about, cooing.

The flight surgeon had no explanation. I wrote about the baffler for a national magazine, and none of its readers volunteered an answer. So I suspect that geese, too, can and probably do fly at times two or three miles high, maybe even higher, with no trouble.

It snowed for a time today, just enough to whiten the grass. Then the clouds thinned, the sun came out, the snow vanished and it was a comfortable day. By noon the snow was gone and all but forgotten. This afternoon I went fishing on the river and caught a fair enough string, including a big rock bass that fought like a largemouth. The chill gave him added energy, just as the cold water makes a brook trout twice as gamey on a line in April as he is in June.

But Fall fishing isn't half the fun that Summer fishing is. I don't like to fish with a jacket on, and today I had a sweater beneath a windbreaker. I prefer to fish with nothing on but a pair of khaki shorts or stagged-off dungarees, with the sun hot on my back. Half the enjoyment of fishing, for me, is in the feel of sun and air. When I have to bundle up, I'd rather walk and let the fish go their own way. So today was probably my last fishing day until next Spring.

Two of the farmers on the hill road have been putting Winter bustles on their houses. They put up low fences of chicken wire two feet out from the house and packed the space between with leaves. Thus they have insulated against the cold that otherwise would creep in at floor level. In earlier days every farmhouse was so insulated in the Fall, sometimes with sod heaped at the sills, sometimes with sawdust, most often with leaves. Even so, the floors were often cold and drafty, and if anyone doubts it let him examine the antique kitchen chairs. Most of them show well-worn front rungs, where Grandmother hooked her heels to keep her feet up out of the floor draft.

Long before rock wool and other manufactured insulators were on the market, men in cold climates learned to use natural insulation. Some were laughed at when they filled the space in their walls with sawdust, but that worked fairly well; it was the method used in building icehouses, and it could keep cold out as well as in. When I was a boy an eccentric sheep-rancher built himself a frame house and packed the space in the walls with well-dried sheep manure. In that dry climate the sheep manure dried into pellets of cellulose with little odor. That sheepman's house was as warm as a "soddy" in Winter and just as cool in Summer.

NOVEMBER

Iᴛ ᴛʜᴇ ʙʟᴜᴇ ᴊᴀʏ were one of those migrants who stop in for only a few days each season, he probably would be known as an exotic bird of unusual beauty. Some jays do migrate a little way, but few places in their range are ever without them. The jays and the crows keep the Winter landscape alive and lively.

I watched a jay this frosty morning and he was the perfect caricature of the pompous alderman of the old school. His feathers were fluffed against the chill and he sat and scowled. His vest was snug across an ample breast. He even seemed to have a series of chins, and his crest was a kind of avian topper which lent a degree of dignity—until he opened his big mouth. A jay rasps, always indignantly. The climate, the landscape, the meals, or the company always seems to be demanding criticism. He flocks with his kind, but he seems to quarrel incessantly.

But there is this to be said for the jay: he has an immaculate air. The white cravat at his throat, the white bars on his wings, the white edging on his tail, are crisply white. The blue of his wings is a clean, rich blue, particularly against a gray Winter sky. He has an air. He can sit stock still and strut.

Yet, for all his pomposity, he does have frivolous moments. On a lively morning I have seen jays play tag in the tangled branches of an old apple tree, a fascinating game to watch. And when nobody is in sight a jay will occasionally whisper a sweet little song, soft, melodious and almost sentimental. At such times a jay seems to me a character actor, always cast as the colorful villain but with a deep, secret yearning to play the young, romantic lead.

Fall

IT WAS A COLD AND DRIZZLY DAY and Pat spent all morning dozing here in my study, luxuriating in comfort. But after lunch I sent him packing. I told him to go out and get some exercise. He went to the door readily enough but when I held it open he took one look outdoors, looked at me and seemed to shake his head. But out he went, just the same. Ten minutes and he was back, wet and muddy, asking to be let in. He practically accused me of cruelty when I said "No!" and to save my own face I put on boots and a raincoat and went for a walk with him. When we came back I let him in, just as he had expected I would.

Dogs are inveterate optimists. They confidently expect the best of life. Yes, I know there are whipped curs that dodge and wince and slink away; but they are broken dogs with no spirit left in them. The country dog that has had even normal care expects the world, his world, to be a pleasant place. He will accept short rations, if need be, but he continues to expect the full meal. He will suffer rain and cold, when forced to, but he approaches the door with confidence, no matter how wet or muddy he is.

I do wish it were possible to train a dog to shake himself, when he is drenched, out on the porch instead of waiting till he gets indoors. But that is expecting too much. He probably wishes we had more appreciation of the wonderful odor of ripe woodchuck, in which he rolls from time to time during the Summer. But we make our compromises, both of us, and live comfortably together most of the time. Right now he is in front of the fire, drying and cleaning himself and waiting to see which brand of dog food he gets for dinner tonight.

NOVEMBER NIGHTS ARE LONG AND CHILL and full of stars and the crisp whisper of fallen leaves skittering in the wind. November nights are good for walking down a country road, when the world is close about you, a world drawn in bold charcoal strokes against the sky.

I suspect the reason is that night and darkness simplify the world to a point of understanding. The hill across

the way is any hill, with substance but no detail. The valley has depth but no contours. The river is a path of sky with a handful of stars wavering in the rippled footsteps of the wind. The pines on the mountain are a thick, restless shadow leaping like a hound at the horizon. The house, from a little way off, is nothing but blinking yellow eyes, windows with no walls around them.

This is no complex world. It is a world of simple things, now brought to rest. Who can make complexity of wood smoke, so sharp on the night air? Or the barking of a dog announcing footsteps and leaf-rustle on the road? And what is so simple as a tall maple, all its leaves shed, silhouetted against the sky?

To walk on such a night is to know that the only mysteries are the great mysteries of all time—the stars, the heavens, the restless wind-tides, the spinning earth, and man himself. Daylight and suntime are the time to explore these matters; nighttime and darkness are the time to accept them

and build dreams and poems upon them. Night, when the cool of the year has come, is the time to walk with them and know intimately the bold simplicities.

WE HAVE BEEN OUT PICKING CRANBERRIES, in a bog by the lake. They are a little late this year, and we were later still. We could find only a couple of quarts where there usually are several bushels, enough for the whole countryside to have wild cranberry sauce for Thanksgiving and Christmas.

When I was a small boy I thought cranberries grew in wooden barrels, or perhaps on trees like cherries. When I first came East and drove past New Jersey's cranberry bogs I mistook the scattered blueberry bushes for cranberry bushes. It wasn't until we came here to live that I went into a cranberry bog and found the plants.

The cranberry grows on an insignificant little shrub, less than a foot high. How that plant manages the crop of fruit it often does is one of the marvels of the vegetable kingdom. Sometimes, in a good year, the berries will be so big and so plentiful that the branches are weighted to the ground; and the whole cranberry bog has a bright red gleam beneath the green of the slim little leaves.

You wear boots to go cranberrying, and old clothes. Sometimes you slip into the bog muck up to your knees. We were wary today, though. Professional harvesters use wooden scoops with long fingers to glean the berries, but we use the scoops we were born with, our hands. The berries picked now, with a touch of frost on them, have a sharp tang but nothing like the acidity of those in the market, which are picked greener. We store them in a cold corner of the cellar and they will keep well into February.

WE DON'T LIVE OFF THE LAND DIRECTLY. We buy most of our food and all our clothing. We don't even keep chickens, which some consider heresy; but I cleaned enough chicken houses in my youth to last me a lifetime. Nor do we keep cows, though I can still milk a cow; much of the strength in my hands and forearms came from milking cows and wrestling a walking plow before I was fifteen.

But, living here, we do get a sense of origins and of time and growth, as well as a moderate share of the earth's bounty. When I go to the freezer in January and take out filets of fish I caught in the river last June I feel both wealthy and fortunate. I can go to the cellar now and see jars of raspberry jam, grape jelly, canned pears, apple sauce, strawberry preserves, which came from our own fruit, ours for the picking. The corn in the freezer, and the limas and the asparagus came from this soil, planted by our own hands. The squashes in the cellar were tended by Barbara and me all last Summer. There are a few jars of maple syrup from our own trees. There is even a flitch of bacon, cured and smoked in the old manner by a man I know. It came from a hog we bought and had butchered, not from Iowa by way of Chicago and the butcher shop.

Fall

Living close to origins here, we are seldom unaware of cause and effect. It seems to me that any way of life remote from origins has a weak spot in its foundation, just as any way of thinking which deals with effects without knowing causes is at fault.

Now come those mornings when buckwheat cakes belong on the menu, buckwheat cakes and maple syrup and home-made sausage. The New England grandmother knew it and had her special crock for buckwheat batter, a crock that came out in November and stayed out till April. So did a good many grandmothers elsewhere, including one of my own who was a couple of generations removed from New England. She saw to it that one corner of the buckwheat field grandfather grew for green manure was left to ripen and was threshed and milled. The grayish flour with the unmistakable tang was there waiting when the first hog was butchered and the first sausage made, which was just as soon as the heavy frosts came.

When a farmer grew practically everything he ate, buckwheat was one of his regular crops. It was good for the soil and it didn't take much of a patch to cover his needs. Farmers had been growing buckwheat more generations than you could count. It came, long ago, from the shores of the Caspian Sea, and it was known as a dark breadstuff all through Central Europe in the Middle Ages. From there it went to England, and the first colonists brought it here.

Few farmers can tell you the origin of the name unless they had a German or Danish grandfather. The *buck* comes from an old Germanic word for "beech," probably because the buckwheat seed looks like a miniature beechnut. When it came to this country it followed maize into a batter baked as a thin cake instead of into dough and a loaf. And here it came to that wondrous union with maple syrup and sage-tanged sausage. Nowadays most of it comes in a package, mixed with many other things and labeled buckwheat pancake flour. Few victims of such ready-made mixes know what a real buckwheat cake tastes like. Sic transit gloria Monday morning breakfast.

THE LARCHES, OR TAMARACKS, stand in the woods now like giant candle flames of yellowish tan, tall and slim and symmetrical. They are about to shed their needles, for they are the woodchucks of the conifers, the only ones in our area which "hibernate" in the Winter. Their tufted needles will soon fall in a yellow shower and the bright tan of their branches will stand out against the grays and browns of the Winter hillsides.

As a species, the larches are among the oldest trees of the chilly northlands. They have seen ice ages come and go; the earth has wrinkled and convulsed beneath their roots. And in the briefer time of man the larches have given their strength and warmth to his house and his fire. Their trunks are long and slim and their wood is hard and resinous; they resist rotting and they burn with a long, hot flame. Small wonder that man learned long ago to build on sills of larch and to keel and frame the longboats of adventure with timbers of larch.

Those who would personify it call the larch a cautious tree; but it were better described as stoutly individual. Though it belongs to the family of evergreens, it sheds its needles. A conifer, its cones are inconspicuous and its seeds so small that they tempt only a very hungry squirrel. A tree of the rocky upland, it occasionally invades the lesser swamp and thrives there. In Spring it blossoms inconspicuously in March or April, but it takes its time about putting forth any new needles. All Summer long it is a beautiful spire of green, but by November it is resolutely deciduous. In Winter it shrugs off the snow. Thus it lives to a stout old age.

UP IN THE EDGE OF THE WOODS, safely remote from passers-by, bittersweet dangles its clustered berries, their orange husks now open and the still brighter orange berries within now vivid. They are like late November flowers in the leaf-crisp evening of the year, brighter than the haws of the wild roses, far more generous than the lacquer-red berries of their creeper neighbors, the partridge berries. Bittersweet berries and sumac heads are the baubles and bangles of the brushland.

Bittersweet is a shrubby vine that coils and twines its way up any handy support, but particularly up the seedlings of birch and wild cherry, strangling its supporter but lifting its own head high. Its flowers are of no particular consequence, small, greenish white and lost among the neighbors in flowery June. Its color is saved for the time of ripeness, when neighbors have bowed to the frost. Then the bittersweet comes into its own.

The common name seems to have been borrowed from the nightshade, which came from Europe, is not really a twining vine, and has poisonous berries about the same size but redder than those of our native bittersweet. Those who have tasted them say that nightshade berries are first sweet to the tongue, then acridly bitter; hence, bitter-sweet. But nightshade is *Solanum dulcamara*, in botanist language, and distant kin of the potato. Our climbing bittersweet is botanically *Celastrus scandens*, a Greek-Latin combination meaning an evergreen that climbs. Our native species is no evergreen, but it has an Asian relative which is. Since nightshade is poisonous to cows, we root it out; since bittersweet is beautiful, we let it grow where it will in the woods.

LAST SUMMER'S ORIOLE NEST hangs high in the elm, in plain sight now that the leaves are gone. The orioles, too, are gone, and after a frosty night the nest sways in the morning sun like a gray purse spangled with brilliants. Snow will come, in due time, and fill the pouch where eggs were hovered and hatched. Winter gales will whip at it, and still the nest will remain, anchored to the slender twigs, a fragment of Summer gone and a reminder of Spring to come, of bright plumage and rippling song.

This morning the blue jays were busy pecking seeds from the frosted apples still hanging in the tree beside the woodshed, pausing now and then to proclaim themselves possessors of this November world. Two of the jays flew from there to the elm, perched near the oriole nest, surveyed it from all angles, and began to jeer. Perhaps not at the nest, but that's the way it appeared. A jay builds no such nest, and it is useless

to speculate on why a blue jay lacks the nest-weaver's skill.

I watched those jays for ten minutes, and the temptation was strong to draw broad conclusions about art, industry, envy, song, raucous noises, and the habit of jeering. But such

conclusions are not justified. Birds are birds, and men are men, presumably with their own reasons for being. The orioles came and wove their nest and raised a brood and sang sweet songs, and now they have gone away. The jays did the same thing, in their own way. Who am I to draw conclusions about them? But I do have my preferences.

THE LEAVES HAVE FALLEN, except on the reluctant oaks, and the hilltops lined with ash trees and maples have a strangely trimmed and hair-cut look. Walking up the valley today it seemed to me that the ridge might have been clipped with gigantic shears, so even was its fringe of trees. So

I climbed among the rocks for half a mile to reach the top and see for myself if all the trees up there were of an age. They weren't. When I stood among them I could see that they were the customary growth, young and old and of varying height.

Then I came down the hillside to the valley and looked up once more. There they were, shorn smooth and even against the sky. And I looked around at a dozen other hilltops. All, every hill in sight, had a crew haircut.

THERE WAS A HEAVY WHITE FROST last night, and here along the river we had a spectacular sunrise. Every bush and weed stem was outlined in crystal, every blade of grass was crisp and gleaming white. The posts of the pasture fence were studded with brilliants and the wires between them were barbed with jewels. The garage had a roof with a wondrous geometric pattern, the shingles outlined in frost. The rail which carries its sliding door was crystal from end to end.

Thus was this world at sunrise, dazzling, with the dark, slow flow of the river almost inky.

The sun climbed swiftly. Within an hour the frost began to turn to water drops on the goldenrod stems. The sunward side of the garage roof darkened and there was a drip from the eaves. The grass turned wet and glistening green. But not all the grass. For several hours there were long white shadows across the lawn and out into the pasture beyond, a strange November reversal of the usual pattern. Where the sun did not strike directly the frost remained. The blocky pattern of garage and house and woodshed and barn and corn crib lay on the west side till midmorning. Even more spectacular, the white shadows of the trees, leafless though they were, lay like white ghosts across the grass.

By eleven o'clock they were gone, all those shadows and all the hoarfrost. But for a time we had the white shadow of days to come, the cold, glittering forecast of December and January.

I WATCHED A CROW GO WINGING past this morning and he looked twice as black as he did two months ago. But it was the same crow, or at least one of the same flock, that has been here all year. Maybe its plumage is new, but it is the same color. The difference is in the background, which is now gray and brown and slightly misty today. The crow is no blacker, but he looks so in this new setting. When the snow comes, he will look blacker still.

The same is true of the blue jays which spend half their time filching from the corn crib. They are bluer than the bluebirds were in May. But the blue jay's color doesn't change either. Again, it is a matter of background. The eye is no longer dazzled by the brilliance of a tanager or a goldfinch, and there is little green and no bright blossom to dim the jay's feathers.

Come snow time and the red crown of the downy woodpecker will look brilliant, simply because I can see it so clearly. And the pine siskin's little yellow rump patch will stand out like a yellow warbler in early Summer.

Color becomes relative as the seasons shift. Brilliance is less a matter of color itself than one of contrast. The less there is to see, the more one sees of it. The eyes sharpen as the days turn chill and the woods turn gray.

THE GRAY WIND OF NOVEMBER today whipped the low scud across the sky and sent the fallen leaves swirling through the woodland. Had it been a bright day I could almost have seen a silvery sheen to such a wind; but it is a dull day and it moans and whispers in the big spruce outside my window. There is a chill in the air and the wind has a whetted edge.

This wind of November is almost as restless as the winds of March. But it roars and whistles over the hills from another direction. March wind sweeps up the valley, with a promise of April and blossom. This wind whoops down the valley, with the weight of oncoming Winter behind it.

Put rain in a November wind and it has the lash and bite of a sleet storm. Put a warm sun behind it and it is somewhat tempered, but I know it is only biding its time, waiting for reinforcements. At its best, I never mistake it for the gusts of September or the breeze that brings April.

The pines lean before this wind and make the whole mountainside sigh. Dead branches are torn from popple and ash and hickory; tomorrow there will be a fresh litter all through the woodland. The woods are being strewn with out-worn limbs, to be snow-buried and rotted into the soil whence they sprang. And here on the river the wind piles up an unnat-ural surf, eating at the banks and gnawing at the rooted soil. It flattens the tall grass at the edge of the pasture, and if the hills were less firmly rooted it would flatten them into the val-leys. It is a primal force, this wind of November, one with the tides and the ice and the very spin of the earth.

THE WIND BLEW ALL DAY and all night and half of today, but by this evening the air is almost calm, almost penitent. We walked in the dusk and came back in the dark and noticed how late Autumn had burnished the stars and hung them back in place and closer at hand. Or so it seemed, for there was an intimacy to the evening and to the trees lifting bare branches almost to the stars.

As we walked north the tail of the Big Bear, the handle of the Dipper, was hidden by the first hill. It will be well above the horizon later tonight, for the Dipper swings around the Pole Star counterclockwise throughout the night. But now it is there on the horizon; and the Little Bear, the Little Dipper, hangs from the Pole Star, which is its pivot, like a crookneck gourd from a nail in an old Summer kitchen.

When we turned and looked to the west, there stood the Northern Cross, which some call Cygnus, the Swan. It leans, actually, toward the right, as though about to pitch from the luminous sky, and it will be much brighter later in the evening when the thin moon has set. To the east were the Pleiades, a cluster which seemed to fade, as always, when we looked directly at it, and to brighten when we glanced away and saw it from the corner of the eye, which is a trick of night vision.

Stars everywhere, the Milky Way like a daisy meadow in full bloom. And so close that if we had climbed to the top of Tom's Mountain we surely could have reached up and touched a star or two.

WE HAVE BEEN OUT SURVEYING the wild berry crop and we brought home a few specimens, just for pretty, as Barbara says. A branch or two of black alder with its vivid red bunches of berries and a couple of branches of baneberry, both the red and the white variety. We also tasted the winter-green tang of the checkerberry, and we found the cherry-red cluster-berries of the jack-in-the-pulpit and the even redder partridge berries. The birds have pretty well stripped the miniature grapes from the Virginia creeper and the inky pur-ple-black berries from the red stems of the pokeweed.

Fall

The partridge berries, which botanists know as *Mitchella repens*, seems to have been more fruitful than in years. I have heard it said that the partridge berry forecasts the coming Winter—few berries, a mild season; many berries, a hard Winter. To me, that reasoning is backward: many berries are plain evidence that the season just past was favorable for fruiting—good weather, many blossoms, and busy bees and small butterflies pollinating those blossoms. That, like a good many superstitions, about the stock market and horse races as well as the weather, is based on hindsight rather than anything resembling reason. You might as well say that because a farmer harvests a good corn crop he will face a rough and rugged Winter.

I'VE BEEN TRYING TO FIND OUT what kind of Winter we're going to have, but I haven't had much luck. The almanacs offer their usual forecasts: "Snow and ice, or maybe nice . . . Wind and sleet and chilly feet . . . Cold and raw, then January thaw." Mildly amusing, but pretty much double talk. And the men at the weather stations talk about averages and norms and refuse to be put out on a limb; though they don't say so in so many words, I think they simply don't know. And the old-timers around here, most of them, don't make forecasts any more. "Those atomic bombs," one of them said, "changed everything." The fact is that he doesn't seem to care too much, because he plans to go South and visit his married daughter right after Thanksgiving.

Charley did come up with his own forecast. I had heard it before. Every year, in fact. "The river will have to freeze over three times," Charley always says, "before Winter's over. Twice before Winter really settles in. It always has. One year it froze and the ice went out *four* times, but that's unusual." I've checked on Charley's theory ever since we've lived here, and only once has it failed.

Since it was warm and sunny this afternoon we got in the boat and went upstream a few miles, to look for signs ourselves. The only signs we saw were new muskrat holes. The new holes were high up the river bank. It takes no great store of lore to guess that the muskrats expect high water before Spring. And that's not particularly new. The river always rises with the Spring thaw. So there's nothing to do but wait for the river to freeze over three times. After that it should be Spring, and we'll know what kind of Winter it was.

THE COLD BEGINS TO DEEPEN and I went up the mountain today to look at the pipeline from the spring. It was laid many years ago, and I can only guess at its course, but if I know anything about that mountainside the pipe lies close to the surface in a good many places. The rocky core of the mountain is close to the surface and I am sure nobody blasted a trench to lay that pipe.

I found the line where it crosses a gully and it was out in the open there. Spring and Summer rains had washed the gully so deep that six feet of pipe were revealed. I carried stones and shoveled dirt and built a dam across the gully, covering the pipe and facing the dam with flat stones so it would protect itself. I hope that any freshets will deposit more silt over my pipe there. With good luck, and by leaving the faucet running at the watering trough, the line won't freeze even if the frost strikes deep.

I like to work on the mountainside at this time of year. The wind whispers in the hemlocks, the sun strikes warm through the leafless maples, and the chickadees seem to like company. Partridge berries are bright beads underfoot and Christmas fern is untouched by the frosts. There are beds of club moss and ground cedar and ground pine.

And Pat thinks it is a holiday. He isn't interested in such prosaic projects as covering a pipe. He finds a rabbit track and runs the mountainside, voicing his excitement. In a few days I'll come up here with him and bring the shotgun, and we'll see if we can get a few rabbits for the freezer.

THE WEATHER is "making up," as they say, making up some kind of change, and probably not for the

better. We have had good weather for some time now and are
due for a change. It looks like rain, to me. We have had little
dew the past few mornings, and none at all this morning. As
the old rhyme goes:

> When the morn is dry, the rain is nigh;
> When the morn is wet, no rain you'll get.

When it didn't rain before noon I spent the afternoon
cutting firewood. The chain saw takes a good deal of the labor
out of that job, particularly for one man working alone; but
it still isn't loafing. Several times when I took a breather I

went down and looked at the boat, wondering if I should haul it out of the water now. The bank is high and steep, and the only way I can get the boat out is with a block and tackle hitched to one of the big maples. Charley or Albert would help, but they are busy and I hesitate to ask them. But if it rains the river will rise. If the water rises enough, say three feet, I can haul the boat out easily. Being only a twelve-footer, it weighs less than 200 pounds.

I finally decided to wait and hope for rain and high water. And I finished with the wood. I cut half a cord and got it all stowed in the woodshed. And then I began to wonder if my decision about the boat was right after all. It might turn cold, the river might freeze over, and we might get a foot of snow. Then where would I be, with the boat frozen in and snowed over? But by then it was too late to get the boat out tonight.

No DEW AGAIN, and still no rain. But I refused to be panicked into hauling that boat out the hard way. Besides, Pat practically said, in so many words, "How about those rabbits? They're getting downright insolent. How about it, Boss?" So I took the 12-gauge and we went up the mountain. And, to prove his point, Pat picked up a scent just above the pasture. I took my stand and waited, listening to Pat's wonderfully melodious voice. He trailed that rabbit halfway up the mountain before it turned and came back. And then I heard a slight rustle of brush off to my left and a moment later there was the big, fat cottontail, going just fast enough to keep ahead of the dog. He crossed in front of me, not twenty yards away, and at my shot Pat came running. We had our first rabbit.

Pat trails rabbits entirely by scent, as any good rabbit dog does. I've seen a rabbit jump almost under his nose, but he paid no attention to where the rabbit went until he picked up the scent. The whole idea of hunting with such a dog is based on a rabbit's way of running in a circle, returning to the place where he was flushed. The dog keeps on his trail, the rabbit keeps moving, and the hunter who takes a stand near the place where the rabbit started usually gets a shot. Nose trailing is rather slow, and the rabbit runs only fast enough to keep fifty yards or so ahead of the dog.

Pat put up three rabbits one after another. One ran in, as we say, took refuge in a hole under an old stone wall. I got the other two. Then, just before noon, when we were working through a thicket of cedars, I heard Pat utter a strange yelp of discovery. Two yelps, then silence, then a quick whimper of pain and a growl of anger.

I hurried toward the little hollow beyond the cedars and found Pat pawing at his muzzle, pawing, darting into the brush, backing out and pawing at his muzzle. He heard me and turned, literally bristling—his nose was feathered with porcupine quills.

I had a leash with me. I snapped it on Pat's collar and tied him to a sapling. Then I found the porky, a big fellow, in the brush and finished him off. I went back to Pat and pulled a dozen quills out of his muzzle; but he had a whole mouthful of quills in his gums. I pulled what I could, but most of them were broken off. So we came back down the mountainside, Pat still on the leash. Hurt as he was, he still wanted to run rabbits.

I got a pair of pliers and pulled what quill stubs I could reach, but he needed more help than I could give. So we took him in the car and went to the veterinarian, who said he'd have to give Pat an anesthetic, put him under, to get all the quill stubs out. We left him, though he obviously thought we were deserting him in his time of trial. We went back and got him this evening. The effect of the drug was still on him. He staggered and was bleary-eyed, and when we got in the car he whimpered softly and lay with his head in my lap. We brought him home and put him to bed in his house. It had begun to rain, but I was scarcely aware of it.

It RAINED ALL NIGHT and was still raining this morning when I went to let Pat out of his house. He heard me coming and was at the door demanding his freedom. I'd thought he might have a hangover and so sore a mouth he would lie around, an invalid, all day. Not a bit of it! He came out leaping and barking, rolled in the wet grass, shook water all over me, and raced me to the back door. He had a full appetite when I gave him his snack for breakfast. Then he settled down here in my study, as though nothing had happened. But I hope he hasn't completely forgotten that porcupine and what it did to him. He will meet other porkies.

Meanwhile, the river rose and the brooks were rushing noisily down the mountainside. It's a strange river, peculiarly responsive to flood conditions. Normally it lies like a lake along here, broad and deep and with a current of less than two miles an hour. It has little fall, though half a mile below here it spills into white-water rapids and begins to assume a proper mountain-stream character. When heavy rains come it rises swiftly, sometimes as much as three or four feet in twenty-four hours. Fortunately the banks are about ten feet high in front of the house; it has been out of those banks only twice in recent years.

This evening the water had risen two feet and covered my dock completely. I remember a year ago, when it threatened flood and other streams swept away bridges and Jim and Juanita were marooned here for a long weekend. They were singing, "River, Stay 'Way from My Door." But I don't expect a flood. I moored the boat to a post up the bank a little way, on the first ledge above the river. Another foot of rise and I can haul the boat out with one hand.

THE RAIN CONTINUED ALL NIGHT and most of this morning, and I put on boots and a raincoat and went out to slosh around in it, across the pastures and along the brooks and down to the river bank. Barbara likes to walk in the rain, but not merely to slosh around in it, as I do. The rush of a brook holds no fascination for her and rouses nothing approaching ecstasy. But she recognizes my delight and knows it for what it is—the exultation of a dry-country person in water that runs ankle deep across the land. I get an almost sensual delight in watching a brook come boiling across the pasture in flood.

I was out for two hours, and though the rain was chill and I got fairly wet, it was well worth it. I was communing with water, with one of the elements, and I felt as frisky as a fish. I wanted, but lacked the small-boy obliviousness, to build a toy water wheel and set it in the brook back of the garden, just to watch the paddle wheel spin.

Soon after lunch the rain stopped and I put on my boots again and went to the river bank where the boat was moored. The river had risen so high that I slid the boat out onto the first step-off of the bank. I hauled it onto the grass with one hand, slid it on up the bank a little way, tethered it to a tree, and am all set to bring it the rest of the way tomorrow and stow it for the Winter. I am feeling a little smug tonight.

MARGARET AND ALLERTON came over this afternoon and we sat around the fire and talked, and I thought how a hearth calls for a small company, for companionship.

A hearth fire is a wasteful thing, in terms of economics. But so is much of the talk that generates around an open fire, perhaps; it seldom settles big problems and it never pays the taxes. Much of it, like the heat from the logs on the andirons, goes up the chimney. But when you have said that you have pretty well exhausted the case against the simmering log and the slow talk beside it. There still remains the reflected glow, which is its own excuse and needs no defense.

There are times when quick heat and sharp words are among the world's greatest inefficiencies. Some things—and friendship and understanding are high among them—mature best by ember light and in a small company. It is doubtful that mob rule was ever inspired by the gleam of a hearth fire. The tinder of violence and fanaticism requires a bigger flame and a larger arena. Philosophy and faith are companions at the hearth, and ever have been.

There are better ways to heat a house, but neither love nor friendship is too much concerned with economics. Man built a home around a fire, and there the family grew. To his fireside man brought his friends, and friendship grew, and understanding. So hearth became home, and home became heart. It has little changed over the centuries. What greater friendship or understanding is there than that which stands, back to hearth, and faces outer cold and darkness unafraid?

Fall

THANKSGIVING, and I am thinking today of the early ones here. When they had given thanks for life, for loved ones, for the purpose that had brought them here, they went about their tasks. The dusk of Winter was early upon them, for Autumn was at its end.

Summer had not been easy, for it was a time of labor; but they had given thanks for that, too, for the chance to labor for themselves. And Autumn had not been easy, for it was a time of garnering, of gathering the small harvest from the woods and fields; but they had been thankful for harvest, for the chance to lay up substance that would sustain them. And now Winter was at hand.

They went about their tasks, cutting wood and snugging houses and caring for the beasts. The simple work, the drudging work, of living. And night closed in, the long night when ice would fringe the river and the trees in the forest would sigh in the toothed wind. The women spun, the children carded wool, the men carved patiently at new porringers and wiping rods and yokes for the cattle. The hearth fire eased the darkness and drove back the cold a little.

And one, it seems to me, looked up from his wood shaping and said, "We have made a clearing in the forest. Another year and we will see a larger clearing. We have made a beginning in a hostile wilderness."

That is the way I see the picture. Beginnings are the most difficult, next only to the dream itself, which is the great beginning of all enduring things. They had the dream, and now they knew that it would endure through the Winter and live on, and on, and on.

NOW IT BECOMES CLEAR that it isn't the little pleasures of the country that make life worth living here. It is rather the big assurances. The little pleasures are for the casual visitor; but one must live with the wind and the weather and know the land and the seasons to find the certainties. The flash of a goldfinch or the song of an oriole can delight the senses; but the knowledge that no matter how sharp or long the Winter, they will be back next Spring provides an inner surety. To see a hillside come to leaf and flower is to know a particular ecstasy of beauty; but to walk the gray Winter woods and find the buds that will resurrect that beauty in another May is to partake of continuity. To feel the frost underfoot and know that there is both fire and ice in the earth, even as in the patterned stars overhead, is to sense the big assurances.

Man needs to know these things, and they are best learned when the silence is upon the land. No one can shout about them. They need to be whispered, that they may reach the questing soul.

I SAW A MOLE come to the surface of the ground out in the middle pasture this afternoon. I was standing there, not ten feet away, when he appeared. He came up like a submarine surfacing, shook himself, nosed the air, went a little way in the open, not more than three to four feet, and plunged underground again. I would change the figure. It was more like a dolphin surfacing, then diving again. Whether the mole struck some underground barrier and came up to detour, or what happened, I do not know. But there he was for a moment; then there he wasn't. It was a mild day and there was little frost in the ground, so the mole's shovel-like forepaws could scoop out a hole in no time at all.

The mole is probably the most ravenous of all animals. It has a digestive system that assimilates food so fast that if it has nothing to eat for as little as twelve hours it will starve to death. It will consume its own weight in worms and grubs in a day. Contrary to popular belief, the mole does not eat bulbs, grass roots or anything of the kind. It is carnivorous, living almost entirely on worms and insect larva. One scientist found the remains of 150 beetle grubs in a single mole's stomach. The damage done by a mole in a lawn is caused by exposing the grass roots to the air, an inevitable result of the mole's search for grubs that often live among those roots. The "mole damage" done in a flower garden is nearly always done by field mice which use the mole's burrow as a runway to reach plant roots or bulbs. Mice eat roots and bulbs. The mole merely provides them a means of access to such provender. So the mole is not the criminal; he is merely an accessory before the fact.

I WAS OUT IN THE CRISPNESS of a chilly early morning, today, and went to a small, shallow pool at the lower end of the pasture. It is the kind of quicksilver pool that mirrors naked willow brush and the bright berries of black alder. Under a moon, it mirrors the stars and a small, inverted sky. This morning it had the touch of Winter upon it.

Frost lined the willows and beaded the grass. The bright berries of the black alder were doubly red against the black branches of the bush, Christmasy in their brilliant contrast. And on the water were the long, sharp ice needles with which the night's late hours had been knitting an intricate pattern of crystal. Some of those needles were a foot long and slim as any knitting needle. Had there been even a breath of wind to ripple the surface they would have been broken to bits. But the shallow pond was glass-smooth and the ice needles lay in an intricate crisscross pattern on its surface.

It requires still, cold hours to form such needles, with the temperature not too low. I seldom see them. But when the night is precisely the right temperature, somewhere around 25, and the air is breathless of breeze, sometimes they form. If they form early in the night they increase, knitting stronger with each hour, until the whole surface is covered. Then I find only a scum of ice in the morning. What I saw this morning was that rare, tentative stage that happens only a few times each season. Tonight the temperature has fallen another five degrees and tomorrow morning the pool will be iced over, edge to edge. But I saw the miracle this morning, the crystal needles, which are cousins of the snowflakes.

AUTUMN EBBS AWAY INTO WINTER, but there is flow rather than ebb in the unseen wind tides that now lap at the hills and send their invisible breakers to hiss softly in the upper woodlands. They are the tides that curl about this earth, forever restless and eternally moving, tides that obey some subtler master than the moon.

As I sat beside the fire this November evening I could hear those tides sucking at the chimney, hear the swish of their unseen waves breaking against the corner of the house, feel the quiver of the panes shaken by the breakers of this vast, invisible ocean. I sat and listened and I could hear the rise and fall of the wind waves, the rush of one after another in crescendo until the peak had struck its battering blow. Then there would be a pause, a gathering of new force, and again

the succession of waves began, to build once more to climactic height and fall away again in the darkness.

Night is the time to hear these tides, a night when the moon is late and the stars are dim with the scud which I imagine is the spray of wind waves crowding swiftly one upon the next. I have lain in bed and listened to them and been lulled to sleep as by the rush and boom of the ocean itself. But I have seen the wind-tides, or thought I have, at dawn and at dusk, at this time of year, breaker-white. They go rippling through the pasture and across the open knoll beyond with its tall red-bronze grass. They swish through the underbrush beside the river with the sibilant song of cove water being crowded up an inlet. They bow the naked maple tips with the murmuring hiss of moontides on rocky reefs.

Fall

Seeing and hearing them, I know that I am a shell-less sea creature living on the bottom of an ocean of air, a kind of elemental newt endowed with comprehension.

EACH YEAR AT ABOUT THIS TIME comes a day when I go out into the raw air, feel the frozen ground underfoot, and look north apprehensively. I say to myself: What if this should be the year? What, I mean, if this should be the beginning of a new Ice Age?

It is a fantastic thought, and I know it. No new Ice Age is going to come overnight. All evidence indicates that pre-

vious Ice Ages were hundreds of years in coming, with a slow accumulation and advance of the glaciers down from the polar regions. There was ample warning for those who heeded it. Birds and beasts simply moved a few miles south each year, and whatever men were here retreated likewise. The temperature drop was gradual, a few degrees a year. Some even say the advance was at least as gradual as was the eventual retreat of the ice, and some estimates indicate that it took 10,000 years for the glaciers to melt back from the area where I now live to their present habitat north of Canada.

But, as I said, there comes a cold, dismal day, when I stand and look to the north and think that there were mammoths-here once, and perhaps saber-toothed tigers and more than likely polar bears, all of them frowning at the ice sheet,

225

which they knew all their lives. Can it be that I and all my kind are itinerants who dwell here between great cycles of refrigeration? In relation to the age of the earth, we have been here only briefly, possibly between the pulses of some strange, rhythmic chill.

I look, and I shiver, and I come back inside and know that I am only rounding out another November.

THIS HAS BEEN A CHILL DAY, despite full sun. The crisp maple leaves rattling down the road in the gusty wind were the cold-stiff fingers of Autumn clinging to the memory of Indian Summer.

Winter does not wait for the solstice, nor does it come in the night and settle down, firm-rooted, to take over the days and weeks unrelieved. Winter creeps in, possessing a night or two and the day between, then retreats, only to come again. It

frosts the valleys, and day eases the frost; it spangles the air with a few flakes of snow, then whisks them away before the ground is whitened. It rattles the door, then hides around the corner when the sun streams warm through a south window. Winter is as tentative as Spring, but as inevitable.

Late November brings an end to full-fledged Autumn. The lasting warmth, the balmy days, the hazy in-between time, seldom endure much beyond Thanksgiving. Then it is that the pines and hemlocks stand out in cold-season strength of green; then the white reach of the birches is clear and clean against the sky. The squirrels have stripped the nut trees of their fruit, the bittersweet has dropped its orange seed and left the husk. The goldenrod is a sere brown curve in the wind and the dead oak leaf flutters, rattling in the quiet night.

The season changes so slowly that I must pause and listen to hear the silence. Autumn creeps away in sandals woven of milkweed floss; Winter makes no noise until it owns the land.

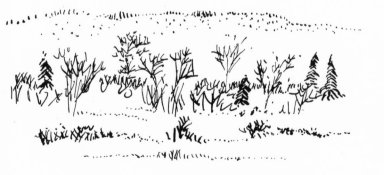

DECEMBER

THE TEMPERATURE on the front porch was 16 above zero when I got up at 5:30 and the highest it reached all day was a chilly 22. But I had outside work that must be done. I had to secure the pipe and faucet at the watering trough, make sure they do not freeze and burst.

I had delayed this much too long, for the faucet was frozen tight. So I got out the heating tape, a length of electric heating element well insulated, and wrapped the pipe with it and ran a weatherproof extension from the garage and plugged it in. Half an hour of warmth and the water ran free. Then I attached the thermostat and set it at 35 degrees and wrapped the whole arrangement with strips of old inner tube to keep out the wind and water. And that job was finished for the Winter. Thanks to electricity and the simple laws of expansion and contraction embodied in the thermostat, there will be warmth on that pipe when needed.

How simple is that arrangement compared to the elaborate and inefficient efforts we used to use to keep pipes from freezing. Only twenty years ago pipes were packed in straw and bound in burlap, and even then they often froze unless a good stream of water was kept on the move through them. And the watering troughs for farm animals had to be de-iced every morning and several times a day. Now a simple heating element in the tank prevents the ice. Gone, too, happily, is the old hand pump that had to be thawed with a steaming tea-kettle of water every morning. I doubt that there is a farm within ten miles of me that still uses a hand pump.

My watering trough is a Salisbury kettle, a hemispherical container four and a half feet in diameter and made of cast iron more than an inch thick which rings like a bell when tapped with a hammer. It weighs, I am told, more than a ton. It has two trunnions and on one side, midway between the trunnions and two inches from the top, is a drain hole. It carries a foundry mark: Salsby, 1807. It is an antique. There are quite a number of them in this area, but the going price for them isn't very high; they are rather awkward to cart home in a station wagon or a wheelbarrow.

I asked around, when I first came here, trying to find out these kettles' original purpose. They were cast at one of the local forges a century and a half ago; this district, in those days, was an iron center and made armament for the Revolution, but the industry died out long ago. Nobody seemed to know much about Salisbury kettles except that they probably were used in some local industry.

Then, a couple of years ago, I found my answers—in Colorado, of all places! There I met a man who came from New York and was an authority on whaling. When he learned where I lived he spoke of the old Salisbury iron furnaces. And he told me the furnaces had a part in the whaling industry of the early nineteenth century. "They cast the trying kettles," he said, "which the whalers used to cook the oil out of the blubber. They hauled them over to the Hudson river by ox-team, and the whalers who sailed out of Poughkeepsie and other towns there bought them. Set them up on the deck of a whaling ship in a brick furnace. That's, what the trunnions were for—when they'd cooked out a load of oil they tilted the kettles and drained off the oil through that hole in the side, tossed the cooked blubber overboard and started all over with fresh blubber. They carried a full cargo of wood for the fires on their way out, and replaced it with barrels of oil on the return trip."

So that's the reason for my watering trough, my Salisbury kettle. This one was flawed, and probably the others I see around were also flawed. One of the trunnions on mine is only about an inch long, too short to support it on the brick furnace. So it was a foundry discard. And now it sits in my barnyard and Albert's cows drink out of it all Summer long.

THE COLD CONTINUES. A few more days of it and there will be ice on the river. A week of temperatures in the 20s brings ice on that water. Two weeks of 20-degree temperature and I can walk across the river.

Old-timers tell me that in their youth the ice was seldom less than five inches thick, often ten, and that the river usually was iced over well before Christmas. Charley tells of putting up ice here, sawing it, drawing it, hauling it to the icehouse, packing it in sawdust so there would be ice next Spring and Summer to cool the milk and keep the meat. That wasn't too long ago. Charley's not an old man, only a few years older than I am.

But I find that I can discuss ice-harvest with Charley and know what I am talking about. I, too, helped cut and store

ice. It was during my freshman year at college. There was a pond on the campus which froze early and deep. Student labor was recruited to help with the harvest, which was used by the medical school to preserve cadavers for dissection. There was an icehouse near the medical building and for at least a month

I spent every afternoon wrestling big cakes of ice in that ice-house and, occasionally, helping with the sawing. That ice helped pay my way through college.

I had all but forgotten that phase of my education until Charley and I began talking about the river ice. But when he spoke of the ice saws, the way the cakes were skidded onto the wagons, the struggle to get those cakes into the icehouse, the way it was packed in sawdust, the bone-chilling damp inside the icehouse, and even the fog when the workers warmed up a bit—then it all came back.

SNOW CAME DURING THE NIGHT, the fine, dry snow that packs hard, and it continues this morning. There is about five inches of it on the ground and the trees stand stark black against it. The river is a black current flowing through a white valley. But the ice is forming. In coves where the current is slack the ice already reaches out twenty feet from the shore.

First snow really should be damp and clinging. It should line the trees, every branch and twig, and the pines should bow formally under its weight. There should be a night of snow followed by a morning of sunlight to give the transformed world a proper dazzle.

But this snow is not that kind. It is cold and dry, and it lies only briefly on the trees, whipped away in white swirls as the wind gusts through them. And there is no sunlight today to give it glitter. This is a gray day, a sky full of sifting snow and a white earth where the drifts slowly gather behind each rock and fence post. The wind is mild, never reaching more than fifteen miles an hour, but it has a bite. The snow plow hasn't yet come through, but Albert went up the road with his truck and the snow swirled like a cloud around him and his tracks drifted full soon after he had gone. It is a white, un-blemished world, a cold world where even the blue jays are huddling in shelter.

The big spruce outside my window sighs and quivers and has its own snowfall, the fine snow coming down in periodic clouds, shaken from its branches by the gusty wind.

THE SNOW CONTINUED through yesterday, but the fall diminished by dusk and stopped completely before we went to bed. When I looked at the thermometer at nine o'clock it was eight above zero. When I got up this morning it showed exactly zero. The air was still, so calm I could hear the crackling of ice a quarter of a mile up the river where the current swirls around the island and there is still an open patch. Opposite the house it has frozen completely over and the night's wind sifted the new ice with snow. The eye finds no river at all, only a shallow ravine with a white floor.

The sun rose clear, so now I have my sparkling world, so bright it hurts the eyes. But it is a distant sun cutting only a small arc of the sky. Now, two hours after sunup, the temperature has risen to five above zero, but if it tops ten all day I shall be surprised.

I was out soon after sunup, shoveling paths, and Pat came barking and puffing steamy breath and full of frolic. Pat loves snow. He thrust his nose into it, snorted, blew a cloud of crystal, then lunged into it like a swimmer making a shallow dive. He rolled and wallowed and got up and shook himself, then rolled again. Then he stood, nose quivering, and tested the air in all directions. This, he decided, was a good world. He barked once more, just to hear the echo, and dashed down to the river, sniffing for tracks. Then he came back and asked for his snack of breakfast. I finished the paths and fed him, and we both came here to my study, I to work, he to drowse in comfort. It's a day either to work or go prowling on the mountain, but I have a job to be done here. Besides, I doubt that it will get above ten outside all day, and I have to get used to the cold by degrees. I've already had a lungful of the day.

I WAS WRONG. Yesterday afternoon the temperature got up to twelve above zero. Then it tapered off again and at bedtime it was two below. Barbara and Pat and I went for a walk in midafternoon and the snow whined underfoot. That is one of the coldest sounds I know, colder even than the boom and creak of expanding ice on a lake.

I am glad we had the fall of snow before the cold clamped down. Snow is nature's insulator for the roots and bulbs. Weather scientists have taken accurate measurements of this, and one record shows that at a time when the temperature was 27 below zero at the surface it was 24 *above* zero only seven inches below the surface of the snow, a difference of 51 degrees! Chronicles of exploration in the mountain West have a number of stories of men trapped in blizzard and killing cold who saved their lives by burrowing into the snow.

The blanket of fallen leaves in the woods provides some protection for the plants there, but I doubt that a foot of sodden leaves is half as effective as six inches of snow. Certainly the worst of Winter killing occurs during snowless cold spells. And a part of the leaf protection is a result of slow decay, which generates a small amount of heat. But that decay, like all bacterial activity, is slowed down in the presence of cold—so when most needed it is least effective. I know that all the farmers dread a snowless cold spell. A few years ago we had two

weeks of below-zero weather with no snow on the ground and it heaved the ground and broke off the roots of many fields of alfalfa, ruining them.

The cold began to abate today. In early afternoon the temperature had risen to 20 above zero, and tonight it stands at 10.

THE DEPTH OF OUR COLD is passing. The temperature touched 30 today and the snow began to melt. One reason for this melting even with the air temperature still below the freezing mark is the warmth remaining in the earth. The snow melts from underneath and the drifts soften and sink. There is also a surface melt by evaporation directly into the air, especially when the air is dry and there is a hint of a breeze. The moving air absorbs the moisture and carries it away, and the drifts slowly diminish.

I doubt that there is a more beautiful curve in all nature than that of a snowdrift fresh-formed by the wind. I went out on the hillside today and could trace the path of the wind by the shape of the drifts. It flows with remarkable fluidity, shaped not only by the contours of the land but even by a grass clump or a weed stem. And there are no angles to it. Only curves.

I once visited a laboratory where tests were being made in a wind tunnel, and to demonstrate the flow of air my guide injected a few puffs of smoke into the tunnel. At once, the flow of the wind became visible in the most magnificent swirls around the test models suspended there. I see something of the same kind in the drifted snow, except that these curves and swirls are frozen into tangible shapes. Here motion is caught and held, frozen motion of a grace and lightness beyond man's devising. My hillside today was a whole gallery of abstract forms, more beautiful than those in any display of free-form sculpture I ever saw.

THE SILENCE IS UPON US, no fly-buzz or bee-hum anywhere, not even in the attic. A month ago a few sluggish wasps were fluttering at the windows there and dive-bombing the electric light. Now they are somnolent or dead. And outside the dawn clamor of the crows no longer echoes; only an occasional lone caw is heard. Blue jays, for the most part, go about their business in blue silence. The chickadee is the most vocal bird hereabout, and though he sings a brief, sweet note his loudest sound is the tap-tap-tap as he cracks a sunflower seed on the feeding station.

The owl hoots among the hemlocks up the mountainside occasionally, and now and then we hear the fine-spun yapping of a fox. But their voices only punctuate the silence, which lies deep in the valley where the frogs, not so long ago, thumped the darkness. Even the brooks are muted, frozen into inaction.

The woodchuck sleeps. Chipmunks drowse in their fluff-lined beds. Gray squirrels go chatterless about their treetop rounds. The silent rabbit avoids even the rustling leaf.

December's sounds are earth sounds and the sound of the chilling wind, the swish of drifting snow. Sometimes in the night I waken and hear a faint groan far up the mountainside, as though the rocks were moving in their beds, nudged by the slow expansion of the silent frost. And often I hear the slow crunch of ice on the river. The year wanes, but it does not creak on its hinges.

OF ALL THE WINTER BIRDS I KNOW, the clown of the lot is the nuthatch. Not that he shows any sign of conscious clowning; far from it! The nuthatch is as serious a bird as you will meet at any feeding station. That is a part of his absurdity. He is short and fat. His bill is ridiculously long, esthetically speaking, and upturned. His tail is too short. So is his neck. And his beady black eyes are set so close together that he looks nearsighted. To cap it all, he doesn't know that a bird doesn't go down a tree trunk headfirst. Not knowing, he turns his stubby tail to the sky and blithely walks down head-first, searching for bugs in the bark as he goes. Maybe other birds can't do it, but the nuthatch can and does.

And his voice! Technically, and by ornithological definition, the nuthatch is a songbird. He has vocal organs. But what does he do with them? "Yark, yark, yark." Slightly petulant, questioning. No melody. Just "Yark, yark, yark," always in the same key, always the same note, whether he is gloating over a fresh piece of suet or warning a chickadee to stand off. In Spring the nuthatch does have what passes for a song, something like "Too, too, too," but as toneless as the yark-call, though in a different key.

None of this is to belittle the nuthatch, an exemplary bird if there ever was one. He is not quarrelsome or noisy or pilfering. He is a good neighbor and a welcome Winter guest, and he eats his full share of noxious bugs the year around. But he is a funny bird, nevertheless.

WE GROW A FEW HERBS, and when I go to the attic now I meet fine old fragrances, the tang of sage and rosemary and thyme, principally, but also the essence of dill and basil. Thus we preserve, on a small scale, some of the arts of the old herbalists. It is nothing like the drying rooms of an herb grower not far from here who makes a business of such flavors; but even there I miss some of the old standbys from the open fields. The old art, and much of the old knowledge of useful wildlings, fades and vanishes.

Who gathers yarrow today to dry and steep for a stimulating tonic? Who dries hoarhound to brew a tonic tea in April? Boneset once provided a hot infusion relied upon to break up a cold or ease malarial fever. The wild cherry can be found in the woodland, but few gather its bark to dry at home and steep for a mild sedative. Pennyroyal once provided a remedy for colic. Who uses it now, fresh from the field or attic? And dittany—once it was the cure for "anything in anyone." Dittany is now an all-but-forgotten herb.

Unknowing, we do get some of the more effective herbs from the drugstore under new names. Science does catch up with the old arts, even though it does leave some pleasant trappings behind. Science makes the best of the old herbalists look like fumbling amateurs. Grant that. But what sweet-scented memories can be roused by a shot of penicillin? There

was a time when just the smell of boneset tea could cure a cold. Can the smell of antihistamine do that? The answer is no, and both Dr. John and Dr. Jim agree, though they have little faith in boneset tea. But I find that both of them prescribe rhubarb and soda for an upset stomach.

OUR SNOW IS ALMOST GONE and the ice has broken up on the river. The weather has settled down to gray cold, night temperatures in the low 20s, the brief sun warming the daylit hours just above the freezing mark. The low places in the pasture are heaved by frost which crunches underfoot and the brook near the garden is a leaping thread of black water between its ice banks.

I have been calculating and have proved to my own satisfaction that December is the shortest month of the year. True, December has thirty-one days; but can you call days those hurried little spans of daylight? By generous total, December has only 288 hours of daylight, and that includes those times when the sun sulks behind a mass of clouds all day long. Even March can muster that many hours of daylight in twenty-four days. And June does that well by us in its first nineteen days.

What is a December day, anyway? Nine hours of daylight, with a few minutes left over at each end to turn the lights on and off. And fifteen hours of darkness. With a moon, to be sure, and a great many stars. But darkness, just the same. The countryman does all the morning chores by artificial light and does the same in the evening. The city worker or commuter sees his home only in darkness or at best in the murk of dawn or dusk. Only on four weekends, most years, does he have a chance to watch the sun dart across the southern quadrant of the sky.

Here it is the tenth of December, and by sundown tonight we will have had only ninety-two hours of daylight, about the same amount that June will bring in its first six days.

OF ALL THE LEAFLESS TREES in my Winter landscape, the most eye-catching and spectacular is the white birch, particularly when seen against the grays and browns of a snowless hillside. It has a grace of line, a slimness of bole, a clean, sleek look that is sheer beauty. I have one clump, at the far corner of the middle pasture, that has seven trunks growing from a common root, and each trunk is at least a foot through at the butt, several of them a foot and a half. (This birch clump, of course, doesn't really belong to me at all; it belongs to a family of gray squirrels and has been theirs for years.)

From the earliest days, the white birch has been a warehouse and source of elementary necessities for both the settler and the woodland wanderer. Its bark makes usable paper, tinder for fire in the wet woods, provides nourishment enough to keep a man or a beast from starving; and from it came the canoe, shaped and sheathed by the tough, enduring bark itself before man adapted cedar and canvas and, eventually, aluminum, to the same purpose. Wigwams were roofed with that bark, by whites and Indians alike, and buckets and boxes were made from it. In springtime the rising sap of the white birch was boiled down, like maple sap, for a syrup and a sugar that sweetened the woodsman's diet and disposition. The white inner wood, easily worked, provided a whole cupboardful of wooden ware for the pioneer and is still used for everything from spools to bowls.

I can't imagine these hills without the white grace of the birch against the gaunt Winter hillsides. Other birches have their own virtues, but the white birch is the noblest of them all. In Spring it rouges the gray hillside with its buds, in Summer it is a whispering canopy of shade, and now in Winter it is simply beautiful, white beauty in a drab gray world.

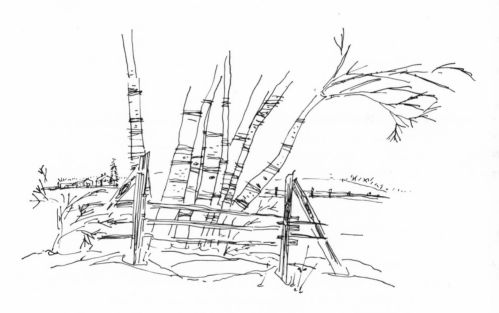

I HAD TO GO DOWN TO THE CITY on a bootless errand and it would have been a lost day had I not met a dour stranger on the train. He was my seatmate and he asked my business, and he said sadly but firmly that there could be no worth-while writing or art or even philosophy in this era of trouble and uncertainty. Rallying to dissent, I cited the days of England's Queen Elizabeth I, which were not only a time of tremendous ferment and achievement in the arts and in human thinking but were also times of tremendous troubles. The Spanish forces were overrunning Europe and threatened momentarily to land on the English coast. War was a matter of daily concern and London was a hotbed of speculation and seditious plot. Old moorings of religion and simple certainties were gone or going. The universities were full of dissident talk. The royal court had its doubtful loyalties.

Yet out of this ferment came strength and greatness, and out of it came lasting art created by big and questing minds. There were those of uncertain faith, certainly; there were also Shakespeare, Spenser and Bacon, and there were Frobisher and Drake. Industry throve. Bondage of human beings diminished. Human rights were increased. True, there was cruelty and poverty and neglect; but by the standards of that day, the only way to appraise the period, great achievements were made. There were tremendous challenges, and there were those to meet them.

I did not persuade my unhappy seatmate, but it was good to have to rally these facts for myself. Too often we forget the substance of the history we once knew without pausing to find its meaning.

LAST NIGHT we went out to walk on the frozen roads and when we came back I looked at the charts and found what I had suspected. Daylight now is almost at its minimum for the year. It will shorten only another two minutes or so between now and the Winter Solstice. The evening change, in fact, has already begun, for the year's earliest sunset is now past. Sunrise will continue to lag for another two weeks.

Thus the year balances its accounts, and what I said a few days ago about December's daylight stands only as a facetious comment. In our latitude we know that each year brings the time when not only the candle but the hearth fire must burn at both ends of the day, symbol not of waste but of warmth and comfort. It is for this time, if we live close to the land, that we lay up the firewood and the fodder. Now we pay for the long days of Summer, pay in the simple currency of daylight. Hour for hour, the accounts are now balanced.

And yet, the short days provide their own bonus. The snows come, and dusk and dawn are like no other time of the year. We come to a long Winter night, as last night was, when the moon rides high over a white world and the darkness thins away. The full-moon night is as long as the longest span of sunlit day in midsummer. And the snowy world gleams with an almost incandescent shimmer.

Year to year, we remember the short days and tend to forget the long nights when the moon stands high over a cold and brittle white world. Not only the moon nights, but the star nights. Who would not cut wood and burn a candle for a few such nights each year?

THE CHRISTMAS FERNS remain green in the woods, bright patches of foliage which tempt the gatherer of holiday greens and remind me that anemones whitened a certain place last April and that violets purpled a particular spot.

There are a number of evergreen ferns but this one, usually called *Aspidium acrostichoides* by the botanists, belongs in the old legends about the Nativity. Among the other wonders of that night, all the plants mingled in the hay in the holy stable put forth their blossoms in celebration. All, that is, except the ferns. And, say the legends, because the ferns failed to blossom and add their fragrance to that holy scene, they were condemned never again to bear flowers.

Thus the legends. But there must be more to it than that. Still thinking in terms of legendry, I believe that there must have been a frond or two of fern in the stable that tried to bloom that night, a few fronds which managed to turn green in celebration. It was the best they could do, being ferns. And since the utmost one can achieve is all that is ever asked, shouldn't the lowly ferns have been rewarded, even meagerly?

No legend of the Nativity should dwell on punishment, not even the legend of the ferns. They tried. They did their best. And that is why, it seems to me, some of them, like the Christmas fern, have their green fronds to offer in celebration now.

WE WENT OUT TODAY to gather greens to deck the doorway, the green of life in the midst of Winter, symbol of hope and faith reborn.

One need not go into the history of the custom or investigate its adoption as a part of the Christmas ritual to understand the aptness as well as the beauty of the evergreen tradition. The pine, the spruce and the hemlock, as well as their more venerable kin, the ground cedar, ground pine and club moss, know no leafless season. For them, there is no time of naked exposure to the gray winds and the white frosts. On their boughs and branches the green of life and continuity remain for any eye to see, throughout all the months and all the years. Small wonder that the ancients turned to the evergreen when the day shrank to a few hours of feeble sunlight, finding in its undiscouraged green new strength for their own belief that no Winter lasts forever.

And even the most ancient of the ancients must have known this, for the pines have been on earth more years than I can count without turning to the charts of geology. Fifty million years, some say, and others say a hundred million years, dealing in numbers which, in terms of one man's life, lose all meaning. The first man saw the pines; put it that way. And when man first saw them, the pines were already old.

So we went forth today and brought in the evergreen boughs of pine and hemlock, and festoons of partridge berry and ground cedar, feeling a kinship with enduring things. They help us to remember, and to believe, and to catch, if only fleetingly, a sense of hope and understandable eternity.

ANOTHER LIGHT SNOW came in the night and this morning Barbara saw two grouse at the feeding station. She couldn't believe her eyes, but there they were, the two of them pecking away like barnyard hens, fluffed against the cold. They looked as big as Leghorn hens as they sat hunched in the feeder, crowding its ordinarily ample space.

They had come down from the mountain where we occasionally see them, driven down by the snow, no doubt. Friends of ours twenty miles from here have grouse in their woods that come down to their house occasionally in Winter but never feed there. They prefer to perch in the apple trees and feed on buds, to the detriment of blossom and fruit. But our friends prefer to have the grouse, and I notice that they always have plenty of apples, too, when harvest comes.

Our grouse are skittish. Not because they are hunted, for we never hunt them; they are too rare a bird in this area to be taken for the pot. They came this morning and fed, and when Barbara moved, there in the living room, to get a better look at them, they saw her motion and flew away. Now the chickadees and tree sparrows are back in their usual place. But now that the grouse have come once, they will come again. This is the first year they have come to the feeding station, though we have occasionally seen them out at the corn crib searching for kernels the jays and the squirrels left on the ground.

ONE OF THOSE STRANGE, violent little storms swept across the lower end of the valley yesterday and took down half a dozen trees. One of them was in a dooryard, and when we passed there this morning the whole place was changed by the absence of that one tree. We lost no trees here, but I am remembering the time when we lost a big maple from another dooryard in such a storm.

There is something about the loss of a tree that almost defies explanation, particularly if it is in a dooryard or at a familiar roadside. We were far less aware of that tree standing than we were after it had gone. Yet everything around a tree is affected by it, the grass, the bushes, the birds, even the insects. Even the paths we used had adapted themselves to the tree's presence.

Then the tree was gone, and every time we looked out

the window or passed that end of the house we were aware of
the absence. The sound of the wind was subtly altered. When
snow came, it drifted differently. The next Summer's shade
had an unfamiliar pattern. The next Fall's colors were altered. Yet when we walked we still followed, by habit, the
path around the spot where that tree once stood.

It made good firewood, but there are few subtle memories in an armload of split maple for the hearth. There is no
shade, no Summer sigh of the wind, no oriole or robin song.
There is nothing but firewood, and eventually ashes. And we
went to the window again and looked out and saw strange
stars through the gap where the tree had stood. It was almost
as though we were looking through a hole in the roof of the
house.

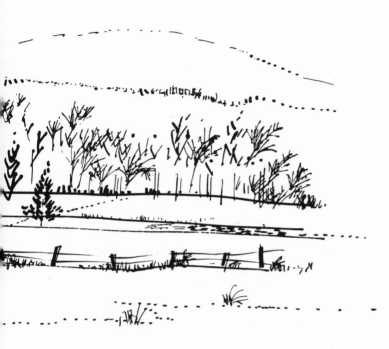

As FAR BACK as the race memories and ancient legends of mankind run, the Winter solstice has been a time of questioning and wonder, followed by rediscovery of basic certainties. To see the daylight steadily shorten and the nights lengthen and deepen with cold, was to feel the approach of doom. To see the sun stand still and then swing north once more was and still is to know that the cold gray of Winter must pass, that hope and belief are neither futile nor foolish.

Hope is easy and belief is simple in a warm green world. Winter is the time when man most needs the securities of un-shaken certainty, whether it is the Winter of the soul or the harsh Winter of the year. And as surely as the Winter solstice brings some understanding of his universe, the spiritual sol-stice brings to man some understanding of himself. He seeks securities, and the more he seeks the more he must know that there are no new securities anywhere, but only the old ones rediscovered.

So comes the time of rediscovery. For though I may define security in a dozen different ways, the ultimate definition leads to the inner man, to myself. There must lie that certainty which gives life its meaning; and there also lies doubt, the depth of cold and darkness. I must know Winter if I am to know Spring and Summer. And here is Winter, with its own wondering and its quiet and its own discoveries, its solstice and its turn.

WINTER STARLIGHT has the deep fireglow of eternity, the unending gleam of wonder. To walk abroad on such nights is to walk in the midst of infinity. There are no limits to either time or distance, except as man himself may make them. I have but to touch the wind to know these things; for the wind itself is full of starlight, even as the frosted earth underfoot, starlight and endless time and exalted wonder.

My eye is caught by the red-gold star we call Arcturus, and wonder grows. Even as the ancients, I strain for a closer look through this peephole, this spark-burn in the blanket of night, hoping for the slightest glimpse into the dazzling brilliance of Beyond. I turn to the star called Betelgeuse, even redder than Arcturus, and I accept the factual truths of the astronomers and yet wonder if they constitute the whole, the ultimate truth. Time, and distance, and wonder—and I walk up this valley in the midst of eternity.

Star after star—the night is filled with starlight, and the Milky Way is a whole sky-drift of mingled stardust. It is as though the star-studded wind were forever blowing across the deepest darkness, forever and changing only with the repeated seasons. Tonight it is thus, and tomorrow it will be a little changed, but only in relationship to me and my sense of time, and the next day another small notch of change. Yet another December will be the same again, as it has been before and still before.

Winter

I wonder and watch the Winter stars, and there is starlight in my very puffs of life-breath. My shoulders lift toward the stars, for I, too, am a part of this eternity.

THE ICE IS ON THE RIVER AGAIN. It began in shards and sheets of ice drifting down in the slow current, forming fragile bridges where it massed. Then there was another night of cold and there was slush between the shards and along the bank. Yesterday was cold and today there is a sheet of crystal all across the river which dances with glitter when the sun strikes it. The flow is still there; if I break the ice near the shore I can see the movement in the dark water. But it is a hidden flow. The casual eye sees the river stilled, locked again in Winter.

It is so clear, so simple, this ice, that one forgets that ice carved these valleys. Ice was the great knife which shaped these hills, ice after the fire had died away. Ice, crystalline water, one of the simplest solids and yet, in crystal, close akin to granite. Raise its temperature five degrees and it flows away. Raise it twenty and, on a chill day, it steams, becomes a cloud. A snowflake, feather light, or a glacier, or a river no longer open to the sky. Ice.

The river flowed in this ice-shaped valley and Winter night closed down and the river at dawn was only a gleaming highway for the wind. I look at it and I stand face to face with my land's beginnings, its primal force, its ice.

NOT THE LEAST of the wonders we celebrate today was the simplicity surrounding the Birth itself. A carpenter named Joseph went with his young wife up from Nazareth to Bethlehem, the town of his fathers, to enroll for taxation as the governing Romans had ordered. Joseph and Mary arrived late and weary to find that the inn was crowded; so they took shelter in the stable with other late-comers. Second-best, but humble travelers could not choose. It was shelter. And there in the stable the Child was born.

Thus the simple beginnings. Add the shepherds on

the night hills, the appearance of the angel, their journey to the stable, and it still remains one of the least adorned of all the great stories we cherish. It is as simple as was the Man himself and His teaching. As simple as the Sermon on the Mount, which still stands, in its essentials, as the summary of the belief of free men of good will everywhere.

There were the night hills with the little town among them. And in a stable there was born One who came to speak to multitudes about freedom and justice and fundamental right. One who spoke in a simple tongue, in terms of the beasts of the land, the birds of the air, the lilies of the fields, and man's responsibility to man. The kings and captains were marching up and down the land, in full panoply, even as He was being born. But it is His simple words that endure, not theirs; and it is the Birth at the stable that we solemnly commemorate, not the gathering at the crowded inn.

THE SUN STILL STANDS away off there to the south, even at midday. We have passed the solstice, but change comes slowly. This is the time when the ancients checked their measurement of shadows to be sure that the change had come. They performed their incantations, and they celebrated when the length of a shadow had shortened by a finger's breadth. That proved that the days were beginning to lengthen once more.

We are wise. We take it on faith, believing that because there was a yesterday there will be a tomorrow; that last year and last Summer are sufficient proof that another year, another Summer lie ahead. In so doing we have lost a measure of the wonder and the deep-hearted thanks for the continuance of our accustomed way. Perhaps we, too, could do with a bit of shadow gazing. Or at least with a little silent speculation. And we might offer consequent thanks.

Water, we know, flows downhill. But only if it is water. Not necessarily if it is ice or steam. Lower the earth's temperature by a few degrees and there would be no flowing water. Shift the earth's axis a trifle and not only would the temperature and the seasons be altered but the atmosphere as well. Change the atmosphere and life would have to change or perish, all life from lichens to the human animal. And this earth has a mental and emotional axis as well as a geographic and celestial axis.

The ancients wondered and measured shadows. We take it on faith, as we do so many things. Perhaps we would do well, now and then, to take a look at our own shadows.

WE HAVE COME INTO A SPELL of clear, cold weather with a bright sun and the midday temperature rising to around 20 and dropping at night to the neighborhood of zero.

We went for a walk this afternoon, up onto the mountain, and we saw again the colors of Winter. It takes time, after the colorful Autumn, to bring the eye back into focus; but Winter, too, has its spectrum, once the eye and the mind accommodate.

The bare tree trunks show every tint of gray and even shades of red. The grays on an ash bole or a maple or a beech are of infinite variety and shading. The browns on an oak cover the whole range, even to the light tan of the leaves the oaks are so reluctant to let fall. The trunks of the cedars are full of red, if you pause to look. The brightest red of all, of course, is in the seed heads of the sumac, which still stand waiting for the hungry birds.

The leaf colors in the damp drifts are now leached to a variety of browns and tans which, as Winter progresses, will slowly mat into the slow decay of leaf mold. The brightest tans we find, in fact, are beneath the pines. Up near the springhouse is a clump of white pines which practically tents the earth, and beneath them is a needle mat six or eight inches thick, the accumulation of years. It stands out today an almost golden tan, in part perhaps because the sky is so blue and the cumulus clouds so white.

There is little snow left down here or in the pastures, but on the mountain there are drifts two feet deep where the shadows lie and the brief sunlight cannot penetrate. They are like miniature glaciers building up to feed the brooks of Spring.

IT IS FOUR YEARS TODAY since Pat adopted us. I should like to sing a birthday song for him, or make some appropriate gesture; but I doubt that he cares much whether I do or not. He greeted me this morning with his usual delight, and when he came into the house and Barbara and I patted him with a bit more than the usual warmth and told him we were glad he came to stay, he accepted it with a proper dignity, then went to warm himself on the rug in front of the register at the foot of the stairs. It is no special day to him. All days seem to be rather special to Pat. Which is something other dog folk will understand and nondog folk will probably set down as a peculiarity in us. So be it.

Winter

Each year at this time I have the feeling that if I am ever to have understanding of the great mysteries, this is the season. The Winter landscape, when I look upon it in a glance, seems to have arrived at the ultimate of simplicity, stripped to essentials. Is it possible that life, too, comes down to its ultimates at such a season?

Then I walk a little way and I recognize the deception of my glance. So fundamental a thing as the wind carves so simple a thing as a snowdrift into ever changing form. Even the blue shadows across the folded fields shift their pattern and color from minute to minute, perceptibly from hour to hour. And I know that the ice is slowly but surely changing the pattern even of the rocks.

Time does not cease. Change does not end. There is no place where I can stand and say, "This rock is unchanging; this moment is endless." Nor is there any place in life where I can stand and say, "This is what I am, complete and unchanging." There are forces beyond our willing that beat upon us, and the best we can do is stand against them, firm in our own faith and conviction. We who would reach the ultimate of simplicity and understanding must first accept our own relationship to change and time. There is our certainty, there the final simplicity, and no calendar's year-end, no season, no prolonged moment, can ever change it much.

The calendar's year runs out. On the chart we begin a new cycle, another sequence of days to add up into weeks and months and, in the end, another year. Thus we mark it off, for man must count his hours and days and bring mathematical order, at least, into his life.

So we come to a place in time where we try to pause for a moment and draw a tally line and, if we would be honest, try to reach some appraisal. But it is no more an ending than is a sunset. Tomorrow comes; and yesterday, last year, hands on its unfinished business. The wind does not pause on the stroke of midnight, nor are the stars altered in their courses.

253

Even the clock which man has made to count seconds continues to tick them off, one by one.

There are new beginnings, perhaps, but only in the mind of man. I can look back and appraise the past, and I know that here is another unit of my time in which to do some of those things to which my conscience drives. Life itself is change, and here is a means of measuring that change. Because I can think and remember and have the capacity for learning, I look back for comparisons. I need the reassurance, the belief, that comes from such a summing up. I need the knowledge of time ahead.

But no year ends on a calendar's page. Change knows no season nor numerical calculation. And even those who would tie time to the sun and the stars must know that the nadir of the year is past. The sun swings slowly north, in our way of seeing it; days lengthen; the season of life renewed, which we call Spring, is already established in the earth as among the stars.

JANUARY

We walked the new year in, as is our long-standing custom. New Year's Eve parties have little savor for us. I still don't know how it happened, but some years ago we were at such a party and I looked at my watch and it was eleven o'clock. Barbara was across the room. Our eyes met and without a word I knew that we both wanted to be away from there. I turned to our hostess and said, "It's been a good party, but we have to go." Then Barbara was beside me and she said, as though carrying on my thought, "You don't mind, do you, if we leave?" And before the startled hostess could answer we were gone. We drove home and, still in party clothes, we went for a walk, the two of us alone with the night. We returned to our house at the stroke of twelve and stood there in the starlight.

Thus we set a pattern. It has meaning for us which needs no words of explanation. We usually spend New Year's Eve at home, but if we go elsewhere we return home before midnight. We dress for the weather and go out for a walk. Sometimes we walk in biting cold, sometimes in snow, and a time or two we have walked in a howling storm. Pat walked with us last night, and it was a brittle night with frost in the air spangling the starlight.

Indians called this the Wolf Moon, knowing well the time when fangs were eager and hunger drove the pack. Most of the wolves are gone, but the fangs remain, fangs of ice and cold, the great primal forces of Winter's depth. The wind courses the valleys and harries the hills, and the long nights have sharpened its fangs. The ice lies deep.

In some lands there are mountain barriers to the Winter wind, but our geography has no such design. Our mountain chains, for the most part, lie with the wind which moves down from the north. The great valleys merely funnel the gales so that they howl unfettered and roar out across the flatlands until they have run themselves down. Our Winter winds have few barriers. Even the trees stand naked, to sigh and moan as the wind whips through them, freighted with snow and ice or merely freighted with cold. And the hills lie open to the elements.

Ice sheathes the ponds and clogs the streams. It thrusts at the banks with its own fangs. But more than that, it gnaws at the hills. It thrusts a hidden fang into the granite of the hilltop and rips the rocks apart. Ledges that can defy all other elements begin to crumble away beneath the ice, which can come from as impalpable a thing as a wisp of mist or as fragile a thing as a snowflake. Ice, the sharpest fang of all, and the most persistent.

The Wolf Moon, they called it, listening to the howl of the pack in the Winter valleys. And the howl I hear tonight will be the wolf howl of the wind in those same valleys, the voice of primal forces at work in the Winter world.

Esthetically, the Franklin stove has little to recommend it. Its antiquity appeals to some, but not to us. It sits there in the living room, a black box with brass knobs and a strange smoke dome which acts as additional radiation. Connoisseurs say it is a rather rare one, but of that I am no judge. It was here when we bought the house and since there was no fireplace and I like an open fire I refused to close the deal for the house without the Franklin stove.

Ben Franklin invented this stove, or its prototype, no doubt after years of aggravation (B. Franklin himself used that word) with fireplaces. He simply devised an iron box which stood out in the room and radiated heat in all directions—a fireplace, so to speak, open to the room on all sides. I cannot provide statistics on its efficiency, but this Franklin stove throws three times as much heat as the best fireplace I ever owned. Two small oak logs will simmer in it all evening and warm the whole living room. It draws well. This one has ledges in the firebox where one could probably suspend a basket in which to burn coal or coke. This stove and a wood-burning cook stove, I am told, once heated this house all Winter long. It could do the same now in an emergency.

Last night as I sat in front of its fire I could imagine the shade of Old Ben standing in front of it, with his bald head, his bifocals well down on his nose, his hands clasped behind him, smiling at me. Smiling and saying, "So, my fire-box endures even today. Strange, what a man's need for comfort will prompt him to devise!"

LAST NIGHT BROUGHT A LIGHT, fresh snowfall, and this morning I went out to see who lives around here. Many of my co-inhabitants had left their marks. Out by the garage were field mouse tracks, dainty as lace. Two of them had met and gone together to investigate the base of a forsythia bush, for reasons obscure. Then they had gone separate ways, one across the road, the other half around the garage, then into some runway beneath the snow.

Near the corn crib was a maze of squirrel tracks. The squirrels had been up the crib's side, taking corn. How a squirrel does it I do not know, though I have watched many times, but he can turn an ear of corn tightly packed against the mesh of the crib and get at fresh kernels. I have tried it, thrusting my fingers through the mesh, and I can scarcely budge an ear. But the squirrels had been there this morning, tracks all over the place. I thought there had been a dozen of them until I followed the outgoing tracks and found that there had been only three.

At the edge of the pasture I found where a skunk had walked, leaving his long-footed tracks. Walked, not run. A skunk can run surprisingly fast, but he seldom does; he has other means of protection. Crossing the pasture, I found rabbit tracks. At first they were leisurely, exploratory. Then they were wary. Then they indicated flight. Not far away I found the reason, the dainty, in-line, catlike tracks of a red fox which had come up the valley, skirting the brush. The fox had seen the rabbit, but too late. He had paused and gone on. Had I followed his tracks half a mile I should probably have found that he breakfasted on field mice. But I came back, instead, for my own breakfast.

It is snowing again today, and according to the radio they are having a sleet storm seventy miles to the south of us. If it continues, such a storm can do tremendous damage and cause endless inconvenience. Sleet is one of the most insidious of all Winter hazards. It creeps in gentle as rain and twice as treacherous. It coats the roads, creating the first hazard. Then it coats the wires. And finally it coats the trees with ice which increases upon itself. Limbs begin to fall. Wires come down. Confusion and peril mingle. The complexity of our way of life ensnarls itself in its own coils.

We lived for some years in that area now being sleeted, in a house eight miles from town and wholly electrified. In one sleet storm we seemed to escape unscathed. The sleet ended with our trees intact, our wires unbroken. But two miles away one maple tree was borne down by the ice. It came down across the power line. Wires snapped.

The consequences of that one tree's fall were enormous. It blocked the road. Those who could have cleared the road were long delayed because of the ice. Traffic itself began to create a jam. Repair men trying to reach the broken wires were caught in the snarl of stalled cars. Within a few hours a truck skidded on the ice and knocked down a utilities pole, severing the wires at a second place. Not only we, but a hundred other families, were without power or phone, and in consequence without heat, without light, without cooking facilities, without water. Then a wind came and brought other ice-sheathed trees down. It was three days before emergency repairs were made. Meanwhile, a thousand families huddled around fireplaces, cooked there, melted snow there for water, suddenly thrown back on the slender resources of their own ingenuity in a kind of neo-primitivism. And all because an unforeseen combination of rain and cold air had coated the trees with half an inch of ice.

THE ICE STORM TO THE SOUTH continued throughout yesterday and this morning there are reports of damage and distress, power lines down and traffic stalled. We have been fortunate here. We have six inches of snow and no ice, and life goes on uninterrupted.

We are fortunately situated, even should such an ice storm come. It is not by chance, of course. The people here have known Winter in its worst aspects and have made a compromise between convenience and self-sufficiency. Our house is not unique, yet we have a gravity flow of water, we cook with what is called "bottled gas," and we have the Franklin stove for heat in an emergency. Should the power be cut off, we could still eat and drink and maintain a degree of warmth. And the same is true of most of the farms round about. The dairymen would have to milk by hand, a long, tiring job but one they have done before. They would have to use oil lanterns and oil lamps, and the chunk stoves would have to be set up in a hurry and fed with billets from the woodpile. But that, too, would only require turning the calendar back a few years.

Those who live close to the land admit the possibility of such emergencies and are equipped to face them. It is those who live midway between the land and the city who are trapped, not only by circumstance but by their own alienation from the simplicities. City living has ill equipped most of us to face the still untamed vagaries of wind and weather. But we are slowly developing a new and considerable fraction of the population which in the not too distant future will be somewhat at home at the edge of the country. Winter and ice are probably the most rigorous and demanding of all the teachers from whom we shall learn this new way of life.

CHARLEY HAS BEEN CUTTING SAWLOGS, and when I drove twenty miles on an errand today I saw three other farmers at work in their woodlots. It's mid-January and the moon is in the last quarter. I mentioned that to Charley, and he as much as said he was cutting logs, not moonbeams. But according to the old lore he couldn't have timed it better. His logs will be seasoned to make good lumber, straight planks and flat boards.

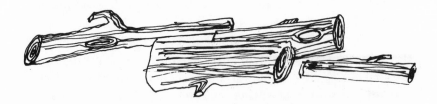

I dug this information out of an old book, and I can't verify it by even the veterans of the sawmill business around here. But according to that old book the original meaning of "seasoning" a sawlog was to make sure you cut it at the right season. And the season was governed by the moon as well as the month. Timbers cut during "the old moon in January"— some said February as well—"will stand straight and true." But if you cut your logs "when the moon is full, timber fibers warp and pull."

Maybe there's nothing to it. I don't know. All I know is that the old barns, the really old ones, and the fine old houses indicate that the men who chose the lumber knew what they were doing. The lumber in them is usually good lumber, straight and true, after all these years. How much the moon's phase had to do with it can only be guessed, but there's no denying that the wood was seasoned to perfection in most instances.

Maybe farmers cut sawlogs in January because it's a slack time and because there's snow on which to skid them out. Maybe that's the only reason. I don't know.

NOBODY SEEMS TO KNOW just why the snowbird is called a junco, but junco is the scientific name and is more and more used as the common name. There are various origins for the word *junco*, one meaning a reed, one meaning a seed. But even the ornithologists hesitate to pin it on the Latin for seed, for many birds are seed-eaters.

Anyway, there is the junco, the snowbird, in a dark-gray full-dress suit with white bosom, tails neatly piped in white. He is beautiful against a snowy background, and while I hesitate to suggest that an esthetic sense dominates his habits, he certainly thrives in snow country. Sometimes it seems that it takes a snowstorm to bring the snowbirds, for they come wheeling in flocks as a storm approaches. They came to our place last Fall, however, even before the robins had left, well before the first snow.

Technically, they are of the same family as the sparrows. This is easy to believe when one sees and recognizes the young snowbirds; in juvenile plumage they look, at a glance, like adult song sparrows, streaked and speckled. And the adults have a little song that reminds me of the more melodious sparrows, a trill a good deal like that of the chipping sparrow. It is never a loud song and sometimes it is elaborated into a soft warble with song sparrow echoes.

The snowbird is congenial but cautious. A whole flock usually winters on our hillside, and they come with a swoop of dark wings to feed on crumbs or seeds. They prefer to feed on the ground, on seeds knocked from the feeder by the sparrows and chickadees. They commonly nest just north of here, and they seldom go far south in the Winter. Western varieties— the ornithologists have argued over twenty or so of them— travel as far as Alaska.

EVEN UNDER AN OVERCAST SKY, a snow-covered night is not a night of darkness. It is a time of black and white and gray, all faintly aglow; and once the human eye has accommodated to it there is much to be seen and even more to be sensed. But it is seen and sensed in different terms than by daylight.

First, it is a world without shadows, for what light there is comes from the snow-covered earth rather than from the sky, a reflected light. Trees are stark outlines. Bushes are vague shapes. Snowdrifts vanish in a common blur that has no small contours.

When one has accepted this shadowless world on its own terms, the next thing that strikes the consciousness is the absence of color. True, there is no color to the human eye at night, but in this world of strong contrasts one is more aware of this than on a Summer night. What we see in darkness is seen with other vision than we use in the daytime; the daytime part of our eyes blanks out and night vision takes its place. Our night vision is simplified, color sensitivity sacrificed so that we may gather every bit of the thinner light now available. Our night eyes gather in contrasts so that we can identify shapes, whereas our daylight eyes bring us color and detail. And the best of our night vision is from the corners of the eyes, not straight ahead. On a star night I have difficulty seeing the dim stars if I look directly at them but find them easily if I look a few degrees to one side and use the edge of my vision, as it were.

We walked last night in a snow-clad world under a starless sky and all our senses were busy. We saw less, but we apprehended twice as much as we would have been aware of at high noon on a Winter day.

Winter

THE CHICKADEE is a delightful bird. I speak, of course, of the black-capped chickadee of these parts, which flits about the woodland all Winter, congregates in the pines and makes even bitter days warm with song, twitters near the house even in a snowstorm, doesn't sulk when caught in a cold, driving rain. The chickadees are regular patrons at our feeding station just outside the living-room window and they sing and twitter between gulps of peanut butter, suet, sunflower seeds and bread crumbs.

The way of a chickadee with a sunflower seed is marvelous to watch. He holds the seed beneath his toes on a hard surface and hammers at it, woodpecker-wise, with his sharp beak. One slip, one miscalculation by a small fraction of an inch, and he would clip off a fragile toe. But that slip never seems to happen. He simply chips at the seed's hard shell until he cracks it, then he gulps it, twitters a paean of praise for the good life, and reaches for another seed.

The chickadee could travel south in Winter. He has close kin who live in the South all year around. But the soft life is not for him. He also has a cousin, the brown-capped chickadee, who lives in the far North, which probably proves that he comes from a sturdy family. The black-cap stays where he is, competes successfully with snowbird and blue jay for food, and survives as a happy companion. He doesn't even take to the deep thickets for long in the worst weather. He lives all over the Winter landscape, brightens dull days with his modest song, and makes the best of what comes his way.

THE JANUARY WIND has a hundred voices. It can scream, it can bellow, it can whisper, it can sing a lullaby. It can roar through the leafless maples and shout down the mountainside, and it can murmur through the white pines among the granite ledges where the lichens make strange hieroglyphics. It can whistle down a chimney and set the hearth-fire to dancing. On a sunny day it can pause in a sheltered spot and breathe of Spring and violets. In the cold of a lonely night it can rattle the sash and stay there muttering of ice and snowbanks and deep-frozen ponds.

Sometimes in January the wind seems to come from the farthest star in outer darkness, so remote and so impersonal is its voice. That is the wind of a January dawn, in the half-light that trembles between day and night. It is a wind that merely quivers the trees, its force sensed but not seen, a force that might almost hold back the day if it were so directed. Then the east brightens and the wind relaxes; the stars, the wind's source, grow dim.

And sometimes in January the wind is so intimate that you know it came only from the next hill, a little wind that plays with leaves and puffs of smoke and whistles like a little boy with puckered lips. It makes the little cedar trees quiver, as with delight. It shadowboxes with the weather vane. It tweaks an ear and whispers laughing words about crocuses and daffodils, then nips the nose and dances off.

But I never know, until I hear its voice, which wind is here today. Or, more important, which will be here tomorrow.

Winter

I LIKE WINTER for two gustatory reasons—soup and stew. I can eat soup every day of the Winter and well into Summer, and I can eat stew any time. Right now I can smell the soup kettle simmering. In it, I am sure, is a soup made from a recipe that started out, long ago, as a recipe for minestrone. But it has been altered and expanded, over the years; now it even contains *frijoles*, Mexican beans, for instance, and it has twice as many onions as it began with. Its base is beef stock, but it usually contains chicken broth too. Sometimes it has scraps of ham in it. But no barley, I insist. It is remarkably savory and it improves day by day, as long as it lasts. I am hungry, just smelling it and writing about it.

Barbara also makes the best potato soup ever served, and with proper persuasion she makes a potato-and-onion and potato-and-leek soup better than any others I have ever known. And her stews are perfection, based on choice cuts of lamb or beef, not on scraps or leavings. She has even used sirloin steak for stew meat, which may be heresy to some but is luxurious eating to us. Stew is not an economy dish in this household; it is choice eating, made from prime ingredients and seasoned with careful pinches of judiciously chosen herbs, just enough to enhance but never mask the basic flavor. And cooked with the skill of genius.

I have tried to make stews from Barbara's recipes, on occasion, but they never turn out like hers, either in look or flavor. She adds a mysterious something. She cooks for the nose and the eye as well as for the palate and stomach, which is the mark of the artist. I didn't marry her for her cooking, but it is a splendid dividend.

WE ARE HAVING THE JANUARY THAW, which comes like a friend long remembered, like a warm greeting in a crowd of strangers. It lifts the heart and strengthens faith, it breaks the Winter cold of discontent. It can also breed a whole week of sniffles.

No one can predict the January thaw or even say for sure that it will come. That is a part of its delight, the sweet happiness of surprise. Cold has congealed the world. The wind was edged. Then, overnight, change came. It crept down the valley. The sun rose clear and beamed with benevolence. The sky had cleared to crystalline brilliance. The wind was friendly and the air this morning had a palpable warmth. The thaw is here.

Whether it lasts a day or a week, it is as though doors were opened suddenly and there was Spring in the next room. Spring, and crocuses and red florets on the swamp maples. There is almost the breath of violets on the air this morning. I am carried away. I listen, absurdly, for the hum of bees and look for the flash of a bluebird, the strut of a robin. I wonder if the sap has begun to rise. Are the buds swelling? How about the catkins on the birches and the popples? Will there soon be purple mouse-ears on the lilacs?

No. I know none of these things is going to happen yet. They'd better not! But Winter, I know again, doesn't last forever. Through the open window behind me I smell something that is not Winter at all. It is the faintest breath of Spring, over a dozen hills and still far away, but Spring just the same.

AFTER THE FIRST exuberance of yesterday's warmth I have begun to mistrust this thaw. The pastures are soggy with melt and the brooks coming down the mountainside are loud with leaping water. The river has risen six inches overnight. The roadsides are awash with the melt. The temperature today touched the high 40s, almost reached 50, much too warm.

But when I went to the garden and tried it with a fork I found hard frost only three inches down. That is reassuring. That frost will not ease away with a few warm days, and it is that frost which will hold trees and bulbs in check and spare them ultimate damage and even destruction. There is too little sunlight yet to lure much activity, despite the warmth of the air. Growth responds primarily to length of daylight rather than to temperature, certainly not to temperature alone.

Severe damage seldom comes from a thaw in January

and the subsequent freeze, which can be as severe as any in the whole Winter. The worst damage comes in March or April when, after the daylight has lengthened and the sap has begun to rise after a week or two of mildness, buds swell and even tentative activity begins. If a severe frost occurs then it may be disastrous. One year March was like April and April like a bitter March. Apple blossoms were caught with their sepals down and leaves with their bud-scales open. There was little fruit that year and many trees suffered. So I am glad to find plenty of frost still in the soil. I hope it stays there two more months.

THE THAW CONTINUES, but my testing fork still finds hard frost only a few inches down. The mildness, however, had us going through the new seed catalogues, and before the day was out we had planted and brought to harvest a marvelous garden.

One thing about a catalogue garden, it is planted, weeded, sprayed, dusted, and even harvested without one substantial ache of a muscle. And there are no failures. Flowers bloom true to color. Every tomato plant bears big, lush, ripe, full-flavored fruit. There are no woodchucks raiding, no rabbits, no squash borers, no bean beetles, no Jap beetles. And no mosquitoes.

But such a garden is rather unsubstantial, come mealtime.

THE THAW IS OVER. It frosted again last night. The temperature was down to 20 when I got up and it barely reached 30 all day. And just in time, too, for we were getting Spring fever and wanderlust. Now we can settle back and get to work again.

But the days are growing longer. Sunset now comes nineteen minutes later than it did the first of this month. Sunrise is only four minutes earlier, but that totals up to twenty-three more minutes of daylight.

The countryman knows the time, but he is already

thinking ahead to April. Charley stopped in today and said he and his hired man were building a new trailer wagon to use with the corn picker. That means that Charley is thinking all the way to October, not only to corn-planting time but to harvest time. And Albert came up to say he thought we'd better get some fence posts out now, before Spring work begins to pile up.

After all, we are past the middle of January and we probably won't have more than about eight more weeks of Winter. One year, of course, we had Winter right up until May, three of our heaviest snowfalls in April. But that was unusual. We look forward to April as the beginning of Spring, and April isn't too far away now.

FENCE POSTS are one of the few harvests for a farmer in the Winter. We grow our own, those slim, straight cedars that fill the open patches in the woods and constantly try to creep out into the grassland of the pasture. The best stands of them are on the brush land just below the rocky ridges, an area that the outlander would consider wasteland.

The trees are red cedars, technically junipers, and their wood rots slowly. In the Fall they have small blue berries, dark blue with a whitish bloom, and the birds eat the berries and plant new cedars with their droppings. So now, when Albert cuts cedar posts, he thinks particularly well of the birds. They relieve him of one essential job of planting.

Albert is on the ridge today, and I was up there with him for a time. It's good to feel the bite of a sharp ax and to hear the lingering echo in the crisp air. As we cut the cedars, the jays began to congregate to see what was going on. Then the chickadees gathered. We had quite an audience. And yet, we were at home there, cutting posts and trimming them, and even the birds seemed to know it. There was less complaint and more companionship among them, as though they didn't mind having company.

A farmer is a little like a tree, actually, rooted in the soil and living with the seasons, shaped by the weather and patient with the years. And as we worked I thought that maybe no man should quarrel too much with the world around him. Good things grow in odd places, and what's poor land for one crop is good for another. It depends on what a man wants and needs. Crop land needs good fences, and fences need posts, and posts grow where crops for market won't grow. Maybe it all evens out. It seemed to, in a minor way, up there getting out posts today.

I can think of only one way to improve the order of things. If the birds would only plant cedars along every fence, and if the cedars would grow as well there as they do up on the ridge, we could cut our posts where we need them and save time and energy hauling them down from the mountainside. But I guess that's asking a little too much.

THERE IS A FICTION that living with the land somehow fixes one, mentally and emotionally, in a conservative orbit. The fact, as I find it, is that knowing both Summer and Winter earth and Summer and Winter sky gears one to change. How can one ignore change, deny its inevitability, when faced by change day by day and season by season? No two days are the same, when you face them whole; and facing them, one must himself change somewhat. Trees grow. Valleys deepen. And there is the horizon, the wide blue sky that has no boundaries. In Winter, especially, the boundaries are all here on the earth and most of them are man-made.

There have always been two major problems—man and man, and man and earth, his environment. Neither problem stands alone. And the false solutions always turn out to be

the ones which ignore that eternal kinship. So, too, with the
false philosophies. But for those who would understand, there
are the times of clarity and simplicity. Especially the times when
Winter hills are naked and Winter sky is wide, inviting exploration. There is a time when the boundaries we set up for
ourselves are a little less constricting. Man and man, and man
and earth, stand forth more clearly.

The clarity of the Winter sky holds its own challenge.
It promises change, and it invites the mind to match that
change. Whatever conservatism is bred there is the conservative belief that change may be slow but it is inevitable.

WHEN I WALK NOW, or even look out the win-
dow, I see the trees stripped to their essentials. They stand in
bare bones, except the conifers, and I can see the source of
their graceful Summer shapes.

That elm against the sky, which in Summer is a great
green feather-duster—see how the sturdy trunk divides some
distance from the ground, then divides again and yet again. It
reaches upward, widening like an inverted cone, and all its
branches point toward the sky.

That scarlet oak—it has a trunk almost three feet
through. With my eye I can follow that trunk to the very tip
of the tree. But its branches start not ten feet from the ground
and they reach toward the horizon. There is a tree as broad as
it is tall, and rounded, even in Winter, like a great dome.

The ash, whether white or black or red, is essentially a
tapering trunk with whorls of lesser limbs—a pole with slender
branches now, a svelte and graceful tree in full leaf.

Maples tend to branch as do the oaks but with more lift
and less spread. The sycamores down the road near the river
bridge shine as though perpetually frost-patched, and they
divide like the elm and branch like the maple, reaching out in
all directions. The sour gum, of which we have only a few, is
a central stem with a hopeless tangle of branches crisscrossed
on each other, a veritable confusion of a tree when it has no
leaves.

Winter

But of all, perhaps the most beautiful against the Winter sky is the flowering dogwood with its horizontal limbs that reach skyward at their tips and form a fine lace pattern of twigs. The dogwood is a picture tree, Winter or Summer.

THE TREES HAVE BEEN interwoven into man's history in a hundred ways. They have provided not only fuel and shelter but dyes and medicines and all manner of comforts and conveniences. This is natural, since most early men were forest dwellers; they learned early to use what was at hand.

Take medicine. A decoction of willow leaves was the best of the early substitutes for quinine in treating malarial and other fevers. Butternut bark made a tea for a mild purge. The sap of the white birch was supposed to be "healing" for lung complaints. The inner bark of the tulip tree made a tea which was a "powerful tonic" as well as a satisfactory vermifuge. Tea made from the spice bush was good for chills and fevers. A decoction of sassafras bark was a warming stimulant and sweat-producer for breaking up colds. Snuff made from dried witch-hazel leaves stopped nosebleed. Sumac tea was a powerful tonic —though some sumac is as poisonous as poison ivy. A decoction from elderberry leaf buds made a powerful purge. A tea brewed from root bark of the dogwood was another substitute for quinine.

The dyes are well remembered by the old-timers. The pink inner bark of the hemlock made a dull red. Butternut bark or red sumac made black. Inner bark of the black oak made yellow. Leaves of the black locust produced blue, and their flowers made a yellow.

White birch bark, when used to make canoes and boxes and containers of all kinds, usually was laced together with white spruce roots and waterproofed with balsam sap. Poison ivy juice made ink. Not only maple but birch and box elder made syrup and sugar. Willow withes and bark were used for cordage.

Useful? Why, the trees were indispensable!

SPOTTED WINTERGREEN is known to the bot-

271

anists as *Chimaphila maculata.* The *"Chimaphila"* comes from the Greek words meaning "to love the Winter." I find it in the woods all Winter long, brightening the dull days almost as much as the partridge berry, though with its leaves rather than with any berries. The leaves are a deep green with white markings along the main stem and side veins; they have the almost waxen texture of the bays, those bush evergreens that fold their leaves tightly or roll them shut against the cold. But the spotted wintergreen neither folds nor rolls its leaves; it spreads them and takes what comes.

Some call it pipsissiwa, an error by no means grave since the true pipsissiwa is close kin though a larger plant. One might almost call the spotted wintergreen a lesser pipsissiwa, if not too many sticklers were present. And as for the winter-green part of the name, it too allows a good deal of leeway. That word has been applied to two other plants with no rela-tionship at all. One, the so-called flowering wintergreen, is ac-tually a milkwort. The other is the checkerberry, better known in some places as boxberry, a member of the heath family.

Spotted wintergreen is one of the lesser plants, seldom growing more than nine inches high. It flowers, but with reti-cence, an inconspicuous little creamy cup that comes in June. The leaves are the principal charm of the plant, an unexpected beauty in the Winter woods. I found quite a patch of them this afternoon on the mountainside beside a drift of snow turned to ice.

FROM TIME TO TIME I HEAR indignant words about minorities, their plight or their privileges. We were at a small gathering today and I received a fervid lecture on the matter. I listened in relative silence, for it is my experience that people who say they want to discuss such matters don't really want to discuss; they want to lecture. They can be quite boring, when they are not frightening. And it doesn't much matter which minority they are discussing or which side they are on.

I wish such folk would stop their talk long enough to realize that mankind as a whole is a minority in this world of living creatures. We are outnumbered on every hand. Man is here only by sufferance of circumstance and his foothold is essentially precarious. Let the insects, for instance, get the upper hand for a few seasons, or let the bacteria upset the present balance, or let even the inedible weeds take over our farmlands—why, this minority to which we all belong, this race of human beings, would be fighting for existence!

We're a pretty arrogant crowd, we creatures who call ourselves human, and we can't afford to go around splitting ourselves into antagonistic minorities. Yes, I know we've been doing it a long, long time, and we have survived. Now and then, however, we have reduced such suicidal nonsense to a minimum for a brief period and we have profited amazingly in such interludes. Won't we ever learn? Why are we so short on enduring race wisdom and general tolerance of each other? Every time I encounter someone like that fanatic today I shiver a little and think again that mankind's most dangerous enemy really is man himself.

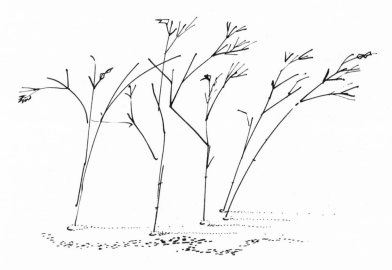

I WAS UP ON THE MOUNTAIN TODAY to check things at the springhouse. All was well, though a porcupine, or some other gnawer, had been at the door. Luckily, it is a thick door, so the gnawing had done no more than splinter it

a bit. But if the animal persists I shall have to take a piece
of heavy wire mesh up there and cover the door with it. That
will slow him up. I doubt that even a slow-witted porcupine en-
joys a toothache.

On the way back from the spring I stopped at an old
apple tree in a little clearing where the white pines are just
beginning to take over. In a few more years the pines will over-
shadow the last evidence that there was once a small orchard
up there. This is the last remaining apple tree and, old as it is
and crippled with rot and wind damage, it is a beautiful thing
in May, full of blossom, and in September its scant harvest of
undersized fruit makes a banquet for birds and deer.

Just now it seems to be a banquet for the partridges. I
examined the lower branches and it seemed to me that the
partridges had eaten at least half the buds. Apple buds are an
important item of their diet now, though it is a mystery to me
how they get much substance or succulence from such tightly
furled little potential leaves. Perhaps it is less a matter of bulk
than of vitamins or some other mysterious food element. We
humans know how insistent can be those hungers which call us
to unexpected foods. When I was a boy the cowboys who had
subsisted most of the Winter on beef, beans and pancakes sometimes rode many miles to town in March just to buy a few cans
of tomatoes. They opened the cans with jackknives and ate
them right there in the street, hungering for vitamin C, which
hadn't even been discovered or guessed at at the time.

Strange, the food memories we have. Looking back to
boyhood, my memories are full of sour-dough pancakes, boiled
beans, bread sopped in coffee, and leaf lettuce wilted with salt-
pork fat and vinegar. I am sure we ate as well as most people
of that day and place, but the vivid memories are of hard-times
fare—cornmeal mush, rabbit sausage, coarse bread made from
cow bran. The really good fare, chicken, steak, and pie, are all
but forgotten.

RAW THIS MORNING, with a heavy overcast, and
there were intermittent flurries of fine snow all day. Pat would

happily have spent the whole day indoors, but I got tough in midmorning and sent him out. He needs some exercise. Half an hour later I heard his voice up on the mountain, trailing rabbits and signaling me that if I would only get a little exercise myself we could have some fun up there. I didn't go, and I only hope he doesn't get into an argument with another bobcat or porcupine.

The first Winter he was here, Pat and the other dog went out the first week and tangled with a bobcat. When they came home Pat was a bit clawed up, a long scratch across his nose and one ear slit. He was pretty well bloodied. Mike apparently had merely stood by and given Pat encouragement, for Mike was unhurt. I cleaned Pat up and salved his wounds, and he lay around for a few days with Mike as his nurse. Mike licked off the salve as fast as I put it on. Mike licked Pat's wounds constantly, and they healed nicely. But the ear was slit and it remains a mitten-ear, as we say. And as far as I know Pat has never since tackled a bobcat, though the cats still live there on the mountain.

I've heard some men scoff at bobcats, call them cowards and say they won't fight unless cornered and that they will never attack a man. Maybe so, but one fisherman I knew still carries scars from a bobcat that dropped out of a tree onto his shoulders while he was walking from one trout pool to another. The fisherman was unarmed and had to kill the cat with his bare hands. He did it, too, choked the beast to death. And still carries the scars.

Another man, who lives in the village and has hunted and fished these hills and streams for years, wants no part of a bobcat and makes no bones about admitting it. A cat rushed him in the woods one day and he had to knife it to death. Not long ago when his wife went out at dusk to bring in a washing from the line a bobcat screamed at her from close by. She called her husband, who couldn't believe a bobcat would come right into the edge of the village. But there it was, in the edge of the circle of light from the back of the house. He went inside for his shotgun, but when he went out again the cat had retreated into the darkness. He didn't follow it, even armed with a shot-gun. He wanted no part of a bobcat in the darkness. And that man is neither a coward nor a believer of old wives' tales.

PAT DIDN'T COME HOME till after dark last night, and I had begun to worry about him. Then he came staggering in, walking almost bowlegged. He was gorged, fat as a tick. He wanted no supper. All he wanted to do was lie in front of the fire and drowse and groan. He had stuffed himself, an absolute glutton.

This morning I took down the shotgun, called Pat and suggested we go up on the mountain. He had slept off his gluttony and was eager to go. I hoped he would lead me to whatever carcass he had been feasting on yesterday. I hoped it wasn't a deer. Pat has never trailed deer, and if he should begin I would have to do something drastic. I'll have no deer-killing dog.

But all he did was lead me far up the mountain, chasing rabbits. It was a cold day and every rabbit he put up ran in, took to a hole. I didn't get a rabbit. Then we came down into the edge of the lower pasture and I started to cross what looked like a sloping patch of thin snow. It was an icy slope covered with half an inch of white, a fact I discovered when my feet went out from under me. I went down with a crash, banging one knee on the ice and banging the other leg with the shotgun as I fell. It was as painful a fall as I've had in years. I melted quite a patch of snow with my language.

I tested both legs, found no broken bones, and crawled off the ice onto the snow-covered grass. And started for home, hobbling. Pat put up another rabbit and made a great uproar, but I wasn't interested. I came on home, painfully. Lord, what a shaking-up I'd got! I felt as though I had fallen off a cliff. And not even a good purple bruise to inspire sympathy—I don't bruise easily.

This evening Albert stopped past and said, casually, that he had butchered out a yearling yesterday. Yes, Pat had been around. He and Albert's dog, Suzy, stuffed themselves pretty thoroughly with the scraps and leavings, Albert said. So. Pat smelled the butchering. Well, he will be eating at home again by tomorrow. And I shall be aching for a week.

A FINE WAY TO END JANUARY, hobbling around the house like an old, old man! If only I had a minor break or a sprain to make it, somehow, legal! I had thought, yesterday morning, that I might get out the skis and do a bit of pasture-skiing. But, I tell myself now, the snow isn't much good. I'll stay here and suffer my aches in silence. But not complete silence. A man is entitled to a groan or two. . . .

Up in the woods yesterday, I was looking at the lichens, which are so much more visible in Winter. They spread over the rocks and they creep up the trunks of the trees. They are maps of strange areas man has never visited, continents almost recognizable, at times, but never quite familiar. Something like the maps we had in the big geography books when I was a small boy, big, colored relief maps with greens and browns indicating mountain and plain. I have all those pictures up in the woods now, and a thousand more, spread out on the rocks.

Looking at the lichens I wondered who first said that moss and lichen always grow on the north side of a tree. Up on my mountain moss and lichen grow on the south sides of the trees, too, and on the east and west sides. More, perhaps, on the north side, but not much more. I suspect that moss and lichen have less of a sense of direction than a sense of shade and moisture. If I were ever lost in the woods and tried to find my way out by compassing on the lichen on the tree trunks I would starve to death or die of old age before I escaped. So much for *that* superstition. . . .

Pat doesn't seem to care a hoot how much I ache, but Barbara just brought me a bowl of fine, hot soup.

FEBRUARY

I WENT DOWN THE ROAD to the swamp this afternoon and found what I was looking for—the first signs of skunk cabbage thrusting up like the first sign of the tulips in our garden. Some of them were up two or three inches, purplish brown with a strong green undertone, fat and primitive. A little later they will begin to open their strange hoods, spathes like eccentric orchestra shells in which will appear the bulb-shaped blossom "spike." Then will come the giant green leaves.

The Old Men of the Swamps are the earliest of all Spring flowers. I have seen them at Christmas time, occasionally, thrusting up through the ice. Often they come in January, and I would have bet heavily that I could find them today in almost any bog. The outside temperature has to be low indeed to discourage them, for they generate their own warmth. The skunk cabbage literally melts its path up through the icy swampland. Those I saw today were surrounded by small pools of open water while all around was ice.

All plants generate a certain amount of warmth through respiration. Since they cannot use it to maintain body temperature, as animals do, they throw it off, as waste. It is nothing more than the heat of oxidation of food in the plant's normal processes. Scientists have measured the heat generated by many plants and found that it sharply increases at the time of blossoming and at germination. So plants too have their time "in heat."

Skunk cabbage thrusting up through the frost may have as much as 27 degrees more heat than the surrounding soil or air and its shape, like a closed conical dome, concentrates that heat where it will do the most good. Thus, even on a day when the air temperature is in the low 20s, as it is today, the skunk cabbage can go right on growing.

GROUNDHOG DAY, and it is my experience that the groundhogs, or woodchucks, have more sense than those who go out looking for groundhog shadows.

February came in kindly, this year, but the woodchucks in these parts have for a long time slept through the first week of February without a worry about the weather. Oh, now and then one may be out by now, but I am sure it is only because he ate one too few meals before he hibernated. And if any woodchuck should come out today he would look for something to eat, not for a shadow. But such mythology dies hard.

I never see a woodchuck out before the end of February, no matter what the weather. Charley says that last year one came out, up at his farm, toward the end of February and seemed to have a hard time of it. We had several inches of snow on the ground and the beast wandered around, hungrily, and Charley's dog saw it and took after it and they had quite a scramble in the snow. The woodchuck, lean from the Winter, could stay on top of the snow, and the dog bogged in, so the 'chuck got away. Charley didn't see a woodchuck again till toward the end of April.

The sun came out for a time this afternoon. I cite it only for later reference: the groundhog could have seen his shadow if there had been a groundhog out and open-eyed. Six weeks more Winter? I doubt it.

OUR SNOW IS GONE, except in the deep shade among the pines and hemlocks on the mountain. I went up there a little way today and the sun was warm, almost balmy, when I got out of the wind; so I sat down with my back to a pine and listened to the song of the tumbling waters of the brook and watched the birds.

I saw dozens of juncos and chickadees, and then I saw two birds among the trees fifty yards away that I am sure were

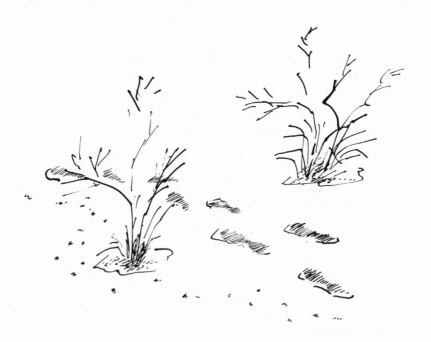

robins. I caught only a quick glimpse of them, but they flew like robins and I thought I saw one flash of ruddy breasts. I sat and waited half an hour, hoping they would appear again, but there wasn't another sign of them.

When I came back to the house Barbara said, "I have been expecting to see bluebirds. In fact, I looked out the window several times, looking for them." But she didn't see any bluebirds. Perhaps it's the weather that makes us feel this way. It was only half dark at six o'clock. We are beginning to be impatient for Spring, as always.

A COLD RAIN TODAY, and yesterday's hopes are gone. Spring isn't just over the hill. Not yet. It's still February.

February rain isn't any wetter than that of March, and February snow isn't any more slushy than that of January. Nor is the sun Summer-hot on an occasional mild February day. They only seem that way because, at this time of year, our weather nerves are right up on the surface. The bad times seem worse and the good seems better than reality.

Winter

It sometimes appears that our forefathers who lived closer to the soil and the seasons were a little more patient. In public print they wrote of February: "Now comes the deepest snow; now we receive the remainderment of Winter." But I have been looking at some of their private letters, and I have another picture of those doughty ancestors. "February," one writes, "is a miserable time. I would gladly pass it by. I long for March, inclement as it is." Another writes, "Patience is a virtue, that I know! but February tries my patience sorely." And in the journals I have found laconic weather records that make chilly reading indeed, cold and wet and disappointing.

They, too, got Winter-weary. They had their troubles, and they were impatient about them, down in their hearts. But, partly because they lived close to the land and understood the leisure of changing seasons, they put up with them and saw them through. Spring was not only a relief from Winter; it was also work, hard work and long hours, planting for the Summer's growth. No year, no season, was without its pains and worries. But there was comfort, even security, in the knowledge of change. No troubles lasted forever, nor did any weather, good or bad. Winter ended, eventually, and Spring came. Thus it was and thus it always will be.

I HEAR THAT THE SOCIAL PLANNERS are after us leisure-wasters again. We seem to be a menace to society. And our reformation depends entirely on our adopting hobbies. It's a sin to loaf. Not a moral sin, maybe, but a sin against society. Besides, the social planners need something to do or *they* will have leisure to waste.

I have tried to run down the origin of the word *loaf* in the sense of taking it easy; but even the lexicographers seem unable to trace it. I have a hunch that it goes back to some language even earlier than Sanskrit, and I also have a hunch that the cryptographers who unravel the mysteries of ancient hieroglyphics will eventually find a clay tablet, perhaps from ancient Sumer, with a social planner's complaint about loafers. The planners and the loafers have been at it for a long, long time.

The heartening thing about it, to me, is that man continues to cherish his leisure and to insist on using it as he wishes. Also, I get great comfort from knowing that some of the best thoughts of all time have been generated by men who would be classed by the social planners as loafers and leisure-wasters. I'd as soon be a member of an ant colony as of a society in which a man didn't dare loaf now and then, just sit and think or, if he chose to, just sit.

FROM TIME TO TIME I have theorized about new-fashioned Winters and climate changes, but when a cold air mass moved in from the Arctic last night and found a warm air mass with plenty of humidity in its way my theories were left shivering and up to their knees in snow. Winter is still Winter. Now I know.

Some of the hill farmers said last Fall that we were just about due for a bone-chiller. They said it rather dourly. And I noticed that most of the folks around used the mild days of December to replenish the woodpile, just as Albert used last June to cut hay on one of the pastures where the cows couldn't keep up with the grass. It's something of a local habit, to make hay and cut wood when they're available. "Hay keeps," as Albert says succinctly.

Folks are using those woodpiles and their extra hay today, and glad they have them. They shivered plenty on their way to do the morning milking, and they frowned at the thermometer at dawn, as I did. But back of the shivers and frowns a good many of us have a feeling of elemental propriety, a feeling that things even out. That droughts end, floods subside, ice melts, and Winter is Winter.

That evening-out process is probably more important than the day-to-day temperature or the total snowfall, for it tends to put a good many things back in perspective. For a time, at least, we know without a doubt or quibble that a good furnace, plenty of oil, and a snow shovel are more important than a machine that can fly to the moon or Mars.

Winter

I HAVE BEEN WASTING my leisure again. I've
been out at the shop going over some planks of native black
cherry which Jerry gave me, thinking about turning a few
shallow bowls on the lathe. But mostly I was doing nothing
constructive, nothing more worth while than admiring the
wood, looking at the grain, speculating on the seasons that
tree knew during its lifetime.

Those planks came from a big tree that grew where
someone wanted to build a road. It was on Jerry's land and
Jerry liked the living tree, but road-builders would rather cut
down a tree than draw a curve. So the tree was cut. But Jerry
got the log, had it cut into lengths and carted to a sawmill.
The planks from it have been seasoning in his garage for several years. And I was thinking today that a few individual
salad bowls might be a pleasant reminder of that tree on
Jerry's and Letty's dinner table.

Black cherry is a hard wood. I have turned it before. It
is harder than maple, but with a somewhat prettier grain and
color, to my way of thinking. These planks are nicely variegated, light wood and dark, the dark the heartwood. I laid out

the blanks for half a dozen bowls, in pencil, but I hesitate to
cut into the wood. A plank has an entity all its own. But as I
looked at one I knew that it had several bowls in it, awaiting
only the sharp chisel to free them from the surrounding wood.
What sculptor was it who said the same thing about a block of
marble?

I laid out the bowls, then went out and watched a tree
sparrow for twenty minutes. Maybe I should have cut into that
plank and got started on something really constructive.

THE SPARROWS make late Winter a pleasanter
time for any countryman. Not English sparrows, the raucous
little city gamins, but American sparrows, the song sparrow,
the tree sparrow, the whitethroat, the pine siskin, the field sparrow, the occasional chipping sparrow. Finches, all of them, in
the big classification of the ornithologists, but sparrows to
most of us. They come to the feeding station, they are busy as
bees on the hillside where the weeds still stand with a few seeds,
and they chatter eagerly in the most untoward weather. On
warm days they sing a little, foretaste of the lively songs they
will be singing after March has made its turn.

In its old meaning, the word *sparrow* meant "to flutter."
They are flutterers, all of them, adept on the wing. See a flock
of them sweep up the hillside, wheel into the wind against a
gray sky, and it lifts your heart. In such a flock I see the
speckled breasts, the solid gray breasts, and the breasts that
seem striped, for the sparrows do not persist in groups of only
one kind. I even see a flash of yellow among them, that bright
little patch at the base of the pine siskin's tail.

They are seed-eaters, all of them. They flock happily to
our feeding station. There they eat millet, mostly shucking off
the outer shell with quick, tongue-rolling, beak-chomping motions. Those papery shells cling around their beaks, like a
small child's oatmeal around its mouth. They eat, and at no
visible sign they all take frenzied wing, fill the air with their
chatter, and swoop up the hillside.

Winter

THE RIVER FLOWS FASTER NOW and the brooks coming down the mountainside leap and gurgle all afternoon. The river is still black, however, in contrast to its icy banks where snow still lies in the brush. But it is live water, refusing now to be confined by ice. And all the water is carrying away, hour by hour, the deep frost of the long night of Winter.

When I walk beside the river I feel the tang of sharp air, morning and evening; but when the sun rides high I know there is warmth ahead. And when I walk beside one of the brooks I know not only the quick movement of water but the surge of forces that will be livening all the earth in a few more weeks. Even the trickles that seep from beneath the drifts on the mountain are live waters, the sustenance for buds and shoots that await a warmer sun. The persistent ice is eaten away. The earth itself gives up its frost to the waters that make their steady way down all the seams and crevices toward the valleys where brooks join rivers.

I stopped past the marsh today and there is a movement of water even there, a slow flow that creeps among the reeds and eases past the root tangles of willow brush. It is there, in the sluggish waters, that Spring will come first, for the marshes generate their own vernal warmth. Frogs' eggs will lie milky in the pools, skunk cabbage will spread its leaves, and dogtooth violets will put forth their mottled leaves and golden blossoms.

But such matters are for later. Today the waters ooze and flow and the ice recedes. The grass beside Millstone brook begins to quicken, but the green is for tomorrow. Today the waters are alive and moving. That is enough for today.

THERE HAVE BEEN BLUEBIRDS around all Winter. I haven't seen them, but Glen and Su, who live just down the valley, tell me they have seen them near their house almost every morning. They come soon after dawn, they say, and perch in a tall tree, as though watching for something—for Spring, perhaps. Then they leave, and if they appear again that day it is at dusk. They return and perch in that same tree again, and look.

Both bluebirds and robins often spend the Winter this far north, finding shelter in the brushy tangles and foraging for food. They almost never visit the feeding stations, yet they survive the storms, the bitter cold, and the icebound feeding grounds. Nobody seems to know just why these particular individuals out of the vast numbers of robins and bluebirds disobey the summons to migrate. It could happen, of course, that from them eventually will evolve a nonmigrating sub-species which will adapt its diet to whatever food our Winters afford. But that is something for the geneticists to ponder.

I noted last Fall that we saw bluebirds here after the juncos had arrived. Perhaps they were of that group which has wintered just down the valley. But we haven't seen them here since November, and I never get down to Glen's place at dawn as I probably would if I were a dedicated bird watcher.

THE BEECH TREES still cling to their brown papery leaves, or at least to a share of them, and March is only two weeks ahead. So do some of the white oaks, making russet splotches in the woods. But when I look closely at the beeches I see lance-tip buds half an inch long, and there are

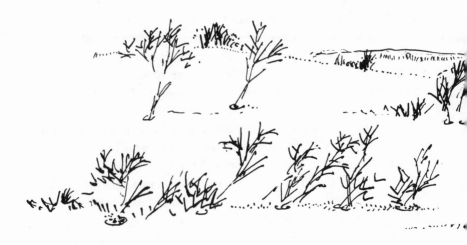

bud clusters at the tips of the oak twigs, more reluctant in their growth.

There is a theory that the clinging leaves shelter the new buds from the rigors of Winter and, indeed, the oaks do cup their buds with the leaf stems. But there is little shelter in the clasp of a beech leaf. Yet it is the beech which swells its buds earlier, so the theory sags under the weight of what I see with my own eyes.

When I peeled back a beech bud today I stripped off layer after layer of soft brown tissue, and at its heart I found a feathery tuft—a twin tuft, in fact—of white, silky catkin-to-be. This will become the staminate flower of the beech, which will appear in May along with the first leaves. The pistillate flowers will also open at that time, but they will be small and inconspicuous; their time of display comes in the Fall, when they have fattened into soft-prickled burs enclosing sweet-flavored beechnuts.

The reluctant oaks are more chary of their secrets. The buds are very small and tightly closed. Even if I could pry into the green mystery I should need a strong glass to identify the nucleus of leaf and flower. They bide their time. But mean-

while both oak and beech cling to last year's leaves, rustling in the wind and keeping their own conservative counsel.

On this mild afternoon the ladybirds were out sunning themselves on the walls and around the windows of the house. Ladybirds, of course, are those small orange beetles with black polka dots on their backs. They have been around all Winter, sleeping in cracks and coming out, even in January, to warm themselves from time to time. If we had ivy on these walls the ladybirds would be twice as numerous, for they feed on aphids, and aphids feed on ivy among other things.

Ladybirds, which technically are *Coccinellidae*, have strange Winter habits. In California they migrate to the mountain tops for the cold season, gathering there in such vast numbers that horticulturists sometimes gather them literally by the bushel, take them to the lowlands, keep them in cold storage until the growing season, then release them to clean the aphids from the fruit and vegetable crops. Brought out of cold storage, they soon return to full life and appetite. And in a minor way they do the same thing here, creeping out of their hiding places, warming themselves in the sun, and starting their Spring cycle of life much earlier than most other insects.

In a way, it is a sign of Spring when they become active. But not an infallible sign. They can and do go back to sleep when the sun goes down or a chilly wave strikes. They can sleep for days, even weeks, as late as March.

Ladybirds are quite harmless to humans and most helpful to gardens. Not as much can be said for some of their cousins. The bean beetles, for instance, and the squash beetles. They, too, hibernate. But not long enough, not nearly long enough.

I say that I hear the voice of change in the sound of running water. Yet this ancient, inevitable shift and change of the elements that comes to any land of changing seasons is basically an inanimate process.

I think of it in animate terms because out of it comes

new life rousing from a period of dormancy. The time of rest is a time of silence, and the time of life stirring is a time of sound, so I think of this change in terms of my own living. We give voice to the inanimate wind and song to flowing water, probably because we would hear voices and listen to music. We are a talkative race and we somehow evolved song out of our emotional heartbeat. If the growing leaves and opening buds made audible sounds we would no doubt hear words and music in them.

WE HAVE HAD A MILD FEBRUARY thus far, and we have waited, almost holding our breath, for it to change. This morning there was the change. I wakened to find four inches of snow. It came in the secrecy of the night. But the temperature was just 30, and it stayed there most of the day, so there was little melting. So I must defer my hope of seeing the first bulb-tips. I have been expecting them to poke through almost any day, at least the white-veined little spears of the crocuses.

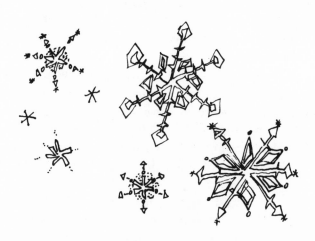

Those who lived here before we came gave us a welcome inheritance of bulbs, to which we have added year by year. What a game of it we played, at first! Nondas had said, with one of those encompassing waves of her hand, "Watch for crocuses there, and daffodils there, and tulips over there. I put in quite a few of them." As it turned out, "there" was a most indefinite area. Daffodils came thrusting up in the grass ten feet from the flower beds. Beside the front porch, where we had thought there were dozens of bulbs, was a thin fringing of crocuses. Beneath the pear tree, where we knew there was a lily of the valley bed, there were also tulips. And squills were mixed with the roses.

The strangest thing of all was to see a patch of lawn turn green before the last snow melted. It turned out to be over the septic tank and it was warmed, like a hotbed, by the hot water from the kitchen sink. Daffodils bloomed there two weeks ahead of those anywhere else. I had expected to find those daffodils up by next week; but now we are snow-covered again.

UP IN THE ATTIC TODAY, looking for a book in the overflow from the downstairs library, I heard a wasp out and buzzing. The sound of a wasp buzz is completely characteristic, far different from that of a fly, for instance. The difference rises from the speed of wing vibration, which sets up sound waves.

The sound waves made by insect wings are the means of measuring the number of wing strokes they make in flight. Some ingenious researcher, with a knowledge of physics as well as entomology, matched the sound of a flying insect with that of a musical tuning fork. Tuning forks are carefully calibrated, the number of their vibrations known. Once the insect buzz was matched with a definite tuning fork, there was the answer to how fast that particular insect moves its wings.

Out of that research came the knowledge that a common house fly makes 330 strokes a second, nearly 20,000 a minute. A wasp makes less than a third that many wing strokes, around 6,000 a minute. Dragonflies, the strongest fliers among insects, are much slower, only 1,600 strokes a minute. All these wing-beats or vibrations are well within the range of the human ear, which can distinguish sounds with as few as 30 vibrations a second and as many as 20,000. Both above and below those rates the vibrations are inaudible to most human ears, though an occasional person is sensitive to sounds above that range, as dogs are. I know one woman whose ears are so sensitive in the ultrasonic ranges that she is physically distressed by the vibrations of a noiseless dog-whistle.

But we can all hear a wasp. And take warning.

THIS AFTERNOON the truckman came to fill the oil tank for our furnace and said that his mother, who is in Florida, reports that the robins which have been numerous there all Winter now seem to have moved out. She hasn't seen a robin in a week. The oil man said, "I guess they're on their way up here. A day like this, you begin to look for them."

Not an hour after the oil man had left I glanced out the window into the side yard, and there was a robin! I went to the window and saw two robins. While I watched, two more came, drifting down like light airplanes to a graceful landing. They looked around, stretched their necks, and made short, quick runs, so typical of robins. Then another. Then two more. And there we had seven robins on our side lawn.

I called Barbara and we stood for ten minutes watching them. You might have thought they were rare, exotic visitors. They found something to eat, though obviously not angleworms, and they ran about the grass as though merely looking over a remembered place, putting it once more in their frame of reference, as the current phrase has it. Then they all took wing, as at a signal, and flew past the apple trees and into the middle pasture. We watched them there for several minutes, then said to each other, "It's coming. Spring is really coming."

IT ISN'T REALLY SPRING; it's only February on somewhat better than usual behavior, and if I were a robin I doubt that I would stay here and wait for it to warm up. I haven't seen the robins today, so maybe they feel the same way about a raw day.

Being a man, not a bird, I went out to the shop this afternoon and turned a couple of cherry wood bowls on the lathe. I was sanding them when I heard a door slam at the big barn nearby. A gusty wind had come up and a latch had come loose. I repaired the latch and while I was there I went up into the loft.

The loft is full of fine fragrance for anyone on a raw February day, mostly the smell of hay and straw. Albert had forty tons or so of hay in there this year, but he has used more than half of it. The hay smell takes me back to boyhood, for it smells of June and hay fields I knew years ago. There is also the smell of oat straw, which I cannot describe but which I can identify anywhere. There are a few tons of baled oat straw there, too.

Old barns, like old people, should have some reason for being. After I had finished the repairs and smelled the fragrances in the loft I went back to the shop. But I turned and

looked at the barn and it seemed to lift its slightly stooped shoulders rather proudly. It is full of years, but it still has a purpose.

I AM NOT SURE how old my barn is, but I would make a guess of at least a hundred years. When I said that to one visitor he shook his head. "It can't be. It has a cement foundation." That man didn't know that Portland cement was used in the construction of the locks for the Erie Canal, back in the 1820s. Most of the barns and houses which date back a hundred years or so had stone and mortar foundations, but that was for economy, not because cement was unavailable. Stone was everywhere and lime and sand were cheap. My barn also has a cement floor, but that could have been and probably was laid in its later years.

Whatever the age of the barn itself, its timbering is even older than the present structure. It is framed in the old way, with beams a foot and more square, oak beams hewn to shape and mortised and tenoned. They came from an earlier structure, because they have mortises in odd places, where no tenons were ever based in this barn. They were, obviously, good beams salvaged from some other barn, and they are pegged

together. The siding is vertical, as on all old barns, and the rafters are shaped only enough to give the roof boards a level support. Some of the floor boards in the loft are old pumpkin pine two feet wide.

A few years ago a passing photographer took a picture of the barn, with a gnarled old apple tree nearby and a broken hay rake near the ramp and won a prize with it under the title, "Abandoned Farm." We got a laugh out of that, but the next Spring I moved the old rake. Nobody has photographed the barn since. Maybe I should have left the rake where it was and kept the barn picturesque.

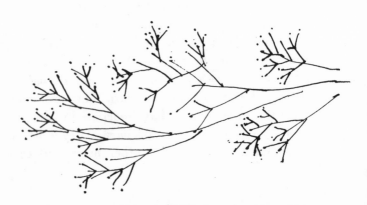

I MET A MAN IN THE VILLAGE TODAY who said he saw a woodchuck yesterday. A lean and hungry woodchuck who probably got out of bed a little too early. Out of bed on the wrong side, too, I am sure. I have yet to see a woodchuck who got out of bed on the right side.

Coming home I caught up with a collie dog trotting down the road. He heard the car, glanced over his shoulder, moved aside and paid me no more attention. And I thought how completely dogs have adapted themselves to automobiles. Not very many dogs get run over, certainly very few in relation to the total dog population. My guess is that fewer dogs are car casualties, proportionately, than human pedestrians.

Do dogs pass on acquired characteristics? I know it is contrary to laws of heredity; but this is knowledge rather than a physical or mental characteristic. Do mother dogs somehow tell their pups that cars are a strange kind of animal that cannot bark or bite but that kill if one get underfoot? Do they tell the pups that cars stay on roads and that if dogs stay at the roadside they are safe? However they learn it, pups come to know early in life that cars must be given right of way. It seems to me that they learn much earlier now than twenty years ago. It may be, of course, that slow-learning strains fail to survive, an instance of the survival of the fittest.

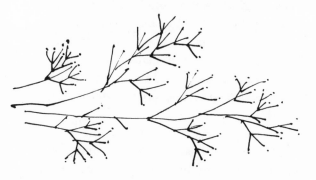

FEBRUARY IS DOING ITSELF PROUD, but I hope it doesn't get delusions of being April, because I am sure March will not be at all like May.

We walked across the pastures and up the mountain a little way and I found a small gray birch with tiny catkins out, not yet turned yellow but out of the bud. It had cheated somewhat, because it was a very small tree growing on a very small island in the brook. The brook water must have warmed its roots and the air temperature must have been raised a degree or two by the water, thus giving it an extra week or two of growing season. But there it was, with small catkins.

In the pasture we saw a pair of common grackles, their feathers gleaming with that iridescent sheen peculiar to their tribe, green and blue overlaying the black in the sunlight. They strutted and poked their long beaks into clumps of dead grass and watched us with beady eyes. They were quite tame, letting us approach within ten feet before they hopped and flew a little way.

I am content with only a few grackles, a few pairs. When a whole flock congregates, particularly in the Spring, they make a din and an uproar. Later in the season I can accept a din, but after the Winter's silence I have to work up to the busy noises of Spring gradually. And there's nothing gradual about a flock of grackles.

THIS AFTERNOON there were ducks on the river. I thought they were ducks until I got the binoculars. Then they were easy to identify as mergansers, which some call shelldrakes. There was no mistaking the males, with their clean white feathers, their dark markings, and their red-orange beaks. The females are a speckled gray and brown, and it was the females that I saw first.

After I had watched them for a time, down at the bend of the river, they came upstream opposite the house and put on a fine display of diving. The mergansers are splendid divers. I watched one old drake upend himself and go under and stay down a full minute. The river at that point is at least ten feet deep, and he probably went right down to the bottom. He came up forty feet from where he went down, and upstream at that, though the river is high and has a strong current.

There were six of them, three pairs, and they were in the water out here all afternoon. Soon, now, they will be quacking loudly at dawn every morning. We see them—and hear them—every year.

SOME OF THE FROST is coming out of the ground. We had reason to take a back road through the woods a few miles from here today and the muddy ruts were treacherous. I thought several times that I was going to get the car hung up on the ridge between the ruts. No wonder that country folk on back roads shake their heads at today's automobiles with their low clearance.

A good many years ago I tried to navigate the ultimate of such roads in Mississippi. I was driving one of those early high-wheeled Oakland touring cars, which could manage most mud roads. But the road I was on had been used by loggers, the ruts had been cut deep by the laden wheels of their wagons and churned to mire by the hooves of their four-mule teams. I managed to stay on the ridges for about four miles, then slid off into those canyons of ruts and there I was. I waited half an hour and a logger came along. He didn't even ask questions. He unhooked his team from his log wagon, flipped a log chain around the front axle of my car, hupped to his mules, and skidded me out. He skidded that car on the greasy mud for the better part of a mile, to a hard road, and wouldn't take a cent for it. "Y'can hep me sometime," he grinned, "if y'ever come back thisaway. Which y'won't, if'n you got good sense."

I went back thataway a few years ago, and that road was a big, broad, blacktop highway. And not a logger in sight.

THE AFTERNOON WAS WARM AGAIN, almost balmy, and the daffodils are showing their tips all over the flower garden. Also dozens of crocuses. Crocus leaves; not a bud yet in sight.

While we were at lunch I looked out into the pasture and saw birds, dozens of birds. They ran like robins. I got the glasses, and they were robins. I began to count. I counted to fifty and lost all count, for they were darting about, busy. There were sixty or more of them, I am sure, and they were scattered all over the pasture and beside the brook. Apparently they had just arrived, for they were searching the grass for food. Those we saw a week ago were scouts or outriders. I had thought they might be part of a flock that wintered here, but now I doubt it. This is a migratory flock, certainly, the flock that comes to this valley each year. They are a couple of weeks early this year. How red their breasts looked in the February sunlight!

This afternoon we drove over into the next valley and saw sap buckets on the maple trees and the curling mist of smoke from the syrup evaporator. When we came home I got out the spouts and the buckets and got down the tub that hangs in the woodshed and scrubbed it out. Our syrup equipment is simple, but it makes syrup. If the weather holds, I shall tap a few trees tomorrow.

It has chilled off this evening. Perfect sap weather, cold nights and mild days.

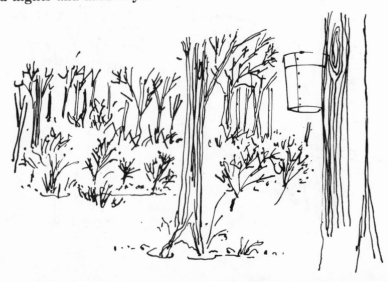

I TAPPED FOUR MAPLE TREES TODAY. To tap a tree we drill a hole about two inches deep, drive a metal spout into it, and hang a pail on the spout. The sap begins to drip. I put two spouts on each tree. That will give enough sap for a gallon or two of syrup and a few cakes of sugar. It takes twenty to thirty gallons of sap to make a gallon of syrup.

The sap flows clear as water, though when I get a gallon or two it seems to have a pale amber tint, so pale it is little more than a shine. And the word "flow" is too strong a word; the sap drips, drop by drop. I timed it this morning and it was coming at the rate of fifty drops a minute, a good flow. By midafternoon we had about six gallons of sap and I began cooking it.

The first year we made syrup I thought of boiling it down on the stove in the kitchen. Layton gave wise warning. The steam would fill the house and, since it is a sticky steam, it would film walls and woodwork. So I built a temporary fireplace of cinder blocks in the yard and used an old wash tub for my evaporating kettle. How right Layton was! The steam rolled up from the tub in a continuous cloud.

Today I set up the fireplace, cut kindling, carried firewood, and as soon as there was enough sap I started cooking it in the tub. By dusk I had boiled down six gallons of sap into a gallon of concentrate, which I jugged for more boiling tomorrow. It had a noticeable maple flavor and a straw color. Tonight I smell of wood smoke and maple-sap steam.

IT CHILLED OFF TODAY and the sap flow slackened, but I cooked down yesterday's concentrate and today's scant run. There was about a quart and a half of syrup when I had finished. The first run is supposed to have the best flavor, so we bottled and sealed it, marked it with the date and stowed it in the cellar.

I have been reading Emerson and Thoreau, and having trouble with both of them, as usual. I wish Emerson had been a better writer and I wish Thoreau had been a better thinker. Thoreau was a remarkably able and patient observer of nature and he wrote a firm, tough-grained prose. But when he begins to prescribe for society he speaks from too narrow a platform for me. And he too often reveals his lack of experience with people and with society. Now and then his solutions remind me of the solutions of those moderns who retreat into primitivism and anthropology and find pat answers in a world that does not exist. Today's answers would be much simpler if life were more simple. But it isn't. It is complex, and it was complex in Thoreau's time.

One thing I miss in Thoreau is an awareness of family problems. Emerson largely ignored such matters, but Thoreau just seemed to lack the knowledge one inevitably acquires, not only of self but of interrelationships, in marriage and under the necessity of assuming responsibility for a family. It seems to me that life is only half lived, experience only half known, without this.

FEBRUARY DOESN'T END; it frays away, or is blown away, into March. A year ago, February went out with a 10-degree temperature and four inches of snow and a bitter wind. This year it is going out with daffodils up four inches. There was a slight snowfall last night, but it was all gone by noon, though a raw wind persists.

The cold weather has stopped the run of sap, but it will resume when the weather moderates.

MARCH

ARCH CAME IN WITH A CHILL. It was down to 15 above zero this morning and it didn't top 25 all day. The calendar shows that it is March, but it might as easily be February. In fact, this day *is* February every fourth year, which proves the fallibility of mathematics in dealing with the days and the seasons. Even the equinox, three weeks hence and the one fixed point of the season, does not really serve as anything but an index of daylight and darkness. The roots and the buds know what is happening, and it is there that Spring will really come, not in the stars.

We saw February this year from only one side. February smiled on us. It's just as well that March came in this way, to make us realize that the seasons can't be too much hurried.

I SAW A CHIPMUNK TODAY, his tail stiff as though it were frozen, scurrying from one stone wall to another. He certainly picked a good time to wake up and take *his* vernal exercise!

Chipmunks do not hibernate, though they spend a good part of the cold months sleeping and are not really active until Spring is well within reach. They build their nests below frost line and they stock up for cold weather with hoards of grain, nuts and grass seed. They eat well and they sleep warm, in nests lined with thistledown, milkweed floss, grass and other excellent mattress and comforter material. I would rather have a few families of chipmunks around—except in strawberry season; they love the red berries—than most of the other rodents.

301

Foxes and cats are the chipmunk's worst enemies, and both of them can be defeated by a stone wall. Every chipmunk seems to have a detail map of all the stone walls in his area. Surprise one in the open and he dives unerringly for a wall, knowing exactly where to find the nearest chink.

I hope that chipper today didn't get his tail frozen. I have seen a few bobtailed chipmunks, but I am sure they didn't lose them to the frost. They lost them in fights, for among themselves the chipmunks sometimes wage bloody and merciless feuds.

THE DAFFODILS have checked their growth. They are cautious—Yankee caution, Mary calls it—and put no more susceptible green surface above the ground now than they can afford to lose. They can take a good bit of freezing without real damage, for if the first shoots are frozen and wither back the bulbs lie and wait for warmer days, then send up new shoots to replace them.

Mary lives on a farm less than ten miles from us, works in the village, and is full of music and pithy talk. She boasts about the severity of the weather in her valley, makes it sound like a northern suburb of Nome, Alaska. When we had our first light snow she had snow "right up to the calf's belly." When there was a scum of ice on the river, her brook was frozen solid, "right down into the gravel." When the last frost leaves the ground and the first Spring rains come she will be out planting peas "in mud up to my knees." And glorying in it. She is the only person I ever knew who sings classical music while she is doing the morning milking. Why? "I like it, and the cows don't seem to mind."

JUST ENOUGH WARMER TODAY to start the sap flowing again, slowly. On the south side of the trees, I am surprised to see. The spouts on the north side of the trees show only a few drops. There wasn't enough sap to justify starting the fire again, only about two gallons, so I jugged it and stowed it in the woodshed. Maple sap will ferment if not kept cold; but no chance of a fermentation temperature tonight. The temperature is in the 20s.

Two of our friends have gone down to the city for a week. They took along a bundle of twigs from their apple trees, the cherry tree and the forsythia, to put in water and watch the buds open. Today we had a note from Letty saying that the forsythia is out and they can see the color in the apple buds. The same mail brought a post card written later the same day the note was written. It said: "Egg cases on apple twigs have hatched a brood of web worms! Spring indeed!"

Well, that *is* Spring. Blossoms, and also bugs and worms.

We went out and cut a few forsythia twigs and added shoots of red-osier dogwood for color. The red osier begins to show its strong red, almost a maroon, on all the shoots. In water it will put forth leaves and be bright and vernal green, little leaves veined like those of the flowering dogwood and soft as silk.

THIS IS THE TIME OF YEAR when our country grandmothers used to mix sulphur and molasses and prescribe it generously. A Spring tonic was needed, something to lift the spirit and tone up the blood. Winter was thought to thin the blood—some iconoclasts insisted that it *thickened* the blood, but the result seemed to be the same—so here came the sulphur and molasses, or some other elixir.

There really was a mixture called Elixir. It was dark brown and it tasted so bad it lifted the spirits in sheer self-defense; unless the lift was manifest there was more Elixir.

And, just a bit later, there was rhubarb, pie-plant in the old lexicon. It, too, had magic qualities, particularly when stewed with a minimum of sugar. Then came the first Spring greens. Dandelions were a favorite, because if one didn't discard the outer leaves they had a splendid bitter taste that must be full of virtue. Any Spring tonic must be bitter to have any authority. That Winter lethargy had to be driven out of the blood stream somehow.

We still use dandelions. But when we pick them Barbara discards the bitter outer leaves. The young, tender, inner leaves are almost palatable raw in salad or cooked like spinach. Whether they have an elixir quality or not, I don't know; I suspect they haven't as much as those tough outer leaves. From my vantage of maturity I now believe that the bitter tonics were less effective as tonics, *per se*, than as a means of driving youngsters out-of-doors, merely to escape taking them. That was where the real Spring tonic was to be found—out in the urge and liveliness of Spring itself. It still is.

DISCOUNTING local conditions of weather, such as March snowstorms, once Spring starts moving north it travels at a fairly regular and predictable pace. The rate is approximately sixteen miles a day. Just for example, if red maples should start opening bud in Washington, D. C., on March 15, which sometimes happens, red maples could be expected to open bud in Baltimore two days later. And, given

normal weather during that period, by the end of March they would be open in the area of New York City. And about six days later they would begin to open here beside my river.

This rate of travel, however, is true only for places of approximately the same altitude above sea level. Another scale of calculation comes into effect when you come to a range of hills or mountains. Spring slows up at the foot of a slope, just as most travelers do. Instead of traveling sixteen miles a day, as it does on level ground, it climbs only 100 feet of altitude a day. Spring may creep into a valley with green grass and violets on a Sunday morning and not reach the top of a 200-foot hill bordering that valley until Tuesday noon.

Last year we saw this happen on our own mountainside, though not as vividly as it did on Canaan Mountain, which we see every time we drive to the village. On Canaan Mountain we could watch the line of opening leaves on the trees climb from ledge to ledge and shoulder to shoulder day by day. Since the mountain rises more than a thousand feet above the

valley, the bottom was green almost two weeks before the green reached the top.

THE SPRING trend of a week ago has reversed itself. Days are raw, nights are cold. We drove around the mountain today, past Lake Washining which should, to my way of thinking, be rippling and sparkling in the sunshine. Instead, it was still half iced over and the open water was sullen and leaden.

Despite the chill, I noticed as we came home that the white birches up the mountainside show a touch of red at their tips. There has been a kind of ruddy cast to them all Winter, but the color begins to warm up now. The birches look like long-handled paint brushes that have been dipped ever so lightly in crimson pigment. It is a heartening sight, and it seems twice as colorful against the background of pines and hemlocks.

MY THERMOMETER showed just six above zero this morning. And I heard that not far from here someone had a reading only two above. How we like to boast of our extremes!

I was once caught in an early September heat wave in the Imperial Valley of California, which can be hellishly hot. On the streets of El Centro there was a thermometer under the wooden awning in front of every store, and the natives were walking along the street looking at every thermometer. I did likewise and found a variation from 128 to 135, the result of varying accuracy in the thermometers. But when I went into a restaurant a waitress exulted, "I hear it's up to 135!" The town's official temperature, apparently, was the highest anyone could find.

But I suppose that once the temperature has risen above 120, a few degrees more or less don't matter much. As for me, the same applies to temperatures in the neighborhood of zero. I have seen it eighteen below zero here in this valley, and it didn't seem one whit colder than it felt at a mere ten below. And this morning I am as unhappy about six above zero as I would be about a mere two above.

I HAVE RESOLVED to pay no more attention to the weather. I will note that it is warmer today, and the sun is shining. But I am looking for Spring now, not statistics. Well, just in passing, I did happen to see the thermometer and the temperature seemed to be up around 30.

One Winter I kept a weather chart for three months, making notations of temperature and barometric readings three times a day and charting them on graph paper. It became such a chore that I finally gave it up. I was going around, just waiting for the hour to take my readings, and I was wishing for sharp changes in the weather to make big peaks and valleys on my charts.

I wasn't cut out to be a meteorologist. But I did find that, over that particular period—and it seems to be true generally—the movements of temperature and barometric pressure are closely in accord. The pressure goes up and the temperature goes down. This is a broad generalization, and there are exceptions; but my chart showed an almost constant relationship. There was, however, a twelve- to eighteen-hour lag of temperature movement behind the changes in barometric pressure. This, of course, applied to Winter weather; there are other and more complex relationships for Summer.

The simplest weather forecasts I ever made were from the weather maps. I found that, generally speaking, the weather in Bismarck, N. D., would reach the East Coast in thirty-six to forty-eight hours. All I had to do was read the Bismarck report and predict that we would have some variation on the same weather late tomorrow. It was about 60 per cent accurate. Then my newspaper discontinued the Bismarck report and I was left to my own guesswork again.

ALMOST MILD TODAY and the sap has begun to flow again. So I collected a few gallons and started the fire under the tub and began making syrup once more.

This afternoon we went down the road to the swamp
and I found pussy willows out. Not the big domesticated ones,
big as my little finger-end, but the moderate-sized wild ones.
The pussy willow pretty well sets the pace for all the Spring
shrubs. The "pussy," of course, is not the blossom of *Salix dis-
color*, to give the shrub its botanical name; the true blossom
comes a few weeks later. This is the bud from which the outer
scales have fallen. It will change into a ragged tuft of yellowish
miniature flowers. Staminate and pistillate flowers are borne
on different trees, as with all the willows. When the flowers
have done their duty, with the help of the early bees, then the
leaves will appear.

All willows have catkins in one form or another, and
many of the lesser willow trees, particularly those on the fringe
of ponds and streams, can compete in a lesser way with the
pussy willows. Even the bearberry willow, which creeps on the
windy slopes of the Eastern mountains, has fuzzy little catkins. So does the even smaller dwarf willow, *Salix herbacea*,
which lives on the mountain summits. The really big willows,
white, black, crack and weeping, have catkins that vary from
furry little tufts to long, slender plumes. And all bloom early.

If pussy willows didn't bloom until May they would
hardly get a second glance. In March we seek them out and
give them hearty welcome.

WE FINISHED the last batch of maple syrup today, bottled it and stowed it away, and we have made four cakes of maple sugar, just enough for flavoring when Barbara needs it.

The sugaring is a simple process, once you have the syrup. We put a couple of quarts of syrup in a big saucepan and cook it on the kitchen stove until it begins to thread from a spoon, keeping the heat moderate to prevent scorching. Once it is cooked to the right point we take it off the heat and beat it with a spoon. I tried using the electric beater on it once and achieved an astonishing mess when it suddenly crystallized, even before I could shut off the motor. No doubt it can be done that way, but I prefer the old way, with a spoon, because I can feel the change in texture at the critical moment. At that point it must go at once into the pans for molding. I can almost hear the crackle as the crystals take shape in a kind of chain reaction. With luck, we get it all out of the cooking pan in a couple of quick gestures. There it cools and sets and within half an hour we have neat cakes of golden maple sugar. The color really isn't gold; it is more of a buckskin, a very light tan.

The sap is still flowing, but we have all we want. I removed the spouts and whittled plugs and drove them into the holes. That will keep the insects out and protect the trees, and when the moisture of the sap swells the plugs they will cut off the flow and send the sap up the tree where it belongs, to make new leaves and new growth. I am always amazed at the quantity of sap that moves up a tree. We take about seven gallons from each spout, and each spout taps only one small area of the tree trunk.

WATCHING AND SENSING the slow, persistent efforts of the green world to achieve leaf and blossom and seed again, I am aware once more of my kinship with all living things. That compulsion for life which animates the world around me created humanity as a species. We all have a kind of racial desire to live. Leave purpose to the theologians, if you wish, and you still face the biological fact. But there is something more than this animate compulsion in man, something which has endowed the species with powers of reason and emotion, thought and speculation. As much a part of man as his powers of vision and locomotion is his impulse to create; and I speak not only of procreation, but of that rarer impulse in the world of living creatures, the impulse to think, to build, to record, not for oneself alone or for now only but for tomorrow and for others of this human race yet to be born.

This attribute is probably unique in man. The bear marks a tree with his claws only to prove his existence here and now, not to help or impress future generations. The wild mother, mink or robin, feeds her young that they may survive, not as extensions of herself but as individuals; and she does it by instinct, not by reason or by social pressure. But man creates his works and sets down his records at least in part because he hopes that life may be easier or better or more purposeful for his own kind after he is gone. Whether he succeeds in his purpose or not is beside the point, which is the innate aspiration of the species. And those who call this pointless and futile are the exception to the race thought, the race impulse, the racial compulsion. They are at war with their own kind and they deny their own racial inheritance.

Two things mark humanity as a species to me: this impulse to build and perpetuate and improve, and the emotional quality which we know as compassion. As I have said before, I find little compassion among the beasts or the birds, except where it relates to the mother instinct and occasionally to the protective instinct of the group or the pair. And I find almost no impulse to improve and perpetuate knowledge beyond basic impulses of self-preservation.

The ironic thing to me is that among my own race the most pessimistic of the intellectuals recognize these impulses but belittle them. They, like the damnation-crying theologians, are a product of this peculiar human possession, yet both the pessimistic thinkers and the damnation-warners refuse to accept its big implications.

THERE WAS A RAW, SLOW DRIZZLE, but Willis and Bobbie drove up as they had planned and Bobbie changed into outdoor clothes and went up the mountain, she and Pat. They were gone an hour and came back glowing and wet to the skin. They had communed with the universe and found everything still in good order. We ate and sat by the fire and talked, the quiet talk of close friends.

Acquaintance is one thing, but friendship is quite another, just as pleasantry is one thing and understanding is something above and beyond. The one is the casual currency of human contact, but the other is a special mintage reserved for exchange between you and only a few choice people. The one is there, always at hand; the other must be earned and then carefully invested or wisely spent.

The rain has slacked off this evening. But it has not been a dismal day. The house still has a glow, and so have we.

THE RAIN RETURNED, but now it is a Spring
rain that slants down in silver streaks and hangs in silvery
gauze over the hills. The river lifts a million hands as the rain
falls and the brook tumbling down the mountainside and
across the pasture has been talking all day. The grass along
that brook is now noticeably green, and when I walked across
the pasture in the rain I saw the clover green again, small
green triumvirates of rounded leaves close to the ground
among the brown stems of last year's grass. As with so many
other manifestations of Spring, I have to walk across the land
and look down, my eyes humbly downcast, to see them. But
my humility was periodic today. When I looked down, the
rain pelted the back of my neck and ran down my back beneath my raincoat. Perhaps that is the way it should be—not
too much humility on a Spring day.

BARBARA SAW the season's first bluebird today. It came and perched in the apple tree that overhangs the woodshed, the one where she saw the wood duck two years ago and couldn't believe that it was a duck, it was so beautiful. She called to me about the bluebird and said, "Now I know that Spring is really coming!" A little later we went out and found the first crocuses in color, not yet open but furled and waiting for the sun to break through the clouds left over from the rain. And the daffodils are in bud. Some of them got nipped in the frosts of ten days ago, but they have come along swiftly since. And the fat-budded big hyacinths are in sight. The grape hyacinths, which do so splendidly, are also well up and budded.

I also found the red first shoots at the base of the clumps of deep red phlox, including a clump I moved last Fall to give a mass of color. And when I took away some of the mulch around the delphiniums I found new leaves there, that delicate yellow-green that is so tentative and so hopeful. The columbines have small rosettes in sight, that deep blue-green that is the coolest green in the spectrum. There are also the reddish green tips of the big tulips, which remind me of skunk cabbage when they first break ground. But how different are the results!

Our Spring is on the way.

WE HEARD THE PEEPERS last night when we drove past the swamp. They always rouse first down there and begin to peep here by the river a week or ten days later.

You can hear the peeper chorus half a mile away, but you can scarcely see a peeper three feet in front of you unless you see him inflating his bubble-throat. The peepers, which are *Hyla crucifer*, have big voices and little bodies. Some of them are no more than an inch long and most of them blend so well in color with their background, be it white bark or brown, smooth or rough, that they become all but invisible. But, come this time of year, you don't have to see them. You hear them, and you try to find some simile for their voices—chime of silver bells, sweet whistle notes, chirps, none of them quite suffices.

The peepers for a time now will be to the dusk what the robins are to the dawn. The robins chatter and scold and whistle and are all over the place. I heard them at five this morning. But the peepers neither chatter nor scold. They simply trill, and their metallic notes have a penetrating ring that is distinctly musical, though the rhythm may be eccentric. Even that is more likely the broken rhythm and the overlap of a dozen peepers piping at once. And though they seem to be all over the place, they are not exploring. They have found the place they want and there they will remain until they have completed their spawning. Thus they have lived their Springtime lives since the world was young.

The peeper's song is only one note in the vast vernal chorus now beginning. It is primitive and ancient, just as Spring itself is very old and very simple.

I WROTE THAT SPRING is very old and very simple, and when I had set it down I wondered at the word *simple*. Yet that is what I meant, and there is nothing paradoxical about it.

There is a vast and detailed quality in any Spring, just as all life is teeming and various, in its origins, its processes, its achievements. Yet basically there is an enduring simplicity in which all living things participate. It is essentially the fact of life. Life persists. It reproduces itself. It animates growth. It evolves into a million different forms. Yet there it is, in a microscopic fleck of matter, in a seed, in an animal. It is a force that has thus far eluded our analysts and researchers, yet it is the very force which animates that search. Life.

And Spring is the periodic resurgence of life. It is the world around us burgeoning with life renewed. It is a season, an astronomical consequence in which we are fortunate enough to participate. The reasons for it may be complex, but the fact itself is so simple, so obvious, that we overwhelm ourselves seeking answers.

Spring is life renewed and made evident to any witness who happens to be there to see. It is as simple as that.

WE CAME TO WEATOGUE seeking a place where we could live in close and constant touch with simplicities and realities. We came not to escape but to return, to find and to know things of which we had been aware all our lives but from which we had been remote for too long. I remember thinking, as we first drove up into these hills from the lower flatlands, of the Hundred Twenty-first Psalm, and thinking that one's eyes should more often lift unto the hills. And every day since we came here we have looked up unto these hills and known a feeling of renewal and freshened strength.

Tom's Mountain is all across the world from the hills the psalmist knew, but it, too, lifts the eye, refreshes the soul and reassures the heart. Living here at the foot of the mountain I have partaken, in some part, both of the mountain's enduring substance and of the constant change of the river which is the mountain's companion. Some of the grit of this soil has gone into me, and some of the sweetness of this water; and some of the patience of the trees, too, I hope. This has become home, my root soil, and I have become a part of the very seasons, which is good.

I look at the mountain now, and I look at the river, and I feel the change of another season. It comes with the deliberateness of time and with the certainty of eternal matters. And here am I to participate in another Spring. Spring, which returns as a promise. And that promise is life and renewal so long as there shall be hills on this earth and a sun to shine upon them. What more can a man ask than life to be lived?